Audio Branding

Brands, Sound and Communication

Kai Bronner and Rainer Hirt (eds.)

Audio Branding
Brands, Sound and Communication

1. Edition 2009
© Nomos Verlagsgesellschaft / Edition Reinhard Fischer,
Baden-Baden, Germany 2009
vertrieb@nomos.de

Layout & Typsetting: Benjamin Troll
Cover Design: Michael Hoppe

Printed in Germany by docupoint, Magdeburg

Contents

D. Basics and principles of Audio Branding

E. Multi-sensory Design

F. Legal Aspects 181

G. Case Studies 203

Glossary 247

About the Authors 255

Index 269

Preface

The volume at hand is based on the German publication of *Audio Branding – Entwicklung, Anwendung akustistischer Identitäten in Werbung, Medien und Gesellschaft* from 2007.

Some articles have been revised, updated and taken over, others are new additions. The selection and combination of the articles is geared towards presenting the topic of acoustic brand management as extensively as possible, in order to provide an extensive overview. Therefore the book is not only suited as an introduction to the topic, but also serves experts as a fundament and reference book.

The book is divided into thematic chapters. The prelude consists of an article that offers an overview of the current level of teachings and development in the area of acoustic communication and an exemplary draft of the Sound Studies degree course offered at the Berlin University of Arts, which also covers Audio Branding as an area of expertise in Acoustic Communication.

The first article of the following chapter B uses examples to describe the importance and function of acoustic signals in every day life, and to what effect sound is used in the media. The second article of the chapter demonstrates the ideas of Branding and brand identity and how a brand can be communicated acoustically by means of Audio Branding.

Chapter C shows how two pioneers from both sides of the Atlantic experienced and participated in the development of Audio Branding.

In chapter D the authors address the basic principles, elements, procedures and methods of Audio Branding. Chapter D also describes the meaning and role of Audio Branding in the modern, digital world of media as well as the possibilities that arise with the new constellation of brands, music industry and music artists.

Acoustic brand signals are essential in multi-sensory brand communication. Chapter E therefore describes the basic principles of multi-sensory brand communication and also displays the contribution made by Audio Branding. Furthermore the chapter illustrates the basis upon and the methods with which consistent and meaningful multi-sensory design is created.

Chapter F deals with the legal aspects of Audio Branding: What legal bases need to be considered and how is the registration of a sound mark implemented?

Chapter G, the last chapter, delivers insight into the practical realisation of different Audio Branding projects, as can be seen in international case studies: What challenges and problems need to be negotiated? And, what kind of possibilities and opportunities are available?

To ensure overall better comprehension, the glossary offers explanations of important terms in the area of Audio Branding, as well as relevant definitions in the areas of musicology, acoustics and branding.

Sound samples belonging to some of the articles and further information about the publication can be found on the website www.audio-branding.info.

We hope this book is a help to those involved in Audio Branding, be it in schooling or as an occupation. The number of academic papers on this topic is increasing and correspondence and the discussion of Audio Branding is growing in international forums and blogs. We would like this publication to further the desire for exchange of ideas and discussions, and lead to more coalescence in the steadily growing Audio Branding community.

We would like to thank those people, without whose interest, dedication and patience this book never would have existed: a big "Thank You" to all authors. We are also very grateful to our publisher Reinhard Fischer for the enjoyable cooperation. We would also like to thank Thom Padlo, Benjamin Troll, Micha Hoppe and Markus Reiner for their support of this project. And last but not least, we are deeply grateful to all those who inspired and motivated us, supplied us with information, encouraged us, proof-read and translated or assisted us in any way and thus contributed to the success of this book project.

The editors Kai Bronner and Rainer Hirt

"If you have nothing to say, sing it."

(David Ogilvy)

A.
Audio Branding and Education in Sound

Education in Sound

Holger Schulze
Universität der Künste Berlin - Sound Studies

1. Why an education in Sound?

Acoustic communication is a new discipline. Over the last ten years one has been able to ob-serve how technical equipment and corresponding societal changes have increasingly ope-ned up new areas of research and educational offerings in the field of sound design. In this sense, acoustic communication is a genuinely global research topic and educational subject. However, newly established courses at state and private educational institutions reflect the different traditions of national and regional education systems; and accordingly orient themselves towards new, predominantly Anglo-American (at present) educational systems and methods of working.

Thus there are two main areas of educational focus – on the one hand, studies are an-chored in the newly established media studies courses of the 1990s – on the other there is an increasing connection with Corporate Design – a field which eagerly seeks new ways of utilising sound and the many senses.

Certainly the educational approach supports a different emphasis. A course designed for a career working with sound should avoid, to a large extent, short-term trends and fashions so as to not be swiftly re-assimilated the way other media and arts offerings in many places have been. It should therefore take care to comprehensively support design objectives in a simultaneously similar but different way than has occurred to date with Visual Communica-tion and Visual Studies.

How is this different from an education in visual design? Acoustic design has only re-cently become a recognised part of course content. A professional and educational profile only emerged as recently as the 21st century. In addition the basic principles of sophistica-ted, considered and well-established visual design had been researched and labelled by the beginning of the 20th century and in the following decades from the middle of the 20th cen-tury they were packaged as educational content. Graphic design became a taught discipline offered widely no later than the 1970s.

Acoustic design and the whole of acoustic communication still face these challenges. We find ourselves at an important junction – since the 1960s individual personalities and groups of scientists and artists have taken on board the stimulus of the avant-garde and 20th century technology and submitted initial proposals for how sound could actually be understood as a matter of design. In this instance first mention must go to the still exceptionally inspirational World Soundscape Project and the discipline of Acoustic Ecology via *Raymond Murray Schafer* and *Barry Truax* as well as *Simon Fraser University* in Vancouver (Schafer, 1993; Truax, 1984). Having said that, naturally all electro-acoustical research and arts centres (such as IRCAM in Paris or STEIM in Amsterdam) were important for the development and education of an aural consciousness and supporting techniques. In this context I'd like to highlight the research conducted by the French architect *Pascal Amphoux* and his Institute CRESSON in Grenoble. This is where subsequently, with reference to and in an extension of the very first meaningful beginnings made by Schafer and Truax, work was done on useful design-focussed theories (Augoyard & Torgue, 2005). The avant-garde explorations of the arts, beginning with the 20th century, connected all these investigations, sociological and ecological research, together with medical, physical and anthropological research and research from communication and media studies to create a new discipline: acoustic communication. It remains neither a recognised nor widespread discipline. Based on the professional practice of sound design in the mass media and by artists and communication agencies, its methodology and professional goals are constantly becoming clearer. It required and still requires action on the part of educational institutions, universities and colleges of Art and Design in order for acoustic design and sound studies to become part of the public domain.

2. Acoustic Communication – An Overview

How broad is the field of research for acoustic communication? According to the eponymous book by Barry Truax from 1984 it could be assumed that it would be a well-known artistic-scientific discipline with a significant body of research and widely included in curricula. However this is only being achieved now (Bull & Les Back, 2003; Cox & Warner, 2004) – not least, for example, with the Technocultural Studies course at the University of California at Davis, founded and run by Douglas Kahn (Kahn 1999). The question is thus: Is there a socially recognised and hopefully also economically motivated requirement for teaching and study involving creative work with sound?

Taking into account historical development in the arts and design in recent years, the answer seems relatively clear in the fields of art and design as well as scientific research. The technical means for sound creation are present in software and hardware; loudspeakers reach us in almost every part of our media-saturated world – in almost any situation. Common sense would dictate that the requirement for sound studies is undeniable. However, establishing new institutional entities requires time as well as more thorough and far-reaching explanation and justification – not least also a financial justification for their institutionalisation.

2.1 Is there a Need for Corporate Sound?

The economic need for a course offering in acoustic communication was investigated in a Delphi study in 2004 conducted by the communications agency *MetaDesign* (Berlin, Zurich, San Francisco). A number of branding experts from large concerns such as *Intel, Volkswagen, Sony BMG, Lufthansa, Siemens, BMW, Allianz, Deutsche Post* and others were questioned. The study's research questions read:

"The study should define:
– What market utility does Corporate Sound have?
– What benefits and risks are associated with it?
– What hurdles have yet to be crossed in order to work efficiently with Corporate Sound?
– What is the expected importance of Corporate Sound now and in the future?"
(Figge, 2005, p. 5)

The realisation – in itself not particularly surprising, yet in its clarity and immediacy actually quite astonishing – resulting from this research was that Corporate Sound (as the commercially most important expression of the work on acoustic communication) is being increasingly accepted as an important subject in these corporations. Corporate Sound seems to be becoming more important for all aspects of brand communication. At the same time a certain lack of confidence and methodological clarity in dealing with sound within professional communication seems to predominate.

In relation to this essay and the question of how working with sound can be expressed and taught, it seems that the following realisation is the most important: it is seen as important that "this subject should also be given a higher value in tertiary education" (Figge, 2005, p.34).

The commercial relevance of acoustic communication – as a broadly based scientific-methodological as well as artistic-creative field of study – seems as a result sufficiently proven by its basis in commercial reality. However there is still one unanswered question: How can working with sound be taught? Are there examples and models available? And to what degree can existing offerings be utilised?

2.2 Are there National or International Examples?

An R&D project conducted by four Masters' students (major Communication in Business and Society) in 2006 at the University of Arts in Berlin performed an examination of the then new course offering Sound Studies / Acoustic Communication. One of the questions *Charlotta Bjelfvenstam, Sabine Halbgewachs, Nicole Köpp* and *Dagmar Lippert* asked was: 'Are there comparable courses on offer in German-speaking countries or worldwide which teach working with sound in as many areas as possible of daily and professional life?'

The study included 21 universities and colleges of art worldwide whose course content could be summarised under the term acoustic communication. They included course offerings in Great Britain (e.g., in London Goldsmith, University of the Arts), research centres in France (IRCAM, Locus Sonus), the Netherlands (STEIM), Austria and Switzerland as well as many individual offerings in America (e.g., Columbia University, University of Berkeley, California State University, Stanford University), Canada, New Zealand and Australia.

Half of the international courses at that time included offerings from the field of applied sound design in the area of Communications. Courses in audiovisual sound design were similarly plentiful while there were a handful of courses in sound art and cultural sound studies. Nowhere were all these individual study paths brought together, though in individual cases two of these four subjects were combined.

In 2006 the situation was similar in Germany and in the German-speaking world: around 14 German tertiary institutions (e.g. Multi-sensual Design in Halle, Darmstadt Technical College Media System Design, Art Academy for Media in Cologne, SAE Institutes in various German cities and the College of Music in Detmold) offered acoustic communication course content. These courses each combine no more than two study paths together - the Anthropology and Ecology of Sound, Experimental Audio Media, Acoustic Conception and Audio Media Design are not taught all together anywhere.

On the one hand this study offers valuable insight into the diversity of offerings in acoustic communication in the German-speaking world and internationally. It also clearly shows that a coherent combination of the four main directions of working with sound (at least in 2006) was still not to be found.

2.3 Conclusions for an Education in Sound

What then is the conclusion to be drawn from these two studies? In the best sense a wide educational offering in the teaching of sound should encompass as many of the topics discussed as possible. It should also include:

– Methods and topics of sound in cultural studies, especially the historical anthropology and ecology of sound
– Working artistically with sound, i.e. experimental audio media
– Practical knowledge of and skills for sound creation – audio media design
– Conceptual skills to plan sonic environments and acoustic concepts

Based on these observations and findings any teaching programme could be influenced in a consequently promising and multifarious way when it's integrated and conceived by different content sources. How then, can one successfully connect these quite heterogeneous elements with each other?

3. Sound Studies – The Hearing Perspective

At the beginning of the 21st century we at the University of the Arts in Berlin were given the opportunity to develop a framework for a programme of study as a state-funded pilot project (Vorkoeper, 2005). The title of the project was "Sound Design as a New Interdisciplinary Subject" (Schulze, 2005). A small team of three employees, complemented by about a dozen lecturers and later also three visiting professors, spent between 2002 and 2005 testing teaching methods and precisely defining adequate course content in 30 workshops and seminars, public symposiums and hearings. Last but not least – and this must be made clear – the management of the University stood behind the development of this potential new study programme from the beginning of the project. We did not need to fight against basic objections but instead could harness the institution's support for developing course content and in planning and research through a process of trial and error.

3.1 Who are the Students?

How did we begin? Firstly, we did not want to develop a new study programme in a purely conceptual way. A city like Berlin – rich with musicians, designers, performers and artists – offers an ideal platform for researching teaching content for a new study programme in acoustic communication. This is why from the very beginning we wanted to learn about the interests; the inclinations and aversions; the themes and practices future students would be looking for.

   We focused our work on the students who had expressed interest – not just on the areas of teaching expertise or pedagogical and course-content ideas, which were already available in the field or the University guidelines, all of which would normally rule such a process of development. Thus we focused our attention on the artistic subculture that is prolific in Berlin. This subculture was the starting point for our development. We included it in countless preliminary talks, public discussions (soundXchange 1-3) as well as in accompanying research. The programme of study had to be exciting, interesting and educational and offer these people a real professional perspective. Professional experience in the area of working with sound, which almost all teachers had, contributed significantly to this.

3.2 New Teaching Methods?

The usual teaching methods such as seminars, lectures or tutorials were prescribed. However our teachers were not only familiar with the teaching methods of a German university but also with teaching further education-type workshops, such as those found at cultural institutes or corporations. Furthermore we were required above all to develop a continuing education programme for musicians, designers or even technicians who would like to educate themselves further about the aesthetically sophisticated but above all conceptual aspects of working with sound. For this reason, from the outset, we acted on the assumption that basic transparency was required to develop new and appropriate teaching methods.

Hearing as a cultural skill demands (not in the least according to the many and didactical-ly effective suggestions from Raymond Murray Schafer) a fundamentally different teaching method in practice and in theory than other well known cultural skills (Schafer, 1993). Differ-ing modes of hearing as modes of design are indeed a departure from common pedagogical techniques and knowledge paths. The Anthropology and Ecology of Sound has this as its purpose (Schulze/Wulf, 2007; Eshun, 1998). These lessons learned must have an effect on the form the teaching takes. In the words of the sound artists and composers *Sam Auinger* and *Bruce Odland* it is about teaching and acquiring a 'hearing perspective'.

"Since the Renaissance we have had an agreed visual perspective and language to speak accurately about images. This we still lack in the world of sound, where words fail us to even describe for instance the complex waveforms of an urban environment, much less what those sounds do to us and how they make us feel. We are lost in a storm of noise with no language for discussion." (Auinger & Odland 1998)

3.3 On-going Open Discourse?

Acoustic Communication as a new study subject is, as has hopefully been made clearer in this paper, at the same time always a subject of on-going research. Students who adopt this new subject quickly move on to the level of current discourse in the various technical disciplines because this is where the path of learning must begin (Kahn, 1999; Morley, 2003). New areas of research such as an historical anthropology of sound (Schulze/Wulf, 2007), audio branding (Bronner/Hirt, 2007) or aural architecture (Blesser, 2006) make this blatantly clear. Acoustic Communication or Sound Studies as a field of study can connect all these research aspects together to create cohesive course content. A course of study conducive to making the audible elements of this world into a truly effective new career can only work with the successful cooperation of theoretical research, artistic practice, design skills and conceptual thought. In this sense I agree with Barry Truax when he writes:

"Much of the work that is needed [for acoustic communcation; H.S.] is educational"
(Truax, 1984, p. 97) [1]

[1] *I would like to thank my colleagues from Sound Studies who worked on this since 2002 – especially the visiting professors Prof. Karl Bartos, Prof. Sabine Breitsameter, Prof. Carl-Frank Westermann – and teaching staff such as Prof. Dr. Martin Supper, Prof. Sam Auinger, Dr. Hans-Joachim Maempel, Dr. Peter Castine, Prof. Dr. Stefan Weinzierl and many others. A very special and personal thank you to my colleague and research assistant Hanna Buhl, M.A. for her support on the project between 2002-2008 and above all for the research she conducted for this paper. I would like to thank Charlotte Armstrong for her translation of my article.*

References

Augoyard, J.-F. & Torgue, H. (2005). Sonic Experience. A Guide to Everyday Sounds. Montreal: McGill Queen's University Press.

Auinger, S. & Odland, B. (1998). Hearing Perspective: Think with your Ears. http://o-a.info/background/hearperspec.htm

Attali, J. (1977). Bruits: essai sur l'économie politique de la musique. Paris: Presses Universitaires de France.

Bjelfvenstam, C., Halbgewachs, S., Köpp, N. & Lippert, D. (2006). Eine Kampagne für den Masterstudiengang Sound Studies – Akustische Kommunikation. Berlin: Universität der Künste.

Blesser, B. & Ruth-Salter, L. (2006). Spaces Speak, Are You Listening? Experiencing Aural Architecture. Cambridge/Massachusetts & London/ England: The MIT Press.

Bronner, K. & Hirt, R. (2007). Audio-Branding. Entwicklung, Anwendung, Wirkung akustischer Identitäten in Werbung, Medien und Gesellschaft. München: Verlag Reinhard Fischer.

Bull, M. & Les Back (2003). The Auditory Culture Reader. New York: Berg Publishers.

Cox, Christoph & Warner, Daniel (2004). Audio Culture. New York: Continuum Publishing.

Eshun, K. (1998). More Brilliant Than The Sun. Adventures in Sonic Fiction. London: Quartet Books.

Figge, O. (2005). Expertenstudie – Corporate Sound als Instrument der Markenführung Berlin: Meta Design.

Jackson, Daniel (2003). Sonic Branding. An Essential Guide to the Art and Science of Sonic Branding. Basingstoke: Palgrave Macmillan.

Kahn, D. (1999). Noise, Water, Meat. A History of Sound in the Arts. Cambridge/Massachusetts & London/ England: The MIT Press.

Morley, P. (2003). Words and Music. A History of Pop in the Shape of a City. London: Bloomsbury Publishing.

Schafer, M. (1993). The Soundscape: Our Sonic Environment and the Tuning of the World. Vermont: Destiny Books.

Schulze, H. (2005). Was sind Sound Studies? Vorstellung einer neuen und zugleich alten Disziplin. In: Vorkoeper, U. 2005, pp. 79-83.

Schulze, H. & Wulf, C. (2007). Klanganthropologie. Performativität - Imagination - Narration. Paragrana 16 (2007), H. 2. Berlin: Akademie Verlag.

Schulze, H. (2008). Sound Studies: Traditionen - Methoden - Desiderate. Eine Einführung. (Sound Studies Serie Vol. 1). Bielefeld: transcript Verlag.

Truax, B. (1984). Acoustic Communication (Series Communication and information science, Melvin J.Voigt, Ed.). Norwood New Jersey.

Vorkoeper, U. (2005). Hybride Dialoge. Rückschau auf die Modellversuche zur künstlerischen Ausbildung an Hochschulen im BLK-Programm "Kulturelle Bildung im Medienzeitalter". Bonn: Bund-Länder-Kommission für Bildungsplanung und Forschungsförderung.

B.

Basics of Sound and Branding

Audio Branding - all new?

Georg Spehr
Freelance multimedia designer, lecturer at the University of Fine Arts Berlin, study course "Sound Studies"

In recent years, the terms audio branding, sound branding, sonic branding, acoustic branding, sound identity, acoustic identity and corporate sound have been increasingly observed in connection with sound design or acoustic design. They describe a process of forming an emotional connection between transmitter and receiver through sound, an associative anchor for recognition, communication of messages, image transfer and image consolidation.

While the terminology may be new, the actual process it describes has existed since man started to generate sound and it is continuously developing. Obviously, we all know the acoustic logo of a car manufacturer which has been booming through the media for more than ten years[1], and for several decades now, we have been hearing the signature tune of a Western movie[2] in connection with a cigarette brand. Specific sounds are created for electronic devices which, due to their properties and conditions, are silent. However, acoustic identities have been around for more than fifty years.

1. Are you sleeping? Are you sleeping Brother John, Brother John? Morning bells are ringing! Morning bells are ringing! Ding, dong, ding. Ding, dong, ding.
Canon for four voices, French traditional, ca. 1860

Bells have probably existed for over 4000 years. The sound of bells has always signified a religious-spiritual as well as a secular context. Mythologically, bells are associated with communication within transcendental realms, and in many religions the sound of bells serves as a link between heaven and earth.

---

[1] *The acoustic logo of the car manufacturer "Audi" was designed in 1996 and got a soft redesign in 2006.*
[2] *The Magnificent Seven, Elmar Bernstein, 1960.*

The many uses of bells include their use as musical instruments, alarm clocks, timers, warning signals and calls for prayer. Their sound was thought to pacify gods, placate demons and confuse enemies and prey. In many cultures, bells play an important role, e.g. in the Alps, they ring in/ring out the new/old year and chase away bad spirits during carnival. Bells also specify a form of phonetic space as the area reached by the sound of church bells encompasses its congregation. In more densely populated areas or cities, the so-called chime order determines the sound of bells to ensure a harmonic sound pattern when bells from several churches ring simultaneously. In addition, the chime order specifies the ringing of bells before, during and after church services, christenings, weddings, funerals etc. Many different motifs and melodies may be created by the number of chimes and the specific tunings, chime techniques and ways to strike a bell. During funeral mass, for example, social status, age and gender of the deceased can be communicated with a specific chime pattern. In the past, church bells were often rung for particular, non-religious events, such as victory celebrations or a sovereign's birthday as well as catastrophes or fires (storm bells).Today, the ringing of bells is mostly linked to churches, with the exception of New Year's bells or regular hourly and quarterly chimes to announce the time. For this purpose, two different bells are generally rung: the higher pitched one chimes the quarter hour and the bell with the lower pitch the full hour. In a 12-hour cycle, 3 pm (15:00 hrs) could sound thus:

DING - DING - DING - DING --- DONG - DONG - DONG

Bell-ringing can also become a synonym or landmark for an entire city. The great bell of the Palace of Westminster clock tower, Big Ben, is one of the most famous landmarks of London. In probably every second TV film or movie, the melody or the low-pitched bells every full hour are used as a London cliché. *BBC Radio* has been using this chime as its signature tune until today. Not only large bells are of acoustic significance. Smaller bells also play a resonating role in every day life. School bells announce the beginning and end of lessons, theatre bells jangle a code to send audience and actors back to their places. Hotel staff are called to attention by the short loud "pling" of reception bells. Cow bells with their unhurried peening remind us of kitschy alpine panoramas and jingle bells are omnipresent at Christmas time, especially in the media.

2. TA TAAH TA-TA TAAH TA TAAAAH TA TA ...
Beginning of the prelude to the "Te Deum" by Marc-Antoine Charpentier, Eurovision signature tune in spoken language

A fanfare is a piece of music with signifying character written for trumpets and horns or the French term for brass- or military music. Many sound transcriptions for a single word, its use and association with fanfare sounds exist. They denote power, major events, important news and certain activities. In many ancient European and Asian cultures, simple natural trumpets were used on religious and military occasions. In the early middle ages, an elongated trumpet was used for military and courtly events. Commanders and kings were announced with fanfares. For centuries, hunters have been using specific horn calls. The start of the hunt is announced by a quick ascending melody, the end of the hunt with a slower descending one. In addition, the traditional "hallali" provides the acoustic branding of the hunters' guild[3]. The announcement "Here comes the king!" is often equated with clarion and trumpet calls, despite the fact that for present day monarchs this type of announcement is now only rarely used. Yet, in many movies and radio plays, the king is announced with a booming "tata". Popular productions for children, such as "Der kleine König (The Little King)"[4], where the story begins with a fanfare, help to keep this conditioning alive.

Heralds use so-called heralding trumpets. This manner of announcing is still fairly popular, albeit not with an actual herald, but for news broadcasts. Comparison of newscast signature tunes used by different TV networks shows that all use tunes which are based on brass instruments, apart from other characteristics which will be discussed later. To start off with fanfares and horns has always been part and parcel of major events such as parades or tournaments. At the Olympic Games, specifically composed fanfare themes are played, apart from the official hymn, to trigger emotions such as excitement, anticipation and team spirit, and to symbolize friendship, peace and unity[5].

Often, resonant brass is used at the opening of a major event especially in TV broadcasts. For over 50 years, the European Broadcasting Union, *EBU*, a confederation of European broadcasting organizations, has been using the prelude to the "Te Deum" by *Marc-Antoine Charpentier* (see article *Synesthetic Design - Building Multi-sensory Arrangements*). While initially this was used as an opener to avoid payments for rights of use, it has since been registered as the exclusive trademark for EBU TV broadcasts[6].

---

[3] *The hallali was originally used to vociferously cheer on hunters and dogs.*
[4] *"Der kleine König" by Hedwig Munck, composition Achim Gieseler, Universal Family Entertainment.*
[5] *"The Opening Ceremony is the occasion of lighting the flame that burns during the Games. The delegations of all the nations participate in a formal parade.The music and choreography intensify these unique moments, which are filled with emotion, and symbolize friendship, peace and unity. (...) The Organizing Committee for the Games in Salt Lake (SLOC) have entrusted John Williams with the task of composing the official theme of the Salt Lake City Olympic Winter Games. He previously composed the themes for the Summer Games in 1984, 1988 and 1996. Mark Waters has been appointed conductor."*
http://www.olympic.org/uk/games/slc2002/gallery/index_uk.asp, 1.12. 2008
[6] *50 YEARS OF EUROVISION, EBU DOSSIERS (2004), p. 36*

However, TV networks apply the principle of fanfares not only to major events. Many broadcasts and TV series have signature tunes dominated by brass instruments.

3. dit dah - dit dit dah - dah dit dit - dit dit - dah dah dah - dah dit dit dit dit dah - dah dit dit dit - dit dah dit - dit dah - dah dit - dah dit dit - dit dit - dah dit - dah dah dit
audio branding depicted in Morse code (dit = short, dah = long)

Industrialization and the discovery of electricity lead to the development of new sounds with such distinct new characteristics that they are still associated with specific clichés, functions or events. I want to focus in more detail on two of these.

Morse code is a method for the transmission of letters and signs. For this purpose, a constant signal is switched on and off. Any medium able to clearly produce two different states (sound on, sound off) may be used. As the actual function of Morse code has become less important, it is used only rarely today. However, as a sound metaphor for communication or news it is regularly applied in the media.
Some examples:
- Symbolic Morse signals are used as openers or separators in short news broadcasts.
- Movie scenes where modern silent communication devices, e.g. satellites, appear are often underplayed with Morse code sound.
- In the past, the signal for the weather report from the German news broadcast "Tagesschau" contained the Morse code for "QAM ~ weather forecast" (−−•−•− −−).
- One of the text message signals of *Nokia* cell phones is the actual Morse code for "SMS" (short message service) (•••− −•••).
- The BBC uses the opening chords of *Beethoven*'s 5th symphony which corresponds to the Morse signal for V (Victory, •••−) as interval signal.
- The signature tune of the German news broadcast "Heute" (Today) contains the Morse code for TODAY (•••• • ••− − •).

Until the 1980s, most news rooms had a telex machine transmitting news in writing. Telex machines produced a rhythmic clicking sound (similar to rapid regular keystrokes on a type writer). This resulted in the coining of phrases such as "ticker news" or "just in on the ticker tape". This brings me back to television news broadcasts. Here, signature tunes generally consist of three audio branding elements: fanfare motifs, Morse code and ticker tape sound[7].

---

[7] *Ticker and Morse code are mostly transformed into a musical rhythm.*

"Tagesschau", Germany's oldest news broadcast, demonstrates a specific form of conti-nuation in relation to audio branding. Created in 1952, its sound has been changed only five times. The biggest change or innovation was introduced in 1956 when the initial signature tune, which was very similar to the UFA newsreel tune[8], was replaced with a novel compo-sition pattern[9]:
1.Gong
2.Anchor speaker ("Hier ist das 1. deutsche Fernsehen mit der Tagesschau")
3.Fanfare motif (TAAAH TAA TA TA TA TAAH)

The gong sound does not only function as prelude, but also as a time signal (it sounds at the exact time of schedule, mostly at the full hour). A time signal consists of a sequence of one or several short acoustic signals to emphasize a specific point in time. On radio, it is often played at the half and the full hour to announce news broadcasts. This acoustic branding is only used sporadically today (e.g. in the German Deutschlandfunk). Time signals mostly consist of short sine-like sounds on seconds 57, 58, 59 and a longer sound exactly at the full hour.
BEEP - BEEP - BEEP --- BEEEEP ---------- "Twelve noon. This is the news..."

Radio as a purely acoustic medium always had to develop specific acoustic signals to ensure recognition. Until the 1980s, German radio stations preferred slow interval signals (with a lot of silence before and after) such as bell sounds (Hessischer Rundfunk, HR), ar-rangements of regional folk songs (Bayerischer Rundfunk, BR, "Solange der alte Peter...") or simply the musical transcription of the station acronym (Sender Freies Berlin: es (E-flat) – F – B). In contrast, the jingles used today are considerably louder, more compact and intricate as they have to communicate content and target group as well as station name and frequency (see article *A short History of Sound Branding*).
Movie studios represent another media section which developed acoustic identification early on. The invention of talkies (or sound movies) enabled acoustic backing of the visual lo-gos at the start of a movie. Arguably, the best known acoustic logos are the fanfare themes (!) of *20th Century Fox*[10] and *MGM*'s roaring lion[11].

[8] *http://www.deutsche-wochenschau.de, 1.12. 2008*
[9] *The changes introduced in 1970, 1978, 1984, 1994, and 1997 are contemporary modernizations, not new compositions.*
[10] *composed by Alfred Newmann, 1933*
[11] *"Leo the Lion" roared for the first time in 1928.*

4. Bond, James Bond.

Sean Connery, George Lazenby, Roger Moore, Timothy Dalton, Pierce Brosnan, Daniel Craig as "007"

A movie series with a strong visual and a strong acoustic branding was launched in 1962. In 23 (official) films to date, secret agent 007 James Bond saunters through the movie world. Alongside specific visual and formal elements, the musical elements are part and parcel of each movie, considerably contributing to its recognition value and the emotionalization of the audience. Essentially, this refers to the core motif of the "James Bond Theme" by *Monty Norman* (1962) and "007" by *John Barry* (1963). Both are consistently played in each movie, e.g. in the opening sequence view through a gun barrel or during action scenes of Bond. The strong audiovisual appearance during the first 20 – 30 minutes of a Bond movie usually contributes most to the recognition value:
- Opening sequence ("Gun Barrel Sequence") - variation of the "James Bond Theme".
- Pre-title sequence (as "opening gambit" or prologue) - background music of sequences with motifs of "James Bond Theme" and "007".
- Title sequence (credits) – specifically composed theme song usually with recurring musical style elements, such as strong dynamic brass sections and integration of the film title in the lyrics.

Theoretically, all three aspects are necessary elements of the diegesis, the narrated world of the Bond universe where the story unfolds, so that the audience can understand it[12]. They are also an integrative part of the trademark "James Bond" significantly contributing to the image[13].

5. New, and not new at all

Many more examples similar to the ones mentioned above exist. In some cases it is obviously debatable whether audio branding was intentional or just developed over time with frequent use. But this is not important. The point is to understand that conceptional and creative use and input of sound is not a fad or a job creation scheme of some agencies, but a process that developed over centuries and which, considering today's ever increasing acoustic inundation and congestion, has become a necessity – not to produce even more noise, but to enable better acoustic differentiation and to reduce noise pollution. On this note, I wish you a sound tomorrow.

[12] *A distinction is made between "extra-diegetic" music (coming from "outside" of the narrated world, e.g. as commentary music or to create an atmosphere, not recognized by the movie characters) and "diegetic" or "intra-diegetic" music (heard by the movie characters, e.g. when switching on a radio or dancing etc.).*
[13] *The music as well as the opening sequence are protected trademarks and may only used in Bond productions of "Eon Productions Ltd.".*

References

Blesser, Barry and Salter, Linda-Ruth (2006). *Spaces Speak, Are You Listening? Experiencing Aural Architecture.* Cambridge Massachusetts & London, England: The MIT Press.

Bull, Michael and Back, Les (2003). *The Auditory Culture Reader.* Oxford & New York: Berg - Sensory Formations Series.

Corbin, Alain (1994) / trans. Thom, Martin (1998). *Sound and Meaning in the Village Bells, 19th-Century French Countryside.* New York: Columbia University Press.

Chion, Michel (1994). *Audio-Vision: Sound on Screen.* Columbia University Press.

Schafer, R. Murray (1977, 1994). *The Soundscape – Our Sonic Enviroment and the Tuning of the World.* Rochester, Vermont: Destiny Books.

Sterne, Jonathan (2003). *The Audible Past.* Durham & London: Duke University Press.

Truax, Barry (1985/2000). *Acoustic Communication.* 2. Edition. Westport, U.S.: Ablex Publishing Corporation.

From Brand Identity to Audio Branding

Karsten Kilian

University of St. Gallen, Markenlexikon.com, Würzburg

"A product without clear and strong branding, is like a set of tones without a melody."
Angela Nelissen (2006, p. 285)

Companies form brands and brands form companies. They capture the identity of a company (or a strategic business unit) and its offerings. If elaborated well, "a brand can transform the way people see the world. It can change perceptions, preferences, and priorities" (Adamson, 2006, p. 219). To reach this level of brand sophistication, a clear brand identity – with a strong linkage to the business strategy – is key. The brand identity is then specified by means of corresponding brand elements, which in turn are combined to actively communicated brand signals, leading to preference and loyalty-inducing experiences with a brand.

1. Brand Identity as Starting Point

A brand identity typically consists of a key word or a short sequence of words that form the basis for the name selection (if still possible) and/or the brand claim. This so-called brand idea is then further specified by two to four brand values. The brand identity of *BMW* illustrates this approach (see figure 1 for details).

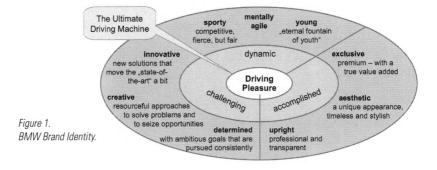

Figure 1.
BMW Brand Identity.

BMW is built around the brand idea of "Driving Pleasure". This idea of "pleasure", which every BMW model is an example of, is clearly expressed in the brand claim "The Ultimate Driving Machine". Interestingly, the original German claim "Freude am Fahren" (Joy of Driving) gets even closer to the original brand idea, whereas the English claim stresses more the source of this pleasure, the engine of the car. However, BMW does not just offer another engine in the market but the "ultimate" one. It turns the car into a "driving machine". The brand core "driving pleasure" is then further substantiated with the brand values "accomplished", "challenging", and "dynamic".

Taken together, the brand identity of BMW sets the brand clearly apart from its competitors, which is one of the four main requirements for a strong brand identity: differentiation. Ideally, all "points of difference" (Keller, 2008, p. 107f.) are managed across all five senses (see article *Acoustics as Resonant Element of Multi-sensory Brand Communication*). For one, the sensory brand messages should be in tune with each other, and even more important, in line with the brand. Only then can a brand create momentum in the market. Second, the identity of the brand should be of relevance to the customers. It should provide connectivity. Driving pleasure is surely linking customers with the brand BMW. In general, successful brands – often reaching iconic status – are mostly established by what Holt refers to as "Cultural Branding". According to *Holt* "successful makes like BMW combine a conventional focus on benefits and quality reputation with cultural branding" (2004, p. 5). Strong iconic brands are oftentimes built around the following seven axioms (Holt, 2004, p. 6ff.):

– Address acute contradictions in society
– Perform a simple story that address these desires and anxieties
– Make these stories reside in the brand, which customers experience and share via ritual action
– Set these stories in populist worlds
– Perform as activists, leading culture
– Rely on breakthrough performances, rather than consistent communications
– Cast a halo effect on other aspects of the brand

When replacing "society" and "culture" with "the industry", it becomes obvious that these axioms can also be applied to B2B markets. In addition to differentiation and relevance, successful brand identities should also be memorable. Their identity should consist of a simple, unexpected, concrete, credible, emotional and – according to the author – (multi-)sensory story, summarized by the acronym SUCCESS (Heath/Heath, 2007). Last but not least, a strong brand identity should provide sustainability with respect to the different experiential touch points and over time. The brand message should be the same no matter where and when a customer interacts with the brand. It should also be maintained over time. Slight adjustments are okay as long as self-similarity is maintained. In this case, the brand identity, also referred to as brand DNA or genetic code, stays intact and with it the value of the brand.

While brand identity is what a company has in mind when thinking of the brand and what it wants customers and other stakeholders to have in mind when thinking of the brand, brand image refers to the customers actual associations linked with a brand. Internally, brand identity knowledge functions as a strong safeguard of the long-term brand strategy. If something is off-brand, it should be clear to everyone within the company, that this should not be pursued any further. Take for example the current trend for energy-saving modes of driving. BMW has addressed this in accordance with its brand values "challenging" and "dynamic" with the 2008/2009 campaign "EfficientDynamics – Less emissions. More driving pleasure" (Kilian, 2008a, p. 1).

2. Brand Elements as Conceptual Units

Once the brand identity has been defined, appropriate brand elements need to be selected in order to help communicate the brand identity. Typically, brand elements are simple conceptual units that mainly make use of one or two sensory channels. Shapes for example can be felt and seen while tones can only be heard and colors only be seen.

In general, brand elements can be divided into primary and secondary elements. While primary brand elements are directly connected to the brand identity and serve to identify and differentiate a brand, secondary brand elements are typically linked to other entities with a knowledge structure of their own in the minds of customers. Thereby, the brand indirectly "borrows" some of this knowledge and leverages these secondary associations to enrich its own brand identity (Keller, 2008, p. 180ff.). Figure 2 provides an overview of the most-commonly used primary and secondary brand elements. In the following two sub-chapters, only brand elements with a clear linkage to acoustics are being discussed in detail. Audible brand elements (written in boldface in figure 2 below) will be discussed subsequently.

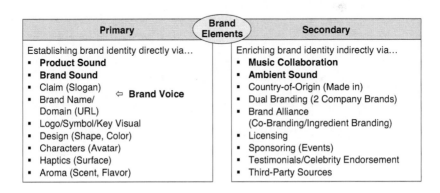

Figure 2. Primary and Secondary Brand Elements.

2.1 Primary Brand Elements

Primary brand elements help establish and sustain the brand identity in the market. The most important primary brand element is the brand name. The name of a company, product, or service takes the role of a mental linkage of all other brand elements in the minds of customers. It is the centrepiece of any brand identity. Therefore, the brand name and its counterpart, the brand claim, both ideally carry the brand identity within themselves. In cases, where the brand name is already in existence or for some reason does not directly relate to the brand identity, this role has to be mainly fulfilled by the claim.

Claims typically consist of short phrases that are being used to communicate the brand identity in a descriptive and/or emotional manner. When set to music, the effectiveness of claims is enhanced. Similarly, intonation, rhythm, and rhyme pattern also strengthen the potency of these short advertising phrases. Furthermore, figures of speech are frequently being utilized to achieve a special effect that augments the level of attention and memory. Alliterations are one typical rhetorical device being used in this context. They designate a repetition of an initial consonant sound, e.g. as in "Don't dream it. Drive it" (*Jaguar*), "Britain's best business bank" (*Allied Irish Bank*), or "The passionate pursuit of perfection" (*Lexus*). Alliterations can also be used with brand names, e.g. *Coca-Cola, Dirt Devil,* and *Magic Markers.*

Taking this a step further, the acoustic pattern of a name itself can carry brand meaning beyond its semantic denotation. A carefully selected brand name can, for example, imitate the sounds associated with a product, e.g. its usage. This phonetic device is called Onomatopoeia. The brand name *Crunchies,* for example, bears in its name the "crack-crunch-crisp" sound that one creates (and hears) when eating this particular brand of potato chips. In the same way, the sibilant sound in the middle of the brand name *Bizzl* anticipates the refreshing feeling when drinking this beverage. Similarly, the name *Taft* acoustically imitates the "tffft" sound when using this brand of hairspray. Table 1 provides an overview of the most commonly used phonetic devices in branding (Keller, 2008, p. 152).

Phonetic Device	Definition and Example
Onomatopoeia	use of syllable phonetics to resemble the object itself (Wisk)
Alliteration	consonant repetition (Mister Minit)
Consonance	consonant repetition with intervening vowel changes (Weight Watchers)
Assonance	vowel repetition (Kal Kan)
Masculine rhyme	rhyme with end-of-syllable stress (Max Pax)
Feminine rhyme	unaccented syllable followed by accented syllable (American Airlines)
Weak/imperfect/slant rhyme	vowels differ or consonants are similar, not identical (Black & Decker)
Clipping	product names attenuated (Chevy instead of Chevrolet)
Blending	morphemic combination, usually with elision (Duracell, short for durable cell)
Initial plosives	b, c-hard, d, g-hard, k, p, q, t (Bic)

Table 1. Phonetic Devices for Brand Names.

In addition to initial plosives, as mentioned in the table above, certain vocals can be deployed to acoustically enhance brand meaning. When adequately applied, they influence our conception of size, shape, and intensity of a branded object. While "a", for example, implies a somewhat larger item, the vocal "i" is typically linked to smaller articles. Soft voiced consonants like "l", "m", "n", "v" and "w", in turn, can support feminine, gentle, and harmonious brand identities, as is the case with *Nivea, Wella,* and *Always.* In contrast to this, hard unvoiced consonants like "k", "p" and "t" can express manliness, vitality, and technology. The brands *KitKat, Pattex,* and *Tigra* are typical examples of this. Table 2 lists further examples of phonetic devices (www.teachit.co.uk/attachments/4071.pdf).

Phonetic Device	Definition and Example
Long vowels	long vowel sounds to create a gentle, languid effect, e.g. a cool wave withdrew down the fading beach
Short vowels	short vowel sounds create a clipped, abrupt effect, e.g. he smashed his fist down onto the box
Soft consonants	soft consonant sounds create a mellifluous effect, e.g. the murmuring pleasure of a lazy stream
Hard consonants	hard consonant sounds create a harsh effect, e.g. the furious witch cackled and spat

Table 2. Phonetic Devices for Claims.

Even when the name is not providing "acoustical" information itself, a transformation into an acoustic pattern can still make the name "sound good". The brands *Moulinex, Schneekoppe,* and *Yahoo,* for example, were set to music, thereby creating acoustical logos that became complements to the employed visual logos.

Besides, brand names are often closely linked to logos. They can be related to the brand name in one of the following three ways: as icons, indexes, or symbols (Solomon, 2007, p. 72). Icons resemble the product in some way as does, for example, the crane logo of *Lufthansa.* Indexes, in contrast, are connected to the brand because they share some property. The galloping horse of the *Ford Mustang* for example conveys the shared property of extraordinary (horse) power. Symbols, finally, are linked to a brand though conventional or agreed-upon associations. The crocodile, for example, we have been taught, is the logo of *Lacoste.* So far, however, there are only few cases, where brand logos have been linked to sound logos. One is *Deutsche Telekom.* Its logo highlights in an impressive way the visual-acoustic linkages that are possible. As can be seen in figure 3, each one of the five tones of the "di-di-di-dii-di" sound logo of Deutsche Telekom resembles one element of the visual logo. While the four dots are all represented by the same tone, the "T" symbol is matched by a sound that is a third higher (see also article *Synesthetic Design – Building Multi-sensory Arrangements*).

Figure 3. Logo and Acoustics in Tune at Deutsche Telekom.

Both, brand names and logos can also become key visuals. Typically, key visuals help a company communicate the brand identity and the brand positioning derived therefrom. In general, three types of key visuals can be observed:
– Brand names (e.g. the writing of *Coca-Cola*) and logos (e.g. *The Michelin Man*)
– Benefit-based imagery (e.g. *Mr. Clean*)
– Pictorial experience worlds (e.g. *Bacardi* Feeling)

Pictorial experience worlds in particular provide – next to their function as identification platforms – a visual environment with which emotions can be conveyed. In most cases, mood-matching brand songs are part of these visual experience worlds. At Bacardi, for instance, the visualized attitude to life – the so-called Bacardi Feeling – is connected to rum and boosted with the brand song "Summer Dreamin'". In the same fashion, *Wall's* (HB, *Langnese, Good Humor* etc. in various countries) has been using the brand song "Like Ice in the Sunshine" for more than 20 years in different versions to accompany their ice-cream experience acoustically.

2.2 Secondary Brand Elements

As we have seen, primary brand elements help establish a brand identity directly and, in some instances, make use of acoustics. Secondary brand elements enrich a brand's identity by establishing a link to other objects. Thereby, brand awareness can be increased and the brand image can be augmented or adjusted. One way of doing this is by stressing the country-of-origin of a brand. Acoustically, this can be done, among others, by using stereotypical music of a country, e.g. German "oompah" music (for brass instruments) or by applying a country-specific language abroad. *Volkswagen*, for example, used the German term "Fahrvergnügen" in the US for a while and *Audi* still to this day, employs the German claim "Vorsprung durch Technik" worldwide (Kilian, 2009, p. 256).

When evaluating primary and secondary brand elements, the following criteria are helpful:
– Memorability (Recall and Recognition)
– Relevance (Associations and their Fit)
– Sympathy (Attractiveness and Aesthetics)
– Transferability (Product Range and Cultures)
– Adaptability (Media and Time elapsed)
– Protectability (Classification and geographic Scope)

While the first three criteria are most relevant for the establishment of a brand, the latter three oftentimes have a more defensive character. They enable a company to leverage already existing brand equity. All six criteria can also be applied when choosing audible brand elements which are discussed below.

3. Audible Brand Elements

In most cases, still, audible brand elements are reduced to jingles. They can be described as extended musical slogans. *Keller* defines jingles as "musical messages written around the brand" (2008, p. 164). If well composed, they contain a catchy hook and chorus that almost guarantees them a permanent place in the minds of listening customers. However, audible branding consists of many more elements today, as this edition indicates. So far, there is not

narrowly defined	Product Sound	broadly defined

• Sound Cleaning
• Sound Engineering /
  Sound Design
	• (Generic) Sound Icons
	• (Interactive) Sound Objects
	  (Functional Sounds)	

Brand Sound	Music Collaboration
• Brand Songs • Jingles • Sound Logos • Brand Soundscapes • Brand Themes	• Music Compilations • Music Sponsoring / Music Events • Product / Brand Name Placement
	Ambient Sound
	• Background Music • Sound Textures

narrowly defined	Brand Voice	broadly defined
• Brand Names • Slogans / Claims	• Brand Voices	

Corporate Anthem
exclusive · · · Right of Use · · · cooperative

Figure 4. Typology of Audible Brand Elements.

a standard term for acoustic brand elements. Instead, the following terms are being used, in most cases synonymously: Brand sound, Sound Branding, Corporate Sound, Sonic Branding, Acoustic Branding, Audio Branding, and Sound Mark.

A common trait of all acoustical brand elements is that they affect us emotionally and increase brand recognition, oftentimes beyond our awareness and our field of vision. The undirected aural sense perceives everything around us 360 degrees horizontally, vertically, and even behind barricades. During a typical TV advertisement, for example, 24% of all viewers are in the room, but do not look at the TV set temporarily, e.g. because they are reading or doing something else (Brandmeyer, 2003, p. 62). It is therefore of utmost importance that a brand always reveals its identity acoustically by mentioning its name and/or another audible brand element. Audible brand elements can be categorized, among other methods, with respect to the right of use a company holds regarding the audible brand element (exclusive or cooperative). Figure 4 provides an overview of the most relevant primary and secondary elements as specified above.

Corporate anthems are predominantly used internally (see article *Case Study: NBL Team Anthem, WWF India*). Their main goal is to increase the level of identification an employee has with the company and its brand(s). While corporate anthems are quite common in some Asian countries, they are not (yet) in Europe. As an example, the corporate anthem of *Nihon Break Kogyo* reached the national charts in Japan. In Germany, there are so far only a few corporate anthems in existence. At the hardware store chain *Obi*, for instance, composer and singer *Udo Jürgens* wrote an anthem for the company called "Mehr als nur vier Wände, an die man Bilder hängt" (more than just four walls, on which you hang up pictures). Similarly, the tractor manufacturer *Deutz-Fahr* uses its own anthem as does supermarket chain *Rewe*. The chorus of the Rewe anthem is as follows:

a little better everyday, with the world smiling back at you, better everyday with you

The anthem not only reflects the ambitions of the company, but also incorporates their claim "a little better everyday" (jeden Tag ein bisschen besser). In the same way, *Henkel*, a leading German consumer goods company, has included its claim "A brand like a friend" in the chorus of its corporate anthem "We together".

While corporate anthems are mainly directed towards the company employees, brand voices primarily unfold their properties externally. As we have seen, brand names and claims are not only primary brand elements but also examples of brand voice. They do not only carry semantic meaning, but phonetic connotation as well. Another example shall highlight this aspect once more: The brand names of *Motorola* cell phones. The brand name *RAZR* not only semantically refers to a "razor" whereby it implies its slim design "like a razor", but also acoustically via the harsh sound of the name. Similarly, the *PEBL* refers to a "pebble", not only semantically expressing its soft-shaped design but also acoustically conveying its "feminine" touch and round, "pebble-like" shape. The same holds true for the *SLVR*, another slim-shaped cell phone, just like a "sliver". In a broader sense, brand voice also includes voices of spokesmen that are as closely connected to a particular brand as possible, e.g. by signing long-term contracts that guarantee some exclusivity. In *Ikea* and *Wasa* TV and radio commercials for example, the speakers of the voice-over have a clearly discernible Swedish accent and thereby noticeably support the intended country-of-origin effect (Kilian, 2009, p. 255f.).

In contrast to this, ambient sound rarely establishes a strong product attribute linkage. Ambient sound can consist of rather simple, chantless sound textures like bird or water tones. It can also, and typically does, take the form of so-called background music. *Muzak,* the leading company in this field provides more than two million songs that they have classified and stored in their database. Besides 80 different business music programs, the company creates for its clients "a custom music experience that's exclusive to your brand" (http://music.muzak.com/solutions). The primary goal of these "sound layers" is to induce an "atmospheric stimulant" for a sales-promotional mood. Ambient sound is also referred to as department store or elevator music. In contrast to "absolute" music, ambient sound typically plays a secondary role for customers in their everyday life. An end in itself is missing. Instead, background music has a supporting effect for the achievement of other goals, e.g. to amuse customers, to put them at ease, to divert them, or to influence them in their decision-making. For this reason, ambient sound is often referred to as functional music. Most of the time, the impact of ambient sound is subliminal providing specialty stores, shopping centres, hotels, restaurants, and bars as well as trade fair stands and office spaces with an unintrusive atmosphere that makes employees and/or customers feel comfortable. While ambient sound might increase productivity of employees, particularly during mid-morning and mid-afternoon times (Solomon, 2007, p. 57), it can make customers stay longer and by doing so, make them spend more money.

While ambient sound is directly linked to sales, music collaboration primarily aims at finding a way to reach the target audience and deliver what the brand stands for. At the same time, music collaboration can lead to desired image transfers as is the case with testimonial or celebrity advertising. With the help of music compilations like *Mercedes-Benz* Mixed-Tapes (see article *Jingle all the Way? Basics of Audio Branding* and *Acoustic Brand Management and the Digital Revolution*), sponsoring of a concert tour of *Alicia Keys* by *Lexus,* or music events like the *Beck's* On Stage Festival Challenge (www.popsponsoring.de), companies try to transfer personality attributes of musicians and bands onto the brand (see article *Bands for Brands*). For this reason, possible music partners are mainly selected according to prevalent music clichés and the music taste of the target group. Likewise, movies, video clips, and commercials are being selected for product placements. Most of the times, however, these placements are carried through rather secretly. BMW for example, has been placing its cars in the entertainment industry for more than 30 years. One of the most famous ones was the appearance of the then new BMW

Z3 in the 17th James Bond film "Golden Eye" in 1995. Thereby, BMW highlighted visually the new roadster design and acoustically its engine power. Three other Bond movies with BMW makes followed. Overall, BMW services 650 projects per year (Hansen, 2008, p. 3). With respect to brand name placement the situation is somewhat different. While some companies might encourage book or song writers to include their brand name in their work, oftentimes brand names are being used without notice. In the US billboard charts, for example, 35% to 40% of all top 20 songs contain at least one brand name (Kilian, 2007, p. 335).

When a brand is appearing in a desired manner in the media, e.g. in a radio or TV spot, brand sound is oftentimes being used. It can take the form of brand themes, brand soundscapes, sound logos, jingles, or brand songs.

Brand songs and jingles can be characterized by their usage of vocals with understandable meaning. While brand songs like "Sail Away" from *Beck's* can – just like regular pop songs – span several minutes, jingles typically only last up to five seconds. They generally consist of a spoken or chanted brand name or claim, for example "*Sa-nos-tol*" (*Altana*) or "Kids and grown-ups love it so, the happy world of *Haribo*".

In contrast to jingles, sound logos can be described as short, mostly abstract acoustic sequences lasting 0.5 to 3 seconds (Lepa/Daschmann, 2007, p. 141). They function as "auditory cues" for the brand. Similarly, brand soundscapes can represent the character of a brand by combining sound objects, sound textures, brand themes and other acoustic traits of a brand. They typically last longer than sound logos, might be set up as infinite loops, and often function as brand-specific ambient sounds.

All audible brand elements, so far, have been surrounding the product, and thus, have been artificially added. Product sound, in contrast, refers to the design of a product itself or its packaging and the sounds naturally – by construction – linked to it. When conducting sound cleaning, certain sounds while using a product are being reduced or eliminated. In contrast, sound engineering or sound design aims at creating a brand-specific sound – a sound that is just right – by adjusting or exchanging certain parts of a product. Think of the sounds of a car engine, e.g. a *Porsche*, where sound engineering is an essential part of the brand experience and obtains up to 5% of the overall R&D investment (Wolfsgruber, 2005, p. 164). The engineers do not only have to focus on engine sound and driving noises, but also on the sound of snapping doors and the "click" noise of different switches inside. They are essential indicators of quality and safety as *Wolfsgruber* (2005) explains very vividly:

"With a saturated "wham" the door falls into the lock. The ear hears safety. The electric window lift does not wheeze "uiuiuiuiui!", but grumbles dynamically "Bzzzzzz!". The ear hears energy. The blinker drums a dominant "Click-clack, Click-clack!" The ear hears control!" (p. 166)

However, sound engineering is not limited to cars. Many other industries conduct sound engineering as well. For example at *Bahlsen*, one of the leading cracker makers in Europe, a development team of 16 researchers works continuously at the optimal sound design for its pastry. When testing their products, the noises that emerge when biting and chewing are being transmitted via loudspeakers into the research lab where they are analyzed in detail (Fösken, 2006, p. 32) since the sound when eating a cracker has a significant impact on the overall evaluation of the pastry, for instance, whether it is fresh and of refined quality (see article *Jingle all the Way? Basics of Audio Branding*). Similarly, *Kellogg's* analyzes the texture of its cornflakes again and again to ensure optimal "crunchiness". Thereby, the company not only guarantees a flavorful product quality difference relative to its competitors but also an augmented acoustic impression that leads to brand preference and loyalty.

When defining product sound more broadly, sound icons come into play as well. Sound icons are the shortest acoustic brand elements. They can be part of the audio logo or the brand song. Typically, they incorporate an actual sound of everyday life or a stylised variation of a generic sound. Thereby, they provide a more or less strong acoustic reference to a product feature as does, for example, the "plopp" sound of a *Flensburger Pilsener* flip-top bottle being opened or the "zzzsch" sound when lifting up the crown cap of a bottle of *Coke* (Bronner, 2007, p. 88f.). Similarly, interactive sound objects refer to short sound sequences that have become popular in recent years with the rise of the internet and because of a shift from analogue to digital device control. While sound objects on websites help users herald an activity or navigate through the menu, they can also replace once existent mechanical sounds of a product that have ceased to exist due to technological advancement. When inserting a cordless *Siemens Gigaset* handset into its base station, for example, a short acoustic affirmation can be heard that informs the user that the handheld is connected to the base station and that the recharging process is activated.

As we have seen, the range of acoustical brand elements is vast. It spans from product sound to brand voice. It can primarily be used internally, like a corporate anthem, or externally like brand sound. In any case, acoustics are of growing importance among the different brand elements at hand. However, it is not until several brand elements are intelligently combined that the brand particularities can be expressed profoundly. We refer to these combinations of brand elements as brand signals.

4. Brand Signals as Communication Content

When several brand elements are combined, complex multi-sensory brand signals are obtained. They communicate the brand identity to all stakeholders, particularly to customers. Four types of brand signals can be distinguished. First of all, the product itself has to be considered, e.g. its design, quality, and functionality. Second, the media, from TV commercials and print ads to outdoor billboards and internet websites need to be kept in mind. Third, people, e.g. employees, testimonials, and customers are relevant brand signals, especially in industrial markets and service-oriented industries. Employees with direct customer contact, e.g. sales and service staff, play a significant role in forming the intended brand image. They act as brand ambassadors. Similarly, testimonials endorse the brand and customers define what image others have of the "typical user" of a brand. Our image of a *Harley-Davidson* biker differs significantly from a *Yamaha* owner as does our image of a *Mercedes-Benz* and a *Jaguar* driver. Finally, surroundings, also referred to as brand environments or brand experience worlds, play a significant role in forming a brand image. Typical examples are brand parks, brand events, and brand stores. Fairs and exhibitions, at which companies are present with their own brand stand, also play a significant role in forming desired associations (Kilian, 2008b, p. 61ff.). Figure 5 illustrates the linkage of brand elements and brand signals and provides a brief summary of the four brand signals mentioned above.

5. Brand Experiences

The brand identity is based on a single brand idea and specified by a set of brand values and corresponding brand elements. These brand-specific elements are then combined to form a set of brand signals which in turn are actively communicated to customers and other stakeholders via the product as well as via different media, people, and surroundings. As a result of this, experiences with the brand might create a new or change an existing brand image. Brand experiences are fundamental not only for the establishment, retention, and directed adjustment of brand-related associations but also for the accomplishment of a brand price premium and brand loyalty. According to *Schmitt* (1999), the following five types of experiences can be distinguished: sense, feel, think, act, and relate.

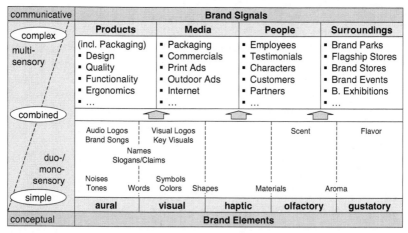

Figure 5. From Brand Elements to Brand Signals.

A "sense" brand experience rests upon sensory experiences through sight, sound, touch, taste, and smell. "Feel" is based on inner feelings and emotions of customers and aims at creating an affective experience linked to a brand, ranging from mildly positive moods to strong feelings of pride and joy. Ideally, brand experiences provide "a steady flow of fantasies, feelings, and fun" (Holbrook/Hirschman 1982, p. 132). Next, "think" brand experiences appeal to the customer intellect, "creating cognitive, problem-solving experiences that engage customers creatively" (Schmitt, 1999, p. 67). They engage customers by providing surprise, intrigue, and possibly even provocation. The SUCCESS factors mentioned above can be applied here, too. The fourth type "act" refers to brand experiences having an impact on bodily experiences as well as on lifestyles, e.g. by showing customers alternative ways of using a product. "Relate", finally, expands the individual experience to joined experiences with others, e.g. to broader social systems like brand communities. They enable customers to interact with other, like-minded customers and, on a personal level, with the brand and its representatives. According to *Löwenfeld* and *Kilian*, the two key brand community experience drivers are mutual member support and brand-member interaction (2009). Figure 6 summarizes the four stages of the brand formation process.

Brand Identity	Brand Elements	Brand Signals	Brand Experiences
▪ Differentiation ▪ Relevance ▪ Memorability ▪ Sustainability	▪ Acoustic ▪ Visual ▪ Haptic ▪ Olfactory ▪ Gustatory	▪ Products ▪ Media ▪ People ▪ Surroundings	▪ Sense ▪ Feel ▪ Think ▪ Act ▪ Relate

Figure 6. Stages of the Brand Formation Process.

As has been shown, one key instrument to help differentiate and memorize a brand identity is acoustics. Acoustical brand elements are an essential part of most brand signals and strongly enhance brand experiences as they affect customers strongly and in a direct manner that oftentimes goes unnoticed (but not without impact). They create sound brand experiences!

References

Adamson, A.P. (2006). BrandSimple. How the Best Brands Keep it Simple and Succeed. New York/Houndmills: Palgrave Macmillan.

Brandmeyer, K. (2003). Zu viel Gefühl. In: brand eins, No. 9, pp. 59-62.

Bronner, K. (2007). Schöner die Marken nie klingen ... Jingle all the Way? In: Bronner, K./Hirt, R. (eds.), Audio Branding, pp. 82-96. Munich: Verlag Reinhard Fischer.

Fösken, S. (2006). Im Reich der Sinne. In: Absatzwirtschaft Marken, pp. 72-76.

Hansen, A. (2008). Spezialist für Auto-Castings. In: Handelsblatt Perspektiven, No. 123, June 27, p. 3.

Heath, C./Heath, D. (2007). Made To Stick. Why Some Ideas Survive and Others Die. New York: Random House.

Holbrook, M.B./Hirschman, E.C. (1982). The Experiential Aspects of Consumption: Consumer Fantasies, Feelings, and Fun. In: Journal of Consumer Research, No. 9 (September), pp. 132-140.

Holt, D.B. (2007). How Brands Become Icons. The Principles of Cultural Branding. Boston: Harvard Business School Press.

Keller, K.L. (2008). Strategic Brand Management. Building, Measuring, and Managing Brand Equity. 3. edition. Upper Saddle River: Pearson Prentice Hall.

Kilian, K. (2007). Multisensuales Markendesign als Basis ganzheitlicher Markenkommunikation. In: Florack, A./Scarabis, M./Primosch, E. (eds.), Psychologie der Markenführung, pp. 323-356. Munich: Vahlen.

Kilian, K. (2008a). Dafür stehe ich mit meinem Namen - Unternehmerische Verantwortung als elementarer Bestandteil einer Marke. In: Die Welt, September 19, Special Supplement „Die Marke", p. 1 and p. 7.

Kilian, K. (2008b). Vom Erlebnismarketing zum Markenerlebnis. In: Herbrand, N.O. (ed.), Schauplätze dreidimensionaler Markeninszenierung, pp. 29-68. Stuttgart: Edition Neues Fachwissen.

Kilian, K. (2009). Klangvolle Markennamen und namhafter Markenklang. In: Bernecker, M./Pepels, W. (eds.), Jahrbuch Marketing 2009, pp. 249-267. Cologne: Johanna Verlag.

Lepa, S./Daschmann, G. (2007). IMES – ein indirektes Messverfahren zur Evaluation von Sound-Logos. In: Bronner, K./Hirt, R. (eds.), Audio Branding, pp. 141-158. Munich: Verlag Reinhard Fischer.

Löwenfeld, F. von/Kilian, K. (2009). Brand communities as experience drivers: empirical research findings. In: Lindgreen, A./Vanhamme, J./ Beverland, M. (eds.), Memorable Consumer Experiences: A Research Anthology. Aldershot: Gower Publishing (forthcoming).

Nelissen, A. (2006). Branding. In: Heilmann, T. (ed.), Manual of International Marketing, pp. 285-295. Wiesbaden: Gabler.

Schmitt, B.H. (1999). Experiential Marketing. How to Get Customers to Sense, Feel, Think, Act, and Relate to Your Company and Brands. New York: The Free Press.

Solomon, M.R. (2007). Consumer Behavior. Buying, Having and Being. 7. edition. Upper Saddle River: Pearson Prentice Hall.

Wolfsgruber, A. (2005). Voll auf die Ohren! In: Focus, No. 41, pp. 164-167.

"It is not rocket science, even if some may mystify
things making the process seem complicated and
therefore more valuable. The process, if it is a
good one, must be logical and plausible."

(John Groves, 2009)

"The approach of using music to connect with
viewers on a deep emotional level rather than a
rational or cognitive level in advertising
fundamentally redefined it as a brand-building
tool."

(Rayan Parikh, 2009)

C.
Beginnings of Audio Branding

Finding the Rhythm: Elias Arts and the Pioneering of Audio Identity

Rayan Parikh
Director of Audio Strategy, Elias Arts

Often when I go to business and marketing events here in New York City or elsewhere and mention that I am directing audio strategy engagements for *Elias Arts*. Some people respond, "What's that?!" while others will often say "Oh yes, Elias totally owns the audio branding category."

In a way, the polarity of these responses reflects the evolution and changing face of Elias Arts over the past 28 years and also bookends the growth of our audio branding approach. During this period, Elias Arts' strategic transition from a commercial music house into an audio identity and branding specialist has been built on its rich legacy and reputation as an innovator in the commercial music industry.

Changing the Game

Elias Arts' origins date back to 1980, shortly after *Jonathan Elias* composed the movie trailer music for *Ridley Scott's* seminal sci-fi thriller *Alien*. Deviating from other scores, Jonathan's work signaled a shift in the crafting of cinematic music and movie trailers. The eerie sound-track created with intermittent klaxons and low frequency tonal elements, coupled with the haunting absence of any vocal exposition or narrative, left an indelible mark on viewers, and the trailer is widely credited for the film's opening day box office success, which totaled over US$ 3 million in its opening weekend in 1979 (which, in those days, was a significant sum of money for an opening weekend). When Elias Arts expanded into writing music scores for television commercials and began applying the principles of cinematic underscoring to television advertising, it quickly established itself as an industry innovator.

The approach of using music to connect with viewers on a deep emotional level rather than a rational or cognitive level in advertising fundamentally redefined it as a brand-building tool. Rather than utilizing music simply as a lock-up for an advertising jingle, Elias Arts harnessed the emotional power of music and sound to tell the story of a brand in a unique and highly memorable way.

Early Elias Arts examples of this approach include an enduring anthemic piece written for *Michelob beer* that propelled Elias Arts' and its composing philosophy to the shortlist of television advertisers. Additional examples include the famous "Moon Landing" rock-themed interstitial that introduced *MTV* to a generation of young viewers in 1981 and continues to do so to this day. Seminal work for *Levi's* and *Perrier* challenged assumptions about brand and advertising music on television by introducing commercial music concepts ranging from world percussion tracks to minimalist modern classical scores. Elias Arts also wrote and orchestrated *Columbia Pictures'* iconic and timeless mnemonic, which won three *Emmys* and has acted as a prelude to movies for over a decade. Delivered by television and cinema screens and conveying powerful brand icons to the public, these seminal works seeded the notion of audio logos and mnemonics in the marketplace and set the standard for the future of the industry as a whole.

The company continued blazing a path for two decades, gathering hundreds of awards for commercial music work and sound design, included numerous *CLIOs, Cannes Gold Lions, LIAAs* and *AICP* awards. Over the course of the next twenty-five years, the company assembled a body of work that encompassed nearly 6000 music and sound projects.

The Genesis of Audio Branding

Early on, the structure of media communications made strategic decisions about the deployment and consideration of music and sound relatively straightforward, which in turn enabled us to deliver clear and compelling audio solutions consistent with our overall vision. Even with the advent of cable television in the eighties, advertising channels were relatively simple; most brand communications were limited to television, radio and print. As the millennium approached however, two major branding industry trends began to surface that brought new challenges, and opportunities, to our company and industry.

The first of these trends was the gradual movement towards the use of licensed music and licensed artists in music for commercials. Licensing, or the use of music or artists that are (presumably) recognized or familiar to a targeted audience, is often considered by agency producers and clients alike to bring instant credibility, attention and resonance to brand advertising campaigns. Additionally, licensing an upstart artist's or band's music can often be less expensive than developing an original score, and production turn-around is almost instantaneous. This coupled with the cross-fertilization of various music genres led to an explosion in the diversity of music available for commercial licensing, especially as many up-and-coming artists began considering licensing to be less about 'selling out' and more about viral publicity for their work. In this environment, many music houses that followed Elias Arts lead in original music for the advertising industry began to shrink, consolidate or close down completely as pressures on the industry intensified.

The second trend was the growth of branding as a marketing discipline: transcending advertising and treating both product and service brands as corporate assets that had to be managed with more attention and sophistication. This trend accelerated as the emergence of the Internet and new digital technologies forced companies to reevaluate traditional advertising strategies and manage new touchpoints for their brands. Following the leads of firms like *Landor Associates* and *Wolff Olins*, a new group of US-based companies began to develop methodologies for their clients that linked brand strategy, brand architecture, design and measurement together in new ways. Large corporations and organizations began to restructure their marketing departments to embrace the new disciplines and processes these companies espoused.

The net effect was that brands, particularly in the corporate and service areas, began to develop more strategically distinct assets supported by brand positioning statements, brand migration plans and communication matrixes. Traditional above-the-line advertising (TV, radio, etc.) became the short-term tactical executions of these longer-term branding strategies. At the same time, marketing dollars that used to go to television were now beginning to be spread more thinly across a wider array of touchpoints that required marketing and branding support. These trends pointed to a fundamental shift in the way corporations were beginning to invest their marketing dollars.

It was at this point, in 2000, that Elias Arts began assembling a team of individuals to alter and broaden the mission and vision of the firm, and seize the opportunities these marketplace shifts created. The Elias ID team was comprised of strategists from diverse backgrounds who worked alongside the resident staff of composers and producers. Starting with the enduring Elias premise that music was truly a universal language and an asset that had yet to realize its full brand-building potential, this eclectic group of specialists at Elias began to develop a systematic approach that sought to help companies understand the emotional power of music as a way to create powerful consumer brand experiences that could reach beyond television and sought to maintain Elias Arts' vision of telling brand stories through music and sound in unique and powerful ways using a myriad of diverse touchpoints.

It was a well-timed strategic shift in many ways. Companies were starting to become more sophisticated about allocating their marketing and media budgets across multiple marketing channels, and the opportunity to break through the clutter using innovative brand experiences was starting to become realized. The work we encountered during this early period of formalizing the discipline of audio branding was generally focused on product design, websites and sonifying other new touchpoints which clients were only beginning to realize could benefit from brand-based audio. In most cases, the market wasn't yet sophisticated enough to recognize that if music was to be evaluated strategically, it needed to connect with a strategic plan for the use and deployment of brand-based audio across all touchpoints.

Several Elias ID client projects from this time period serve to illustrate this paradigm. Elias Arts partnered with *IBM* to develop a set of experiential and functional sounds for the *IBM ThinkPad*, a powerful laptop that was designed to deliver technologically innovative hardware and to meet corporate business users' technology and networking requirements.

We developed a suite of sounds each representing a distinct function and enabling users to emotionally register a particular function in 1-2 seconds. All of these sounds emanated from a single creative brief which was derived from the ThinkPad's brand attributes. This allowed the system to be scalable – the sounds could be expanded to allow for more complex systems or shrunk for specific modular components while remaining brand-based. IBM's success with the ThinkPad is a great early example of how an audio solution was a key component of a user experience, one that paved the way for many other technology companies, like *Sun Microsystems* and *TiVo*, to harness the power of sound in innovative ways.

Our engagements during this time were not limited to sonifying new and emerging touchpoints, but also expanded to helping brands that were eager to leverage the power of music through more traditional channels. As mentioned earlier, licensing had become a common approach among brands as a method to gain instant credibility among consumers through the use of a familiar song or artist. What brands often didn't recognize however, is that this music had to fit the brand and be harnessed effectively in order for the music to support the brand - not the other way around.

A salient example of this is when we were contacted by *Chrysler* to help them deal with the unintended consequences of an advertising campaign they had initiated. In 2003, Chrysler featured *Celine Dion* in their television commercials singing her single "I Drove All Night." The rationale behind this decision was that a high-energy, emotionally resonant song sung by a superstar would help connect prospective customers to the Chrysler brand and products through music.

After signing a reported US$14 million three-year contract with the singer, the advertising was dubbed a "disaster" by many in the advertising press. Many observers suggested that the campaign strategy was inherently misguided; viewers associations with the music were not connected back to the Chrysler products and target demographics, so while the campaign helped sell a lot of CDs, automobile sales at the company after the campaign launch remained generally stagnant.

When Elias began collaborating with Chrysler in 2005 on re-tooling their strategic approach to music, we introduced the idea of a single bookend brand mnemonic that began and ended each commercial. The auditory design of the mnemonic served as both an interrogatory at the beginning, calling attention to the brand and its product's innovative design and value, as well as an exclamatory at the end, when it was coupled with the Chrysler logo and tagline. In addition, a coherent set of subtle, provocative music beds were developed and calibrated to the needs of the particular Chrysler vehicle featured in each of the individual product spots. Specific vehicle attributes like "performance" or "luxury" were dialed up or dialed down to reinforce the key emotional objectives of the spot. When orchestrated in combination with the bookend mnemonic, the approach provided tremendous efficiency and awareness for the Chrysler brand and its products.

The success we had with reviving Chrysler accelerated the use of audio logos as tools among agencies and other music houses, which were met with varying degrees of success. Often the audio logo was created as a "snap-off" that didn't flow with the rest of the commercial, or it was created as a singular expression that did not reflect the emotional context of the spot, or the brand, for that matter. In the case of Chrysler, Elias was able to balance the tactical needs of the campaign with the longer term strategic rebuilding of the Chrysler brand in the marketplace, thereby using mnemonic-based music as a catalyst for the success of the advertisements.

Changing the Game. Again.
Our earlier ID projects demonstrated to the marketplace that music, unlike most visual branding techniques, has a unique ability to connect with consumers on a deep emotional level. But our longer-term goal was to convince the market that when brand-based music is created, it should not only be designed for the unique emotional objectives of a particular touchpoint (a stadium sporting event or a customer complaint hotline, just to name two diverse examples), but should also be approached holistically so that music can link all the ways in which a consumer experiences a brand. This strategic use of audio creates much more powerful, sustainable – and measurable - contributions to many more faces and expressions of a brand's personality.

It became apparent to us that we needed to find a way to create basic brand-based criteria so that music and sound could be evaluated more objectively against the brand, rather than influenced by marketers' personal preferences. From experiences and project feedback early on, we began to understand that the real value lay in finding a way to link brand strategy and music for all involved parties. This in turn, required a whole new lexicon and translation/communication process that fostered a collaborative dynamic approach that in turn helped clients become part of the decision making process and allowed us to participate in the selling in of our entire process within the client organization.

By 2003, our Identity team at Elias had begun to establish a set of deliverables that were able to bridge the gap between our vision for audio branding and the evolving needs of our clients. With this knowledge and perspective, we began to secure clients that were committed to a comprehensive and holistic approach to their audio identity systems.

We developed recommendations to our clients for developing brand-based audio with this objective in mind. All existing points of customer interaction should first be evaluated for both their current and potential use of music and/or sound. Best practices in user design and experience should be analyzed to determine the best use and application of music, sound and acoustic technologies in order to optimize the user experience. The resulting touchpoints could then be sonified by designing and applying a set of unique brand-based principles to the creation of specific audio assets. These audio assets may include an audio signature, a music library, environmental audio or a myriad of other sonifiable applications.

But in each and every case, music and sound would be developed from a proprietary brand-based audio palette so that all experiences a user might have with a brand are interconnected, coherent and coordinated across all touchpoints.

The core deliverable that evolved during this period was a proprietary conceptual tool that helps our clients determine the sound of their brand and defines what the brand sounds like – before we embark upon design. This tool accomplishes several things for us, including involving the client in the audio design process. By participating in conceptual reviews, clients become more comfortable with evaluating music in a brand-based way. Moreover, it allows our designers the opportunity to get immediate and direct feedback from clients, who know their brands best, which then informs the creative team's design work. In this way, when we shift into creation of actual deliverables, whether it is a music-on-hold playlist, an audio logo or functional sounds, designers fully understand the business needs of the creation, and clients are better prepared to evaluate the work; they are well-versed in what their brand could, or should, sound like, and have contributed to the criteria that will be used to objectively assess the work. This component of our process, coupled with other supporting deliverables, began to establish a bridge between the strategy and design process while simultaneously creating a rationale for the strategic process that could be clearly articulated during the sales and client buy-in process. At the same time, clients began to recognize that economies of scale could be realized by looking at audio holistically instead of the manner of execution on a touchpoint-by-touchpoint basis, which further justified the investment in the audio strategy component of the process.

When we formally established a relationship with *Orange Wireless* in 2003 we were able to apply our full process to a strong brand that could only be made better by the development of brand-based audio. As a global wireless brand, Orange had many agencies in different international markets that were responsible for developing advertising that resonated with local consumers. Orange had developed visual and verbal guidelines for their agencies, but music and sound was largely relegated to the local agencies discretion. By analyzing how and why particular markets were using audio to support the brand relative to competitors, Elias was able to make a concrete recommendation to senior marketing management about the need to approach audio more holistically. We developed an audio strategy that allowed for both brand adherence across the globe and flexibility for local markets using our audio moodboards as a baseline for establishing the sound of Orange. These guidelines are still used by Orange as a way to continue to develop brand-based audio for existing channels as well as new touchpoints. The moodboards were also used to create brand-based functional sounds for Orange handsets so that the orange brand experience was not limited to stores, advertising and customer service, but became an integral component of the everyday user experience.

This process was also applied to *Cisco Systems.* Upon the launch of the Human Network brand campaign in the US in 2007, Cisco approached Elias about developing a 'sign-off sound' for their brand in television advertising. Leveraging our process and helping Cisco approach sound more holistically prompted a total reconfiguration of the project into a coherent 360 marketing system that includes television, employee ringtones, product and network sounds, executive walk-on music, and other assets in development.

Our practice continues to evolve everyday, and we are constantly looking for the new challenges that are forming on the horizon. This is particularly critical for nascent experiential touchpoints, such as mobile technologies, Web 2.0 and other virtual brand interactions and experiences. User generated content for viral brand marketing is also a big opportunity and challenge for our clients as they try to draw the line between maintaining the overall brand persona while encouraging customers to personalize their brand experience.

Much of our recent work shows how our audio branding techniques have come full circle to emulate, and add to, the qualities that made those catchy jingles so pervasive decades ago. When music began to be leveraged as an emotional tool, some of the rational qualities of the jingle were displaced. Now that our audio branding systems are designed to be closely and consistently connected with a brand and its brand attributes, they have reclaimed some of that cognitive effectiveness; in fact they work harder for the brand since they do not need to be anchored with a tagline and can exist across a multitude of touchpoints. In this respect, our work combines the best of the jingles with the best of music's overall ability to engage, compel and sustain behavioral change in consumers.

I do hope that as we continue to grow and expand, everyone I talk to at conferences will recognize Elias Arts for what we are doing. But on those occasions when someone hasn't, I am in the fortunate position to give them a few compelling reasons why they should know about Elias Arts in particular, and audio branding in general.

Elias Arts Creative Director Fritz Doddy and Analyst Adin Heller contributed to this article.

A short History of Sound Branding

John Groves
Groves Sound Branding Hamburg

1. History?

I was asked to write a short history of Sound Branding. I felt like a six year old being asked to write his memoirs. Sound Branding hasn't even started walking yet, so what is with the history? Should I write a chronological list of the developments to date? Would it be interesting or useful? I called the man who asked me to write. "Wouldn't it be more interesting if I presented a case study?" I asked, "or if I present our methodology?" I could almost hear him pouting in the silence at the other end of the phone, so I sighed, agreed, got out my laptop and here I am – writing a short history of Sound Branding.

Ok, a short history of Sound Branding

Well, Sound Branding is old and new. It is so old, that the church has it and so new that it has to be explained to virtually every marketing or brand manager. Admittedly, I was one of the first out there on my soapbox preaching about it, but contrary to popular belief, I didn't invent it. Sound Branding evolved out of necessity from the established rules and procedures for visual branding. The eye, for some strange reason, is the preferred organ that brands have used until now as the entrance to consumer's minds. Brands now realize that sound may have been neglected as a communications tool. And things are changing rapidly.

The church, incidentally gave us what was possibly the first true integrated corporate identity with all the trimmings. They have a very clear corporate structure, corporate behaviour (hands together) as well as corporate clothing (Cassock), Corporate headquarters (Rome). And they have a logo (Cross), a brand sound (Bell) – even a brand instrument (Organ)! They also had corporate architecture long before *McDonald's*! But I digress...

2. Where it all started

But they want history! Let the harps play an arpeggio and make the TV screen go all wavy as we go back in time – to the year 1995…

This was the year that I had my first real consulting assignment for Sound Branding. I had used principals much earlier but this was the first time I actually was paid specifically for consulting and advising about the process of creating a Sound Identity and not just music production. When I think about it, *DEA*, as in "Hier Ist DEA – Hier Tanken Sie auf", was possibly the first brand for which I produced a complete Sound Identity – Sound Logo, Brand Song, Sound Icons, Soundscapes, and Telephone – the whole kit. And this was in the dark ages of 1987!

The main element for DEA wasn't a Sound Logo but a Jingle. Having grown up in England there are lots of jingles that were planted in my mind – and some of them are still in my head today. Jingles like " You'll wonder where the yellow went, when you brush your teeth with Pepsodent" and "boom-boom-boom-boom. Esso blue" or even "Now hands that do dishes can feel soft as your face – with mild green Fairy Liquid".

I am surprised that, after 30 or so years, these melodies and lyrics are still so clear. In exactly the same way that the lyrics of all the pop songs of my youth used the melody as a Trojan horse to get into my brain, these sponsored messages are still there available for instant recall – right along side "Hey Jude" and "Yesterday". Amazing! But, I digress…

The WDR

So, back to 1995. We didn't call it Sound Branding then. My contract was for the "development and implementation of Corporate Music for five radio stations and a TV station". The object of the exercise was to define the job to be done (creating a sound that would fit the WDR and be different from the commercial competition), define the method of doing it, write the brief for the production and finally define and control the usage.

At the time, radio stations had problems seeing themselves as a brand and I was not a welcome guest for some of the producers. They feared that, by being considered a product (heaven forbid!), they would be treated in the same way as if the brand in question was a dog food. Actually, the process is virtually identical. Nevertheless, they were aware that, despite them having excellent program content, their conflicting programs and mix of music styles were no longer working. They were losing ground to the new private radio stations in a market where they had been alone for so long. Listeners perceived them as being distant and aloof. They realised that, unless some radical changes were made – not just to the product, but to their image and attitude – they would be losing even more listeners. They decided on a major program reform. The position of each station was musically analysed, redefined or modified and given a clear definition. To do this we needed to make an independent air check. In those days it involved sending two men to Cologne in a *Volkswagen* bus to record 48 hours of all five stations. This was possibly our first Brand Audit.

It was intended that *WDR 1* would intensify its efforts as a youth station, but in the end it was decided they should leave the WDR umbrella and have their own ID (which proved to be a good decision as they have been immensely successful). The second program should be the main middle of the road AC (Adult Contemporary) station. The third would have a classical image, while Station number 4 is now what the Germans would call a Schlager- and Volksmusik-Station, although it is much more. Station 5 became a minority/political type programme but was then re-launched as a Talk Radio.

Having completed this basic restructuring, the individual programmes got juggled about and reassigned to a new slot where they fit better. A Sound Logo was created which strictly adhered to the criteria you will read later. A fitting music style was chosen for each station, with special attention made to keeping them mutually exclusive. Each separate programme was also given its own individual musical profile while consequently including the Sound Logo of the umbrella. I realise that it is impossible to squeeze so much information about such a huge project into one little paragraph and make it understandable. I will cut to the chase and just say that the mission was accomplished. After the reform, the Independent Media Analysis reported that the amount of listeners for *Eins Live* (WDR 1) went from a market share of 3.8% to 11.7% which is an increase of around 300%. Not bad, eh? And the last I heard was that *WDR 4* is still Germany's most listened to Radio Station. Now, I'm not claiming that these results are solely due to the new Sound ID, but as we are talking about a mono-sensory media, it just might have something to do with it! And, dear friends, the main element for achieving this was a simple but sensible Sound Logo.

NIVEA

Another early project was *Nivea*. Here is a snippet of a lecture I first held at the *Eyes and Ears of Europe* annual conference in Cologne on October 1st 1999 (later also for the European Broadcasting Union at the *ZDF* in Mainz). It had the rather dry and lengthy title of " The Neglected Potential – Audio Design as a Branding Tool for Radio and Television".

"A group of products are bound together under the name of Nivea, which was initially a brand name for a hand cream. It was decided that all packaging and communications for this range should use the prescribed CI. Until now, there have been no efforts to get all the products under one roof musically so we have several options. As the music is communicated to the public primarily together with pictures in TV Commercials, one option would be to use the same music for all products and all films. Here I mean the same 20, 30 second recording. That would indeed give us continuity but it would also give us a few problems as well. Firstly, each product has an individual target group. The person wanting to get rid of his acne, for example, would most probably identify himself with another style of music than, say, the person wanting to get rid of grey hair or iron out her, or his, wrinkles.

Secondly, the style & pace of each film would be different, as would be the emotional content. The solution is that every film should get its own music, illustrative or otherwise, with the one common element common to all – the Sound Logo. When used consequently, the image of quality and competence that one expects from the name Nivea will instil a sense of trust in the listener."

Nivea took our advice and the Sound Logo was developed and implemented. Sadly, due to a number of reasons including creative resistance, two unaligned advertising agencies and lack of Brand Sound Guidelines, it just sort of fizzled out...

3. The Sound Logo

Both the WDR and Nivea examples are based on Sound Logos. A sound ID does not however have to be based on a Sound Logo – and having a Sound Logo is by far not the same as having a Sound ID. At the time of writing we are in a transitory phase. There is an acute awareness of the enormous potential that a unique Brand Sound has to offer in brand communications. The problem is that brands are enthusiastically adding ding-dong-dings at the end of their TV spots and thinking they are *Intel*. They will soon discover that it is not that easy.

In a study carried out by *Cheskin* Research and *Headspace* regarding Sound and Brand[1], one of the key findings is that the sound was able to communicate Intel's main brand attributes just as efficiently and effectively as the visuals. The report findings indicate that, when designing the Sound Logo (brand signature), it's critical that existing brand attributes be understood and that sound expresses these attributes. The report concludes by saying that sound can also have a negative impact on brand imagery.

So, what are we hearing here? Two bits of vital information: The first is good news – "Sound alone has the capability to convey brand attributes". The Intel Sound Logo was apparently designed to communicate attributes like energetic & high quality as well as to portray an accurate decade association. The good news means that image building can be done equally well in a cheaper medium – for instance radio. Cool! So, what's the bad news? I'll say it again – "Sound can just as easily have a negative impact on brand as a positive impact." Considering our current state of generic ding-dong-dings, it is obvious that "communicating brand attributes" seems to have been left out of the offending brand's shopping list!

Ok, I'll come down from the barricades. I'm passionate about this and every time I hear one of those things on the TV I almost spill my tea. If things don't change, the Sound Logo will have joined the ringtone as a major cause of environmental sound pollution. But let's think positive. Soon, due to books like this one, maybe brands will be aware of criteria like fit, differentiation and consequent usage. They will discover that good sound will help to make them more identifiable and memorable and thereby contribute to a more efficient communication.

---

[1] *www.cheskin.com*

In plain talk, communications using good Sound Branding will be recognised with less push, which means more and better contact for less money. Eventually a good Sound ID can even become a brand asset but it's a long and bumpy road. Even the best Brand Sounds are useless unless there are agreed rules of usage and methods of enforcement and control. *Nivea*, the worlds 99th best global brand (*Interbrand* - Best Global Brands by Value for 2006) had to learn this lesson the hard way.

Books have a long life. It could be that by the time you are reading this that things have normalized and that all major brands have aesthetic and pleasurable – or at least bearable – Sound Identities. I'll drink to that! (Tea, of course!)

I'll say it again, Sound Logos are nothing new. Strangely enough, the ding-dongs are nothing new either! As a kid, I can remember vividly how the sound of our doorbell triggered a voice in my head that said "Avon calling!" I don't even remember how it got there but the Sonic Mnemonic is indelible emblazoned on my brain.

Another one was the unique chimes of ATV television. Together with an animated graphic, the letters A - T - V unfolded, each accompanied by its own note. As a grand finale, the words "channel nine" came on the screen and were accompanied by three timpani hits – two deep, one high mimicking perfectly the spoken rhythm of the words "Chan - el nine" - dim-dim dum!

3.1 Methodology

As mentioned before, there are forms of Sound Branding that don't use a Sound Logo, such as the Key Sound Elements as used by *O2* and *Gerolsteiner*, but in most cases Sound Logos currently provide the basis for a Sound ID. So, what can be done to prevent a brand that has just discovered the benefits of communicating with sound and music from developing an irrelevant or non-specific Sound ID? The Sound Logo Design and Judgement Criteria is the basis of the methodology that is used today at *Groves Sound Branding*.

It was partly developed from experience gained from working with the world's leading branding companies. Back then, I was amazed at how systematic the approach of such companies was compared to that of the music producer/composer and the kind of briefings we still sometimes get from advertising agencies.

Creative people such as musicians and composers as well as agency people used to shudder at terms like methodology, strategic development and structured process. Things are changing and getting more in- line with the mind-set of the likes of communication & brand managers.

A Sound Logo is a Sonic Mnemonic – an audible mnemonic device that can make associations and links. Some examples are police sirens, the ringing of a telephone, the cry of a baby. We know that sound and music can also communicate emotions and create geographic as well as time-related links. The relationship of sound to colour, although perhaps not so widely known, is well documented by such people as *Goethe* & *Kandinsky.*

But, let's get to work: We have learned that a Sound Logo should ideally communicate brand attributes. What other qualities does a good Sound Logo have to have? The catalogue of parameters may vary slightly from case to case, but importance is usually placed on the following prime criteria. They are primarily the design parameters but they are identical with the judgement criteria for the selection of Sound Design Elements. In the meantime, the following criteria have pretty much become the accepted norm:

3.2 The Criteria

Fit
When talking about "fit", we don't mean fit as in healthy, but more like pertinent or relevant. Match or conform may even be more accurate. It wouldn't hurt if the Sound Logo had relevance to the brand. It's not paramount, but take a look at *Deutsche Telekom* (*T-Mobile*), *Audi* and *Intel*. They are benchmarks and all "fit" wonderfully. Ideally, a Sound Logo as part of a Sound Identity will reflect the brand's values and interpret its attributes into sound or music. If a good fit is not possible or, for whatever reason, not desired, it is very important not to contradict any of the brand's values or its attributes. This will most definitely have an adverse effect. It's like wearing a jacket that's much to big or small or in a style that really doesn't suit you. It's not gonna be flattering!

Distinctive
The Sound Logo has to be distinctive. Otherwise you are not going to be recognised or you'll be confused with someone else. Sometimes so-called "me-too" products want to have an indistinct generic sound – and possibly be intentionally mistaken with someone else. Otherwise, differentiation is essential for all brands, which makes this a very important parameter to get right. Differentiation means being different (surprise, surprise!) – but different from what? Or from whom? This is why it is important to know what's happening sound wise in your market sector – or better in the whole market place. When you know who is doing what, you must be able to quantify the data. This makes things measurable and therefore comparable. Only then can we identify clusters and free areas – and identify the benchmarks. To stay distinctive we recommend protection by registering the Sound ID as a Sound Trademark.

Memorable
Seems logical. Who would want something you cannot remember? This parameter is a little more difficult to quantify, as it is highly subjective. It relies on the talent of a composer or sound designer intuitively creating something that will have the properties necessary for retention by the masses. Being distinct and unique is half way there, but memorability is by definition, the ability of being able to recognise and recall. This is important for building associations. One way to achieve memorability is to be catchy and make what the Germans

call an "ear worm". It's a sort of a mini hit that you can't get out of your head. But one note or even just a sound can be both distinctive and memorable. For instance, the first note of "Sloop John B" from the *Beach Boys* or the first chord from "Hard Days Night" by the *Beatles.* Both are instantly recognisable and unmistakable. They are so emblazoned in our minds that there is no doubt that they are memorable (see also article *Audio Brands and Brand Sounds*). In fact "unforgettable" (Thank you, Nat!).

Flexible

There are two kinds of flexibility: musical and technical.

Musical flexibility is necessary if a theme is to be adaptable enough to be quoted in different musical contexts or styles. Not all melodies have the same degree of flexibility. Melodies containing strange intervals or blue notes will not be as easily variable as simple melodies based on the tonic and dominant notes of a scale. Some melodies in a minor key may be emotionally inflexible. A system has been developed to ensure that proposed themes or Sound Logos conform to certain rules to ensure both tonal and genre flexibility. If it is intended right from the beginning that the Sound Logo will be quoted in different music styles and instrumentations, then flexibility is a must if the Sound Logo is to achieve the desired maximum distinctive and memorability values.

Technical flexibility refers mainly to the choice of audio frequencies. Certain sounds will not work optimally in all applications – listen to the *Philips* simplicity Sound Logo and the *Audi* man & machine Sound Logo. Although both score top marks in "fit" by optimally communicating the brand values, when used in TV, Philips is so sharp that cuts like a knife right between your eyes. And Audi's backwards heartbeat leaves my televisions loudspeakers tongue hanging out – exhausted. What's more, neither of them can work 100% effectively cross-platform as they have limited and non-optimal frequency spectrums to allow them to do this.

So, ideally a Sound Logo should work equally well in all applications and touch points. For a number of reasons, this may not always be possible. Firstly, current and possible future applications must be identified by studying the various touch points. Then, by bringing the relevant touch points into descending order of importance it will become apparent which applications may or may not be compromised.

Concise

A good Sound Logo has to be short and to the point. My team has forbidden me to use the word "synergy," which used to be one of my favourite buzzwords. I wish someone would forbid me to say "less is more", because I hate it! But it applies here. No excess baggage. No waffling around. What good is a 10 notes Sound Logo that will end up having to fit a two-second visual. So for concise, also read "short". *Deutsche Telekom* (*T-Mobile*) manages to get its message across in 880 milliseconds (Yes, we measured it!).

So, we have established that the practice of Sound Branding has existed a lot longer then the term, but using Sound Logos has only really caught the imagination of the marketing community since Intel and Deutsche Telekom (T-Mobile) started having such documented success. At the time of writing, these two Sound Logos are still the benchmark with regard to both design and usage. Let's consider branding in its most elementary sense – marking something to make it recognisable – although not with a red-hot branding iron but with sound.

I have a cartoon in my head of a herd of cattle out on the prairie. Each cow has its individual brand mark on its rump, but acoustically, they are all just mooing. Sound Branding, as a process is able to give the cows that belong to a particular ranch its own unique moo – I mean voice. Ideally, it is a voice that reflects the image or values of the ranch – a voice that makes our sound branded cows stand out from the crowd.

These basic parameters, together with other findings, form the basis of the creative brief for creating the Sound Logo. They are the same exclusive objective criteria that must be agreed to in a creative workshop as judgement parameters.

So remember – "Fit, Memorable, Flexible, Concise, Distinctive". Unless all five criteria are met, it is the wrong idea and it should be discarded. Otherwise there is a big chance of you getting lost in the crowd with the "ding- dong dingers". On the web site of a well-known Sound Designer, a Sound Logo is defined as being "an acoustic illustration of an animated brand logo". I hope I have convinced you that it is much, much more!

4. Creativity – Strategy

Being regarded as a creative person, I am frequently asked the question "How do you always come up with an idea? Aren't you worried that you will dry up?" I now answer "Not any more!" I can remember in the early days when I have walked out of an agency briefing laughing and backslapping, just to find myself later biting my lip in the back of a taxi on my way back to the office thinking "Shit! What am I going to do?"

Then I started reading books on how to be creative, always titled something like "How To Be Creative" (Very creative title?). I learned a few basics that helped me define some of the criteria for approaching the task of composing. It taught me that one must have a structured process to channel the creative energy. It is no good having your net set wide to trawl in any ideas that come. The net must be set very slim so as just ideas that fit the defined criteria swim in. I am well aware that there are other opinions out there.

It would be out of the scope of this article if I try to go too deep into this aspect, but it is important to mention it, as this was the birth point of the development of a structured process for creating a Sound Identity – the process that is now called Sound Branding. Well, elsewhere in this book I'm sure you will find other terms for it, which just proves that the saying "ask three experts, get four opinions" could be true! But we are working with others in our field on developing a common terminology.

5. Intuition versus strategy

I would risk stating that developing anything that will be put to use should have a system. I am constantly surprised to discover how many decisions are made without weighing up the options and analysing needs. Sound Communications, to have optimal effect, cries out for a system. It must be analytical and use experience values and data. But a system should not totally rule out intuition. Intuition, a sublime sense based on buried knowledge and experience should not be confused with guesswork. The sound of a brand is far too important to leave to intuition. Brands need strategy. Nevertheless, intuition is vital for an accurate interpretation of data and statistics. It shouldn't be ignored when making judgement or forming an opinion. Many decisions are made based on the blind trust of data. When you are presented with information suggesting or stating that 1 and 1 is 3, I suggest you double check. There are a number of well documented historic boo boos that have been based on wrong or wrongly interpreted data (see section 'music experts').

But Sound Logo & Sound ID development isn't the only area of Sound Communications that should follow a structured process. Brand & artist partnerships (see article *Bands for Brands*), as well as the development of Corporate or Brand Songs will benefit from a systematic approach. Even the choice of music for a campaign or a single TV spot will be surer if based on existing structured processes and not purely personal preference – or guess work!

6. Future applications

Where can things go? Currently, the buzzword is Multi-sensory Communication. Here we are talking 3S2T – Sight, Sound, Smell, Taste and Touch. So, let's have a look at smell (what?). As we don't yet have Smelly- vision, we will have to consider the product itself, the point of sale – and the packaging. But stop – I'm not going to get into Multi-sensorial Communication, as it is apparent that we are not yet able to optimally use the dual-sensory communication possibilities we have had for years.

So, staying in the sound domain, we have the obvious touch points where sound can be used. But what about the product itself or the packaging? Using the sound of the packaging in brand communications is in itself nothing revolutionary. Over the years we have been involved with it ourselves a few times. The "crinkle-crinkle" of a *Schmackos* dog food bag was an effective Sonic Mnemonic which was built into radio and TV ads in the eighties. The sound of the metal bottle top holder for *Flensburger Pilsner* is still being used today. We also had a hand in the "thwack" of the *Visa Card* and the "Zisch" of *Coca-Cola Light* and more recently, the "draft fresh" sound of *Bitburger* beer.

But, how about the other way around. Taking the Sound Logo or another element of the Sound ID and using it in the packaging? Well, I haven't seen it yet, but there are methods of giving the packaging a sound that could tie in to other touchpoints and become a part of a Sound ID. I have heard of supermarkets with shopping carts that use Bluetooth to trigger small sound chips in packaging or shelves as the shopper passes by. For such applications, a brand's Sound ID is going to have to be pretty distinct to be recognisable.

7. Music Experts

Depending on who is responsible for the music choice, the end result can be very different. There is a danger of directors and creatives over-involving their egos and putting their desire of winning creative advertising prizes above the job of creating an optimal homogeneous and cohesive piece of audio-visual communication.

A common problem is that creative persons are more concerned with aesthetics then marketing matters. They have very little knowledge of the communicative possibilities of music, something that will disappear in the future when Sound Studies become a part of standard schooling. Some may even have the prime objective to be regarded as hip by their peers. (Mainstream? Moi?) I have experienced all the phases – *Yello, Classical, Vangelis, Moby, Buddha Bar, Massive Attack, Fatboy Slim, Cafe Koss* and *del Mar.* Trouble is that, demographically most of this music is elitist and has a minority appeal. It creates an impression of hipness in the mind of the creator but what about the target group? The worm must taste good for the fish, not the angler. If we look at car advertising, which usually sets the standards for aesthetics, we went through a long period of using drum n bass. One brand after another used the same music style, regardless of the brand attributes, the image or their client group. Even if we disregard the desire for differentiation, the creatives are using the same worms to catch all sorts of fish. Even low price, mass market car models have used cutting edge yuppie sounds in their TV advertising that went way over the heads of their potential buyers. The music must fit. Sounds simple, doesn't it? It is actually that simple. The music must fit in one way or the other. Whether the music is chosen to represent the brand or to illustrate a TV commercial, it must not alienate the receptor, or he will just switch his brains to standby and he won't feel addressed. Look at the target group and decide on a style or genre that won't alienate them. Decide on what function the music should have. Put these two things in your briefing and you are well on your way.

Still, marketing managers continue to rely on personal preference to define the sound of their brand. Why is this? Why is every one suddenly a music expert? The *iPod?* Who knows, but fact is there is a lot of over-confidence of decision makers regarding their music communication choices. The choices are often based on personal subjective taste or their own interpretation of the brand's perceived image when it comes to using certain styles of music or sponsoring a specific artist. Apart from the Intel study, there is a wealth of empiric evidence to prove that using the wrong music can actually harm the brand (see also article *Jingle all the Way?*). I suggest we all accept this. For those who don't believe that there is a right or wrong music, I suggest that this evening you create the ambience for a romantic candle light dinner – and put on a CD of German marching music (That'll get you both in the mood!).

Ok, we are only human, but in the present climate brands just can't afford to make errors. Some say that if you are not making mistakes you are doing enough, but make this an exception. Here you can't risk learning by doing, especially considering that music has the potential to become a brand asset and increase a brand's value.

8. Brand Sound Consultants

Some are still sceptical about the concept of Sound Branding, despite the overwhelming evidence of its benefits. Recently, a creative director sneeringly asked me why I think the world needs a Brand Sound Consultant. I answered that there are many areas where I would consider it wise to enlist the help of a specialist. For example, I have a financial advisor, a fitness advisor and an architect. Their experience and knowledge, not to mention passion and talent, have a huge value to me. There is no way I could achieve the same level of expertise in all these fields and I can't afford to make mistakes: Not with my building activities – or my health.

To illustrate the importance of expertise, I like to use the analogy of the architect and the builder because I think it makes it clear what we are up against.

Before we set out to build a house it is always a good idea to have a plan. Except for the lucky few who can allow themselves the luxury of "learning by doing" it is also advisable to have an architect. He will be educated in all aspects of house building and will have had the necessary experience to prevent you from making mistakes. He will be able to make sure that the owners' wishes and preferences are considered at the right time. He will also be able to advise on details that will improve the functionality of the building and possibly enhance its value. When the architect is removed from the equation, the builder will only build the house that the client orders. Sure, the basic requirements – such as floor, walls and roof – may not pose much of a problem. The problems come in making an efficient and effective plan.

What is needed, how will it be done and in what order? Even with a good builder who is helpful and involved, he can't possibly be held responsible for asking the right questions at the right time. Questions like: Where does the sun rise? Is it possible you will have more children? Do you really want the toilet next to the kitchen? The architect also acts as a moderator for channelling the opinions and wants of involved parties. He speaks fluent plumber, carpenter and electrician.

9. The ending

Sound Branding is powerful. The process of developing a sound identity is a set of steps that, when done correctly and in sequence, will greatly increase your chance of getting to your goal quickly and effectively. It is not rocket science, even if some may mystify things making the process seem complicated and therefore more valuable. The process, if it is a good one, must be logical and plausible.

The Sound Branding Consultant has to be clear and understandable and develop a common language with his client. In the end, marketing criteria and brand attributes must be translatable into sound and music. In short, he has to bring objectivity into a highly subjective theme. This role is not a replacement for the composer or music producer. It requires a whole different set of skills, experience and perception.

So, I managed to sneak in a few work examples and a chunk of my life story along with the compulsory history. But Sound Branding is not an absolute science: New knowledge is being amassed every day. The first movers and early adopters have long since been reaping the benefits. It is my hope that books like this will contribute to more effective and efficient sound communications by making guesswork history.

"When it comes to responsible dealings with brand sound in a social context, my appeal is: not everything that can be given a sound, needs one… Responsibility sometimes means: silence takes courage!"

(Rainer Hirt, 2009)

"Sound design is a crucially emotional communication element that has ascended to being an image carry-all, an associative anchor and a source of product differentiation. As a result, the increased awareness regarding acoustic brand management is not a coincidence: analog to binary coding, sound is also a lingua franca, which in itself knows no cultural or linguistic limitations."

(Lukas Bernays, 2009)

"Use and selection of music and sound for advertising and communication cannot be left to chance or the personal taste of a marketing manager. The motto "let's take some beautiful music to make people buy our stuff" is simply not enough."

(Kai Bronner, 2009)

D.
Basics and Principles of Audio Branding

Jingle all the Way? Basics of Audio Branding

Kai Bronner
Sound & Communication, Hamburg

1. Brands with sounds (What sounds?)

What do brands like *Nivea, Deutsche Bank* or *Porsche* sound like? Strange questions? Well, there are actually people who are concerned with such questions: experts in audio branding and corporate sound. But can brands sound at all? Let us approach it from a different angle. Imagine the sound of a Porsche Carrera motor engine. It has its very own sound which can be easily differentiated from that of a *BMW* or a *Ford*.

At BMW, for instance, every model range gets a particular sound profile. But not only the engine obtains a sound design, indicators, electric window lifts, audio cues and warnings are also acoustically optimised.

However, car manufacturers are not the only ones employing psychoacousticians and sound designers. These sound experts also pay attention to other products such as vacuum cleaners, hairdryers and razors. At food maker *Nestlé*, researchers even developed a device – the so-called "Krustimeter" – that allows analysis of munching sounds whilst eating crackers and cookies. As a result, every tested food product gets an acoustic fingerprint and the most promising sound samples serve as benchmarks. A treat and a feast for the ears!

While psychoacousticians and engineers are engaged in designing the sound of the product itself, experts for audio branding and corporate sound primarily concentrate on the sound of a brand. Thus, audio branding specialists create a brand sound for use within a brand's communication activities at points of contact such as TV, radio, internet, on-hold music and trade fairs. A brand sound consultant needs to be familiar with marketing and branding terminology and possess a "sound" knowledge of music and the sound domain.

However, product sound design and audio branding are not mutually exclusive. Think about the start-up sound of your computer or the default ringtone on *Nokia* mobile phones. Modern coffee machines let you know that the coffee is ready by playing a proprietary/idiosyncratic melody.

The Porsche product sound - as well as the sound of the motor engine - is distinct and conveys brand attributes like sportiness, power, drive/dynamics and thus contributes to brand differentiation. Brand attributes and brand differentiation are the main objectives in the work of brand sound experts.

These experts have to create a particular world of sounds that reflect the brand identity acoustically and hold the potential to establish a very distinctive brand sound. They define a so-called Sound Identity (SI) in terms of musical and sound parameters such as melody, instrumentation, timbre, and rhythm which can be listened to in soundsamples and sound collages. The sound identity SI must be strictly observed when creating brand sounds and can also serve as a benchmark in the design process of product sounds.

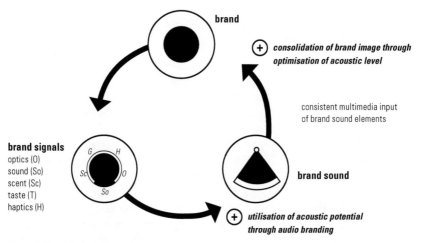

Figure 1. The audio branding process.

With regard to the terms used in audio branding there are obvious corresponding parallels to visual branding. In the sound domain, the audio logo represents the acoustic counterpart of the visual logo.

2. Elements of Audio Branding

2.1 Audio Logo (Sound Logo)
The audio logo represents the acoustic identifier of a brand and it is often combined with an (animated) visual logo. It should be distinct/unique, recognisable, flexible, memorable and fit the brand by reflecting brand attributes. German car manufacturer *Mercedes-Benz* launched its very first audio logo – as recently as November 2007. Rumours are that they had been working on it for years with several sound consultants.

The Mercedes acoustic trademark is a young choir boy singing three notes. As every human voice is unique and sung audio logos are rare, especially with automobile brands, it stands out from other automobile brands, it is recognizable and thus meets the demand of being distinctive. Due to social and communication aspects that I do not want to go into here, both singing and speaking voice are sensory stimuli that we pay highest attention to. Our brains are trained to analyse and monitor voices for rational and emotional semantics (see article *The Voice in Brand Sound*) that make voices so memorable. The Mercedes audio logo combines a human voice with a short melody (three notes) and therefore scores high in memorability. In order to make your advertising slogan become more memorable, add a melody or a voice to it and as a result you will get a well-known brand sound element: the jingle. But we will come to that later.

But what about the fit of the audio logo? Choosing the angelic voice of a young choir boy presumably conveys associations like "guardian angel from above" (safety driving) "The Star always shines from above". One of the major innovations of the new Mercedes brand design states that the visual three-pointed star logo always shines from above. This can actually be observed in the first TV commercials with the new audio logo.

The timbre of the voice is thin and eerie rather than steadfast and clear. In addition, the intervals between the sung three notes (approximately D4-D#4-C4) create tension and dissonance that give a negative impression and make one think of a child in need. Thus, the audio logo would be more appropriate for a children's organisation like *UNICEF*. Whether it fits the Mercedes brand is highly questionable. By the way, the audio logo is a preset sample from a sound library: LULU BOY3 from *Spectrasonics'* "Symphony of Voices".

2.2 Jingle, (Acoustic) Brand Theme

The concept of an audio logo as an acoustic brand identifier is a rather new one and has been developed only in recent years. This is a consequence of increasing awareness of the role of sound in brand management.

The first jingle, a sung advertising slogan, can be credited to *General Mills* which used a singing commercial to promote their cereal brand *Wheaties* back in 1926. The lyrics "Have you tried Wheaties? They're whole wheat with all of the bran. Won't you try Wheaties? For wheat is the best food of man," were performed by four male singers who eventually became known as the *Wheaties Quartet*. This singing commercial was aired on the radio station *WCCO* owned by General Mills. Radio was the medium that spread advertising messages in the form of jingles and the term jingle also became a synonym for a radio station's on-air musical or spoken station identity. Other well-known jingles include "You'll wonder where the yellow went - when you brush your teeth with Pepsodent!" or "This Is The Place To Be - on ABC."

In Germany, the English slogan of the *MARS* chocolate bar "A Mars a day helps you work, rest and play" was adapted and given a melody and thus became a very famous and memorable jingle "Mars macht mobil, bei Arbeit, Sport und Spiel" (Mars makes you mobile, at work, sports and play). After a certain time of exposure to a jingle the link of lyrics and melody become so strong that the lyrics can be left out and will be conjured up automatically in the consumer's mind by the melody alone. The prime function of a jingle is to make an advertising slogan more memorable and less hard selling or intrusive, whereas an audio logo should additionally evoke associations that fit the brand's values and attributes (Jackson, 2003, p. 9). However, there is no strict boundary between audio logo and jingle. The (slightly modified) melody of a jingle or an audio logo can also be integrated into various spots and background music (soundscapes) and act as a sort of leitmotif. When used in this way it may be called brand theme as it creates a clear association to the brand.

The *Mc Donald's* jingle "I'm Lovin' It", which was launched in a global brand campaign in 2003, is a little snippet from the song "I'm Lovin' It" by *Justin Timberlake*. The relationship between Timberlake and Mc Donald's was a cornerstone of the new campaign and resulted in the sponsorship of Timberlake's European concert tour and other public activities. After an initial amount of exposure, the slogan part of the jingle (I'm Lovin' It) was omitted and nowadays, playing only the first part (ba da ba ba baa...) invites the consumer to complete it with the slogan.

Music in general and specifically the partnership with the artist Justin Timberlake enabled McDonald's to establish several marketing activities, such as sponsoring Timberlake's tour and promoting his song and his artistic talent, that all fit perfectly together in terms of a holistic/integrated brand campaign.

Although only a small part of the song "I'm Lovin' It" became the well-known jingle, the song itself played no (substantial) role in the marketing campaign. Thus, it did not become what, in audio branding terminology, is referred to as a "brand song".

2.3 Brand Song

Unlike a mere "commercial song" used only temporarily for promotional purposes, a brand song is connected and attributed to the brand by regular and consistent use in brand communications and eventually becomes a real acoustic trademark. Brand songs may be adapted for special applications or target groups and can get a face-lift from time to time.

Prominent examples of brands that have used such songs for many years in their advertising and communication touch points are two air lines: *British Airways* and *United Airlines*. "Flower Duet" from the opera *Lakmé* by French composer *Léo Delibes* has been representing - in different arrangements - the brand British Airways for more than 20 years. United Airlines' commercials have been accompanied since the late 1980s with *George Gershwin's* "Rhapsody in Blue", which was licensed from Gershwin's estate. In Germany, the song "Like Ice in the Sunshine" has accompanied advertising of the ice-cream brand *Langnese* since the 1980s. In the 2000s, the song was reinterpreted in different musical styles like Hip Hop, Techno, Country and Pop (see article *From Brand Identity to Audio Branding*).

In German advertising history, the commercials of the beer brand *Beck's* are real classics. They feature a green sailing ship as a key visual and the signature song "Sail away" (see article *Acoustics as Resonant Element of Multi-sensory Brand Communication*). The tune was originally sung by *Joe Cocker*, conveying brand attributes like adventure, freedom and manliness with his striking, rough voice.

2.4 Brand Voice

Voice is an essential design element in acoustic brand communication. A voice evokes emotions and associations not only through the singing but also the spoken voice (see article *The Voice in Brand Sound*). Apart from the timbre of a voice – which is affected, inter alia, by age and gender; and in the case of Joe Cocker, is rough – the spoken voice is characterised by rhythm, accentuation, pitch and loudness which are all subsumed under the term prosody. A brand voice represents a brand and thus the perceived character/personality of the voice must fit the brand personality. If you listen to a commercial of *IKEA* Germany you immediately realise that a Swedish company is talking to you as the voice in the commercial speaks with an unmistakable Swedish accent. Diction and way of speaking go well with the brand character of IKEA and the guy in the commercial represents a typical employee of IKEA.

2.5 Sound Icon, Sound Symbol

While the audio logo is a core element in audio branding, sound icons or sound symbols usually work in a more subtle way. Sound icons are short acoustic signals that can also be integrated into an audio logo or a brand song. Sound icons indicate by analogy a certain aspect or feature of the brand benefit. A descriptive example is the opening fizz of a *Coca-Cola* can or bottle, which was integrated into several commercials over the years, clearly demonstrating the freshness of the beverage. In a similar way, the *Kit Kat* crack allows associations with the crunchiness of the chocolate bar.

In fact, a sound icon is the equivalent to what - in the domain of Auditory User Interfaces (AUI) - is referred to as an auditory icon. Auditory icons represent 'everyday sounds' whose meaning is familiar. In contrast, the meaning of the so-called earcons is not known from everyday life as the mapping of the related sound is arbitrary. For example: If you play a quiz on your computer and type in the correct answer the applause sound is an auditory icon, while two short beeps would form an earcon.

As symbolic sounds like earcons are not limited by any similarities they can be designed more freely and with emphasis on their aesthetic properties. *Elias Arts* developed a suite of 1-2 seconds of functional sounds for *IBM*'s laptop *ThinkPad* that emanated from a single creative brief considering the ThinkPad's brand attributes (see article *Finding the Rhythm…*). These sounds – one might call them sound symbols in the audio branding domain – each represent a distinct function and enable users to emotionally register a particular function while being brand-based.

2.6 Brand Soundscape

In analogy to the Gestalt design principle of figure and background, sound icons, sound symbols, brand voice, brand theme, audio logo and adequate sound textures can be combined to form an ambient sound that fits the brand sound identity and reflects the acoustic brand attributes. This brand soundscape is suitable to support the brand experience on websites, corporate buildings, on-hold music applications, brand flagship stores, presentations and trade fairs.

2.7 Corporate Anthem

Apart from the external effects at the customer and business partner levels, audio branding elements can also create an impact within the brand company. Suitable fields of applications include company events, internal company presentations, company staff cell phones with ring tones and mailbox sound design and system sounds on company computers. Application at the internal company communication level can strengthen the identification of staff members with the company and increase the emotional bond between them. This may result in more loyalty and team spirit and increase staff motivation. For this purpose, a corporate anthem is most suitable (see also article *From Brand Identity to Audio Branding*). Apart from a catchy tune, the lyrics – expressing the corporate philosophy – are the central element of a corporate anthem. In Japan and the USA, corporate anthems are more prevalent than in Europe. In Japan, corporate anthems are sung by the members of staff at company parties.

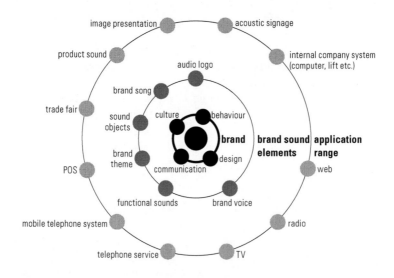

Figure 2. Brand sound elements and their range of application.

3. Music Marketing and Brand Entertainment (Where do brands sound?)

In 1986, *Levi's* started its "Back to the Basics" advertising campaign which decisively influenced the use of music in advertising. The commercials, broadcast all over Europe, used popular and lesser known soul and rock classics which corresponded well with the brand identity of the classic jeans model "501" according to the slogan "originals stand the test of time". The campaign led to a revival not only of the jeans model but also of the advertising songs. Following chart successes various types of cooperation between corporations and the music industry developed resulting in many brand name compilation CDs, advertising hits compilation CDs and other marketing and sponsoring activities of the brand company within the music sector. The already mentioned cooperation between Beck's and Joe Cocker was not limited to the artist's commitment for the advertising song. Beck's also sponsored his 1997 concert tour in Germany under the "Sail away '97" logo. To create a close connection between artist, tour and brand, the tour was endorsed with substantial measures within the framework of integrated communication via various communication channels of the Beck's brand.

Including music in marketing and brand communication is not limited to compilation CDs or sponsoring of musicians. Brands increasingly provide contents and opportunities to reinforce the relationship with consumers and to enhance brand loyalty. The term here is brand entertainment. Due to technical progress, digitalisation and media convergence, the range of audio applications is increasing with many new developments, e.g. podcasts and videocasts, audiobooks etc. (see article *Acoustic Brand Management and the Digital Revolution*). Here, selection and presentation of contents are becoming more important, i.e. form and content adjustment within an integrated communication. In order to benefit most of the brand potential through brand-adequate acoustic design and presentation, audio branding has become inevitable.

Mercedes-Benz – moving music for mobile people

Mercedes-Benz is a brand that combines the opportunity of audio-visual information brokerage with the advantages of brand entertainment.

In June 2004, Mercedes-Benz launched *Mixed Tape*, a platform for as yet unknown music by promising artists. Every eight weeks, a new mix of carefully selected tracks by international, mostly unknown artists is released. Genres range from melodious pop, NuJazz to electronic tracks and relaxed downbeats, quite unlike the usual charts releases and without style limitations. Selection criteria are – in line with the brand values of Mercedes – quality, innovation and uniqueness. The project also offers a platform for newcomers and talented young artists. Everybody can send in or upload his/her music with the chance of becoming one of the artists featured on a future Mixed Tape release.

Since February 2008, the Mixed Tape platform also includes a monthly video magazine featuring trends, styles and news in the context of the presented music with music videos, album tips, portraits of artists and other interesting facts. As a consequence, the connection between brand and audio-visual contents has been meaningfully supplemented by Mercedes-Benz through integration of a mobile playback unit into its vehicles. Thus, an *iPod* can be connected via an interface kit with the car's audio system. Operation and title selection is done through the multifunctional steering wheel, while title navigation is carried out on the display panel.

4. Relevance and Significance of Audio Branding (Why do brands sound?)

Apart from the growing number of communication instruments with acoustic components, audio branding and corporate sound are becoming more important also due to changing economic and communication scenarios. The explosive increase in the number of brands and products calls for consolidated measures and efforts to raise a brand image and to set it apart from the competition.

When brands become visible through audio logos, brand songs and characteristic brand soundscapes, it will be easier to discern and distinguish them from the mass of choices. An advertising banner on the internet, normally ignored or overlooked, can become more interesting with acoustic signals. Maybe one even has to scroll down to bring the sounding banner into view. This will not only attract the interest of a possible customer but also prompt him/her to act, thus considerably increasing the impact of the advertising contact.

The number of communicative brand methods is increasing in the same way as the choice of brands and products is continuously growing. The classic communication methods are supplemented by other activities such as events, sponsoring and product placement. In addition, with the establishment of the internet, novel ways of communication have become possible. Consequently, media planning has become more demanding and provision of the optimum media mix has become even more challenging. Also, no longer able to take in the overabundance of information, the consumer is developing an increasingly negative attitude towards advertising. To ensure that a consistent and clear brand image is nevertheless conveyed, the methods of brand communication must be coordinated in an integrated communication concept. However, purposeful input of music and acoustic branding elements within the framework of consistent acoustic brand management can counter the decreasing efficiency of communicative advertising methods. This is supported by several factors:

– The passive effects of music, which can be used to activate and attract attention, also work with a distracted listener and over several repeats.
– Sense of hearing is non-directive, i.e. while the consumer may not watch, he/she nevertheless continues to listen.

– Musical messages are easier to process than text messages since they require less cognitive effort and can also work unconsciously.
– Through the so-called "visual transfer" a few beats of advertising music are sufficient to evoke the respective commercial in front of the "inner eye". Combinations of radio and TV spots, for example, can initiate visual transfer effects and as a result increase the advertising impact and the efficiency of the communicative method.

Due to tough competition and saturation of brands, almost no differences in quality or function of brand products exist. Differentiation through quality and product characteristics is becoming less and less possible. Instead, brand differentiation is increasingly done through communication and brands compete with each other in a proper communication contest (Esch, 2008, p. 33). In this contest, emotional and experience-driven factors play an ever important role since strong brands also feature a strong emotional bond. And how better to communicate emotion and experience than through music? Imagine the effect of the *Bacardi* commercial without the appropriate sound. This is why relaying of consumer relevant experiences as well as emotional charging of the brand are today's major challenges in brand communication and advertising. The experience profile is becoming more important than the product profile. For this significant reason, multisensory branding, i.e. branding covering a range of senses, is considered one of the central issues in brand communication of the future (see article *Acoustics as Resonant Element of Multi-sensory Brand Communication*).

Results from studies on "musical and voice-fit" demonstrate the significance of brand-congruent acoustic elements (North et al., 2006). Acoustic elements which "fit" the brand achieved significantly better results regarding brand awareness, advertising recall and willingness to buy than music that did not "fit" the brand. Unsuitable music can even have negative effects.

"In association with spoken words music can give a notional sharpness that is head and shoulders above speech itself" (Zander, 2006, p. 478; Rösing, 2008, p.95). However, music can outmatch the effects of impact and expressiveness of images, as demonstrated by the movie soundtrack. In Great Britain, the movie "The Da Vinci Code", based on *Dan Brown's* novel of the same name, had to be toned down to be deemed suitable by the British Board of Film Classification for audiences aged 12 years and over. In fact, this was not due to its violent images but to the movie score. After revision of the audio score – the graphic material remained unchanged – the movie was eventually classified as suitable. The fact that music and sound can have effects that cannot be achieved by images alone may be exemplified by the film adaptation of *Patrick Süskind's* novel "Perfume". In this movie, impact and power of smells and scents are transported mainly through music. The association between sense of smell and sense of hearing is obvious: Both are volatile, have highly emotional effects, recall memories and possess a strong associative character. This is reflected in the language of the movie, where scents are "composed" and base, middle and top notes of a perfume must be tuned like "chords".

5. Coda

When you read the heading of this article, did you hear a tune in your head? Audio branding follows this general principle, namely the linking of acoustic stimuli with associations and meanings as well as stimuli of other sense modalities (visual, olfactory...). Whilst listening to music or a series of sounds I can think of a brand, just as a brand can evoke a melody, an advertising slogan or a jingle in my head. But does the song ("Jingle Bells") whose melody you may have had in your head while reading the article heading fit the article content? The aim of branding is not only circularisation, identification and differentiation of a brand, but also to link positioning contents and to support image effects: Thus, the brand fit of music and sound plays an important role in audio branding.

The manifold application possibilities of music and sound in brand communication, the attainable effects and the advantages of the acoustic sense, which have been exemplified in this article, demonstrate that use and selection of music and sound for advertising and communication cannot be left to chance or the personal taste of a marketing manager. The motto "let's take some beautiful music to make people buy our stuff" is simply not enough (Zander, 2006, p. 478).

In the visual area, experts have long been listened to. It is high time to show as much appreciation to the ears of customers and stakeholders as to their eyes. The often demonised advertising sector will thus be able to contribute its share in counteracting the generally escalating acoustic pollution. And for the future, there is hope for more melodious sound and aesthetically pleasing design in communication as well as products and services.

References

Bronner, K. & Hirt, R. (2007). Audio-Branding. Entwicklung, Anwendung, Wirkung akustischer Identitäten in Werbung, Medien und Gesellschaft. München: Verlag Reinhard Fischer.

Esch, F. - R. (2005). Strategie und Technik der Markenführung. München: Vahlen.

Helms, S. (1981). Musik in der Werbung. Wiesbaden: Breitkopf Härtel.

Huron, D. (1989). Music in advertising: An analytic paradigm. Musical Quarterly, Vol. 73, No. 4, pp. 557-574.

Jackson, D. (2003). Sonic Branding. An Introduction. London: Palgrave MacMillan.

Knouf, Nicholas A. (2007). Encouraging the Expression of the Unspeakable: Influence and Agency in a Robotic Creature. Master thesis, Massachusetts Institute of Technology, Cambridge (MA).

Kilian, K. (2007). Multisensuales Markendesign als Basis ganzheitlicher Markenkommunikation. In: A. Florack, M. Scarabis, E. Primosch (eds.): Psychologie der Markenführung. München: Vahlen.

Luckner, P. (2002). Multisensuelles Design. Eine Anthologie. Hochschule für Kunst und Design. Halle.

North, A. C., Hargreaves, D. J., MacKenzie, L. C. & Law, R. (2004). The effects of musical and voice 'fit' on responses to advertisements. Journal of Applied Social Psychology, 34 (8), pp. 1675-1708.

Ringe, C. (2005). Audio Branding. Musik als Markenzeichen von Unternehmen. Berlin: Verlag Dr. Müller.

Rösing, H. (2005). Musik in der Werbung. In: Das klingt so schön hässlich – Gedanken zum Bezugssystem Musik. Bielefeld: Transcript.

Zander, M. F. (2006). Musical influences in advertising: how music modifies first impressions of product endorsers and brands. Psychology of Music, 34 (4), pp. 465 – 480.

The Voice in Brand Sound

Mark Lehmann
Communications Consultant, Berlin Germany

Audio Brand Identity

We are exposed, daily, to a flood of advertising messages these days – each and every day brands are competing for the customer's attention. The Institute for Marketing and Communications Germany estimates there are approximately 6,000 advertising contacts per consumer per day. However, only a tiny fraction of all these messages will be effective. For one thing, competition requires differentiation. The launch of a new brand has to be carefully orchestrated in order to create a brand identity that stands out and be instantly recognizable in the vast sea of information. A brand has to appeal to all our senses and, thereby, make us feel something. This means focusing only on the visual aspects of a brand is not nearly enough.

Brand identity is sought in a variety of ways – and one is through acoustic expression. In order to successfully establish a brand in today's marketplace, it is almost necessity to acquire an audio identity, as well as a visual one. Music, sounds, and the human voice are all essential elements in successful branding strategies. It is a well-established fact that music and sounds elicit a strong emotional response in listeners, in terms of identifying a brand and its message.

The targeted acoustic orchestration of a brand's launch comes under various names, for example, 'audio branding', 'sonic branding', 'sound branding', 'acoustic branding', and 'corporate sound'. These terms describe the creation of a brand sound as an integral part of an overall communications strategy.

In form and content, the elements of music, sound, and voice[1] are often each treated differently, and music and sound are normally given more prominence. Even though voice is regarded as important, with its sound qualities, it usually takes a back seat to the other two. This is all the more surprising when considering that almost no brand can make do without a voice!

---

[1] *The human voice can be differentiated in terms of the speaking voice and singing voice. We will only focus here on the speaking voice, even though the singing voice functions in much the same way. The singing aspect, with its particular aspects of musicality, needs to be dealt with separately.*

Brands are perceived in very complex ways. Each individual aspect of a brand's message – including (and, likely, even especially) the speaker's voice and the particular expression of his or her voice – can dramatically change the overall impression of a brand, and therefore how it is perceived as a whole.

Because of its very specific role in sound branding, the speaker's voice, however, has to be considered very carefully. Voice, as an element in sonic branding, can lend uniqueness to a brand and enhance its recognition. Voice endows the brand with emotional qualities, so infusing in the recipient the desire to listen more carefully and to absorb the information.

Voice is the audio impulse that is paid the greatest attention. It is especially the tone of voice that impacts human communication in very subtle, yet significant ways. The perception of voice tone is acquired through evolution and social conditioning. The sound of a voice is carefully analyzed by the listener as to its informational content and its communication intent. These decoding processes can hardly be suppressed, a phenomenon which becomes abundantly clear when we are exposed to a spoken language we don't understand. And this is true even when not only the language is unfathomable, but when the cultural conventions too, differ greatly from our own.

Voice Tone and Brand Personality

We are all familiar with the following scenario: a telephone is ringing and someone simply announces, "It's me". The voice of the speaker evokes a series of complex associations and emotions within the listener as to the person's identity, and an image is formed in the mind of the listener about the speaker. These complex associations are not played out on a conscious level. It is quite amazing that people develop these complex images based on so little other information, for example, visual clues.

This is comparable to the visual perception of a person based purely on physique. We associate physique with certain personality traits, which can change to a certain degree as more information is known, yet often without changing the overall impression. In a way, the voice is the audio physique of the person and, like physique, is rooted in every individual's anatomy.

In brand communication, voice without any visual presence, known as the off-voice, bestows its personal aura and unique sound to a brand. This character transference, however, does not only work one-way. Depending on the strength of this pattern, a counter-productive, unintended effect may occur.

This phenomenon can often be observed when widely-known people's voices are used in advertising. The voice of a famous person like, for example, that of the German soccer icon, *Franz Beckenbauer,* may lead to some confusion in the minds of the listeners as to the intended message. Associations in the minds of listeners may, as intended, concern mobile phone technology, but the intended message could be lost in the recipients' own connections to soccer. This distraction – this pulling of the listener away from the message – is known as the "vampire effect", and is further evidence of how strongly a voice can impact brand identity. And, in this case, it may tip the scales in favor of the "brand", Beckenbauer, rather than, for example, the intended mobile phone provider or the financial institution.

This example illustrates how the impact of voices can vary considerably. The perceived personality of a voice depends very much on the degree of its familiarity, and the listeners' experience attributed to or associated with a particular voice. Apart from such 'testimonial' voices, the voices most often used in brand communication are those of professional speakers who convincingly convey desirable qualities of audible expression through their tone of voice and way of speaking. But a particular speaker's characteristic features and the unique identity always shine through. And, as a professional speaker lends his or her voice to a variety of brands over time, it can lead to a kind of overload, an over-familiarity.

When listening to the same voice, over, and over within changing contexts, a certain conditioning unfolds. It can be assumed that the voice becomes increasingly associated with surrounding contextual elements. The recipient or listener forms a pattern of the voice in his mind, and then makes mental adjustments as he hears the voice in different contexts. This image of the voice is very often the result of audiovisual and purely auditory mass-media perception and can thus be considered to a certain degree as especially identifiable, and thus overly identifiable. The voice then becomes too prominent and functions as an audio brand in itself.

The pitfalls of overloading a voice with too many contextual qualities should be taken into account when selecting a speaker, if the brand's sound is to remain autonomous and unique. Voices are used in many different areas of brand communication. The impact of voice, however, is not equally strong in every medium. The speaking voice in brand communication is used mostly in mass media. A focused and brand-specific deployment is necessary in order to be clear about its intended purpose and its target audience.

In strictly auditory communication, like the telephone and radio, voices have a much greater impact than in audio-visual media. The sensory modalities in telephone and radio are limited by the acoustic medium, as no further information is available to help with interpretation. The telephone is a purely audio medium, and it is presently undergoing a renaissance due to new and innovative applications. The relative length of time spent on the phone, and the considerable number of contacts made via the phone, make it a medium for which acoustic design becomes ever more important. For example, technical innovations have supplanted call centers, and we now have greatly improved interactive voice systems. So, here too, the same voice can be heard over and over, and this greatly impacts the perception of the brand identity. The creation of a voice character, the so-called persona, is thus becoming more and more important in the success and general acceptance of these applications.

Brand Voice and Corporate Sound

The distinctive voice element in brand communication is called brand voice[2]. The brand voice stands for the brand's personality (and its values) and is often part of an acoustic signature. The spoken brand name along with the core message will normally receive widest dissemination, as it indicates who the sender of the brand message is. As a rule, these are played toward the end of a TV, radio spot, or movie theater commercial, as an "ending" but they can also be applied in other areas. Often it is a combination of the visual and the acoustic logo, plus the spoken brand name.

The voice has to be considered a key element of the brand identity. Thus, it is strategically wise to really make use of the personality and uniqueness of a voice. This holds true not only for voice but for all acoustic elements that make up brand communication. The auditory experience thus enhances consumers' appreciation of a brand's unique qualities. The process of how this linkage occurs can vary depending on the strategy and direction through which the company markets its brand.

Beyond the subject of brand voice, voices are used in ad campaigns, and this should to be dealt with separately. Whereas a brand voice essentially represents the brand's unique personality, campaign voices also activate and solidify specific advertising messages. Campaign voices generally cannot be used over a longer time period, and their impact and effectiveness very much depend on advertising strategy.

What both usages have in common is that the selected voices add value to the way a brand is perceived. Consequently, a voice's characteristics have to do justice to the brand's identity. The overall strategic direction must ensure that audio identity is solidly established, as well as maintaining consistency across all relevant areas. A brand voice ought to, as should all brand sound, be professionally produced and fully integrated into the wider corporate identity.

A possible strategy to better integrate voice into sound branding is through the creation of what's known as a "corporate voice[3]", as part of an overall "corporate sound". The corporate voice is an element within corporate sound, and it is the conceptual integration of the brand-specific voice. This approach seeks to arrive at distinct voice characteristics through a brand's inherent qualities and values. And, it requires interdisciplinary knowledge and competencies.

The personality of a voice has to be determined and formulated in such a way that it serves as a base for subsequent creative decisions in relevant areas of sound branding.

Such a briefing determines the constants, which are necessary for the creation of voice

---

[2] The internationally-used advertising expression, "brand voice" results from the differentiation of the "brand voice" and "campaign voice". Comparison, Lehmann, M. Voice Branding (2008).
[3] German branding agency MetaDesign, for example, refers to the voice element in its Corporate Sound concept as Corporate Voice.

applications. The creative aspects include the choice of the voice, direction, and script. These aspects influence a voice's effectiveness and are variables in designing a brand-specific voice. It is nearly impossible to evaluate these aspects separately as they all impact one another.

These important interdependencies complicate the conceptual design of voice as part of sound branding. The existence of a corporate voice often overrides 'from the gut', spontaneous decisions when choosing a voice for a particular brand. Brand identity is achieved through consistently employing a brand's values. A brand-specific voice strengthens the brand's impact and image and adds personality. The utilization of voice in this way can make brand communication more memorable, emotional, and authentic. Voice enhances a multisensory brand experience.

References

Bregman, A.S. (1990). Auditory Scene Analysis: The perceptual organization of sound. Cambridge, Mass. et al.: MIT Press.

Eckert, H. & Laver, J. (1994). Menschen und ihre Stimmen - Aspekte der vokalen Kommunikation. Weinheim: Beltz.

Fährmann, R. (1982). Elemente der Stimme und Sprechweise. In: Scherer, K.R. (ed.), Vokale Kommunikation, Nonverbale Aspekte des Sprachverhaltens. Weinheim et al.: Beltz.

Graham, Marcus G. (2004). Voice Branding in America. Vivid Voices, inc.

Hasebrook, J. (1995). Multimedia-Psychologie: Eine neue Perspektive menschlicher Kommunikation. Heidelberg et al.: Spektrum Akad. Verl.

Lehmann, M. (2008). Voice Branding - Die Stimme in der Markenkommunikation. München: Reinhard Fischer Verlag.

Truax, Barry (2000). Acoustic Communication (2nd edition). Westport, US: Ablex Publishing Corporation.

Percy, L. & Woodside, A.G. (1983). Advertising and Consumer Psychology. Lexington, Mass. et al.: Lexington Books.

Audio Brands and Brand Sounds: Relevance of Timbre in Audio Branding

Hannes Raffaseder
St. Pölten University of Applied Sciences

1. Introduction

Timbre is the third human primary sense to perceive acoustic phenomena next to volume and pitch. It enables differentiation between two equally loud and equally high-pitched sound signals. Compared to the colour palette in painting, different timbres, as it were, are the prime material for every acoustic composition. Unlike melodies, accord sequences or rhythms, timbre has initially no consciously designed structures which have to be analysed on a rational level in the process of perception. Therefore, it is often unconsciously perceived and experienced, while at the same time totally immediate and direct. We react to timbre mainly on an emotional level.

Surprisingly, this parameter has attracted little interest in the past. For a long time, prominence was given to, e.g., organisation of pitch, volume or time structure such as rhythm and form of music. The question as to how a piece of music sounds and what instruments it should be played with was less relevant. Yet, timbre in particular can also achieve a substantial effect within a very short period of time and transmit emotion as well as information.

From the increasingly sophisticated instrumentation in romantic orchestra music, the timbre or soundscape compositions of 1960s contemporary music, the easy-listening synthetic to the random, digitally stored acoustic incidents of the sampling technique, the relevance of timbre in acoustic design has grown considerably. The characteristic sound[1] of a singer

---

[1] *The comprehensive English term sound has no German equivalent. It encompasses every sound event, i.e. speech, sound and noise. For the characteristic sound of a band or a singer, timbre is the decisive factor, while timing, phrasing and several other musical parameters also play an important role.*

or an entire band is a crucial factor for quality and success in pop, rock or jazz. Only if songs are performed by charismatic artists with unique, almost inimitable voices and instrumental sounds – undoubtedly the case with continuously successful artists such as *Madonna, David Bowie, Mick Jagger, Sting, The Who, U2, Robbie Williams* –, will they have the desired effect. Lyrics such as "Smoke on the water, fire in the sky" are actually not that captivating to the masses, neither are melody and rhythm of many songs exactly amazing. Hence, the fact that - even decades after its release - we start to drum our fingers or even sing along during the opening bars of a chartbuster such as "Smoke on the water" is mostly due to *Deep Purple*'s characteristic sound. Conversely, songs with no characteristic sound often lose their appeal rapidly. If, for example, karaoke singers try to imitate the original as much as possible, the attempt will obviously fail. What matters is not the original effect of the performed song, but the fun factor.

In some electronic dance music styles, timbre seems to be at the centre of interest, e.g. in drum and bass or experimental techno, where harmony sequences or melodies are dropped in favour of rhythms played with elaborate sounds. The increasing recognition of sound design[2] in film and video is another indication for the growing relevance of timbre. Also, product sound design, i.e. design of the timbre produced by or with commercial items, is turning into an important competitive factor in more and more business sectors.

In the early 1990s, the automobile industry began with the purposeful design of the sound of engines, doors, switches etc. The costs of the necessary acoustic measurement laboratories are about 100 million Euros. This emphasises the relevance of audio branding as well as the fact that corporations consider this expertise strictly as company secrets[3].

Despite these developments, the present expert literature on acoustic media design continues to occupy itself with the relevance of rhythm, harmony, melody and their potential to create suspense, to influence perception of time or to express specific emotions. However, deliberate choice, purposeful input or possible impact of timbre as fundamental raw material of any acoustic design – and thus obviously also audio branding – are still considered more theoretically than practically. Below, general observations on acoustic perception and their role in human communication will be followed by closer analysis of the characteristics of timbre and their relevance in audio branding.

---

[2] *The concept of sound design has several meanings in media production. On the one hand, it includes conception and design of the complete sound track (spoken words, noises and music), while on the other hand, it implies the development of suitable sounds for various products.*

[3] *This refers to a lecture by Dr. Friedrich Blutner during the international symposium „AllThatSounds – Die Tonspur in den Medien", on 27th March 2006 at Museumsquartier Vienna, Austria. Blutner is managing director of Synotec GmbH, a product design company. Cf. Blutner (2006)*

2. "The whole is more than the sum of its parts". The importance of intermodal design concepts

Our senses produce individual stimulus qualities which are normally associatively connected when perceived simultaneously. For example, we can distinguish between "loud" and "quiet" or between "bright" and "dark", but not between "loud" and "dark". Objectifiable comparison or continuous transition between individual sensory perceptions is also impossible. Therefore, our environment can only be perceived in fragments. Our sensory organs are obviously specialised in the perception of such fragments. Only through associative linkage of sensory impressions in combination with earlier experiences is an additional value achieved which enables mental supplementation of missing parts and thus a more detailed description of the environment.

During simultaneous perception of different stimulus qualities we continuously try to develop causal associations. Visual and acoustic sensations not only complement each other, but are also in permanent correlation influencing and overlapping each other. In brand communication, exclusive concentration on the visual level can hardly bring about optimum results. Hearing – not to mention taste, haptics and smell – must be considered much more strongly. However, equalisation of sensory perceptions in a media context may not automatically result in improvement since a lasting increase in quality can only be achieved through cooperation, not just coexistence of different sensory stimuli. As optimum cooperation of all stimulus qualities is always mandatory, intermodal[4] conception, design and production must be aimed for at all times[5] (see article *Synesthetic Design – Building Multi-sensory Arrangements*). For this purpose, the characteristics of the individual sensory organs must be examined and compared to guarantee optimum supplementation of sensory perceptions.

3. Some distinctive features of acoustic perception

In a world dominated by visual sensations, the question arises as to how relevant acoustic perception is at all and hence, what role sound can play in brand communication.

---

[4] *Intermodal means combined analysis, conception and design of the various levels such as form, colour, light, speech, noise, music etc. In today's media production, these concepts are lacking mainly in regard to a combined conception of visual and acoustic elements. Often, even in the purely acoustic domain, association of individual elements is still surprisingly rare. Many disciplines, such as linguistics, musical sciences, technical acoustics etc. deal with acoustic phenomena. In movie production, dialogue editor, sound designer, Foley artist, composers etc. work relatively independent of each other on the design of the sound track. A comprehensive observation of interplay, similarities and differences of the acoustic phenomena of speech, noise and music is still rarely observed in theory and practice.*

[5] *Important suggestions on this subject matter are to be found in the publications by Randy Thom available online at http://www.filmsound.org (as of 30 Aug 2006). Comprehensive approach on an intermodal analysis of the sound track in Leeuwen (1999).*

3.1 The omnipresence of hearing

Unlike the eye, the ear cannot be simply closed. Also, as it is not fixed to a visual angle it receives all audio signals from its environment. Hence, the flow of acoustic information is generally much too complex to be consciously perceived and analysed in total. Usually, the majority of acoustic stimuli present in the immediate environment are perceived only unconsciously. Often, this unconscious perception is erroneously not at all considered as perception. The so-called cocktail party effect describes the fact that even in a relatively noisy environment, people are able to focus on a specific acoustic event. From experience, while we are able to focus our listening attention in a noisy pub without any problem to a single talker at our table, we simultaneously perceive the voices around us as babbling sound. However, if something of interest is mentioned at a neighbouring table, our attention may refocus immediately so that we can listen in on the other conversation. This situation, which undoubtedly has been experienced by many, demonstrates that not only consciously perceived acoustic information is processed in the human brain. Evidently, we also continuously listen to and analyse the allegedly unimportant background noise. Otherwise, any reaction to the words of interest from the neighbouring table would be impossible. Thus, in human communication, an essential role is always played by numerous subliminal stimuli, which at times may not be noticed by the recipient, but which still significantly influence the overall impression.

While acoustic perception always happens automatically, albeit often unconsciously, visual perception requires active looking. Looking at something always also implies looking away from something else. While the visual sensation of humans in a specific environment always depends on what everybody is looking at and what they want to see, acoustic sensations remain more or less the same for everybody. It does not matter whether we want to hear a specific background noise or not. We will hear it as not hearing it is impossible.

Thus, looking is a selective process depending on the individual vantage point, whereas hearing, in contrast, is uniform, encompassing and uniting. Since the acoustic scenario in a specific environment is more or less the same for everyone present, sound signals can have a uniting, collectivising effect. This aspect is demonstrated, for example, by military marches when everybody is moving to the music as if remotely controlled. The same can be observed with dance music in a disco. In speeches by public speakers, it is often attempted to use this acoustic effect. When considering populist politicians or dictators, in particular, it becomes apparent that the actual content of such speeches plays a minor role. The striking timbre of the voice, combined with a succinct speech rhythm and a unique speech melody, literally forces the audience to pay attention.

3.2 Interconnection of formation, event and reception

In its original form, sound energy is inherently volatile. Before the invention of the phonograph by *Thomas A. Edison* (1847-1931) in 1877, storage of sound was impossible. Acoustic events had to be experienced at the time of their formation, i.e. "now or never". If an acoustic sensory stimulus is to be consciously perceived, the concurrence of formation, event and reception requires total attention, active experience and participation from the listeners. The direct, immediate, often strong emotional effect of acoustic events is possibly associated with this fact. According to experience, acoustic events are perfectly suited to transport moods and emotions. Obviously, this is of enormous importance for brand communication. Undoubtedly, music in film, advertising, at corporate events or product launching etc. is often intended to fulfil this function. However, mighty resounding fanfares or "sugary" violins are not necessarily required to lend emotional depth to an acoustic message. Small acoustic gestures are often sufficient to transport a multitude of emotions. For example, a sigh may imply exhaustion just as well as depression, compassion or arrogant rejection. The timbre of the spoken language can also be vital for the meaning of a sentence. Even the slightest differences in individual tones can result in a dramatic change of meaning. Therefore, in acoustic events, a multitude of fine nuances with lasting influence on content and effect can be perceived and distinguished.

Timbre and memory

As sound could not be stored for a longer period, it was impossible to identically repeat a specific acoustic event. Even when acoustic sources as similar as possible were vibrated with mechanisms as similar as possible, the acoustic event was generally different – to a greater or lesser extent. For example, breaking glass, knocking on doors, bird song or live performances of *Beethoven*'s 5th symphony may always sound relatively similar, but never completely identical. Thus, acoustic events were always unique. This may be the reason why specific sound signals can be remembered for a surprisingly long time. For example, many people remember many nursery rhymes even in old age and despite the fact that they have not sung them for many years. And the chartbusters of our teenage years will stay with us for life when many other details from this period of our life will long be forgotten.

In the advertising industry, which is very important for audio branding, it can be observed that commercials with distinctive sounds, spoken slogans with memorable timbres or generally unusual acoustic design are often remembered for years. The relationship between acoustic stimuli and memory has been analysed in several scientific studies.[6]

While these initially appear to reach differing conclusion (Roth, 2005, p. 121), it must be stressed that – due to the intermodal interdependencies – it is not simply a question whether a commercial with music is more memorable than one without.

[6] *A good overview of relevant studies is provided by Roth (2005), p. 251.*

It is not only relevant if, but also how acoustic elements are used. If, for example, background music should communicate a pleasant mood to create a positive attitude towards the product, this music is obviously perceived unconsciously. In order to avoid diversion from the intrinsic advertising message, it must not attract attention. Studies have also shown that an acoustic stimulus may be better remembered that the product name if precise signals and cross-references are established between acoustic elements and content. Thus, sounds can become mnemonic retrieval stimuli for the commercial, the advertising message and the brand name (Roth, 2005, p.127).

As mentioned in the introduction, characteristic sound is a significant factor for quality and success in the music business. This underlines once more the importance of careful selection and design of all sounds and noises used in a commercial. Even years after their release, many songs are recognised within seconds. In an experiment repeatedly carried by the author out with many students[7], the songs "Wonderwall" by British band *Oasis* and "Don't Speak" by *No Doubt* were positively identified by a large majority after the first guitar chord. At first, this is quite surprising as in both songs, the chord is very similar and could set off numerous other songs. Neither rhythm, nor melody or harmonic progress had been developed in such a short period of time. Hence, the characteristic timbre was the only distinct feature in this case. This simple experiment, which was also repeated with several other songs, demonstrates that it is not only "guitar" that is heard. The parameter of timbre is perceived in a highly discriminatory manner where even very fine nuances may be distinguished. The fact that more than seven years had passed between release of the songs and the first realisation of the above mentioned experiment shows once more that obviously, timbre may be retained in memory for a considerable length of time (see article *A short History of Sound Branding*). The frequent playing of a song in various radio stations is often considered as the main reason for this rapid and definite recognition. However, most chartbusters are only played frequently during the first months after their release and after that more rarely. If that was the reason, it should be possible to also remember and positively identify often repeated slogans with the first syllable or at least the first word years after their first release. It should also be noted that this experiment works well not only with frequently played songs but generally with acoustic sounds. The sound of the harmonica from the movie "Once upon a time in the West", for example, is quickly recognised by everyone who has just once seen this movie.

---

[7] *This experiment was carried out by the author during lectures at the Universities of Applied Sciences in Hagenberg and St. Pölten to illustrate the importance of timbre to the students. It was therefore performed for teaching purposes and has not yet been validated scientifically. The experiment was repeated in various terms with about 600 students of media technique. As results were always comparable, these findings and the conclusions drawn thereupon should be included here.*

3.3 Acoustic events as stimulating sensory input

The specific characteristic of acoustic events, namely to attract attention, is of particular importance for brand communication. This characteristic is used in every day life in many alarm signals, such as the car horn, the ringing of a telephone or an alarm clock etc. and is of particular advantage in an environment overcrowded by visual stimuli. Unfortunately, the prevailing opinion appears to favour high volume in acoustic signals. However, delivering a lecture in a loud voice, for example, rarely helps to get the attention of a restless audience. In general, a careful mode of speech with a variety of sound parameters, consciously set pauses or pointedly used quiet speech are much more efficient.

Acoustic events can also stimulate us without demanding an immediate reaction as is mostly the case with various signals. Often, this stimulation happens unconsciously. Again and again, we may catch ourselves unconsciously tapping or even humming or singing along with a piece of music that is being played somewhere in the background. In scientific research on the effects of advertising, the potential of acoustic events in stimulation has been generally recognised and supported by empiric studies (Roth, 2005, p.117).

3.4 Sound as a result of dynamic processes

A sound event is always directly and causally related with stimulus and acoustic source thus unequivocally mirroring their characteristics. Fundamentally, every audible sound signal is always the result of a preceding dynamic process set in motion by a respective exertion. Movement and change are always basic prerequisites for acoustic events. Total silence exists only in a completely static and thus lifeless environment. Therefore, acoustic events are also always an expression of vitality and life (Blutner, 2006). Evidently, this characteristic should play an important role in brand communication. An indisputable relationship between the physical process as cause and the acoustic event as effect can always be established.

These are the decisive differences compared to visual perception. Optic impressions do not change over time unless the observed objects or their environments themselves change. For example, the *Mona Lisa* painted in 1505 by *Leonardo da Vinci* may be viewed effectively in the original. The eye produces, especially in this static environment, highly precise and detailed information on the surfaces surrounding us, from whence the ear can only receive silence. However, visual perception of the movements and changes, whose results can be analysed by acoustic perception, can only be insufficient. Already a few individual images per second convey continuous movement and rapid changes result in blurry contours. Some activities are happening too fast altogether to be properly grasped by visual perception alone. For example, even with close inspection of a pistol the actual shot cannot be detected, whereas the resulting sound is certainly clearly perceived. Therefore, stills and slow motion are applied in the media to enable detailed analysis of specific situations.

3.5 The difficulty in describing acoustic perception

Hence, with the sense of sight we preferably perceive static objects which are also physical, tangible and thus describable. It is generally possible to sufficiently and coherently describe objects with the use of several characteristics (colour, form, size etc.) and relevant object identifications. Since hearing always conveys information on dynamic activities, it is impossible to point with a finger to a sound. Acoustic events are neither tangible objects nor can they represent these (Leeuwen, 1999, p.93). This fact explains why a sufficiently accurate description of acoustic events generally fails, except for signal theory parameters (e.g. frequency, spectrum, amplitude progression etc.). In most cases, not the acoustic event itself but the triggering process of formation is described. Often comparisons are used: "It sounds as if...". These difficulties result in the fact that even in media productions, acoustic events are occasionally still considered diffuse, unspecific, mainly subjectively tangible and hardly objectifiable sensory stimuli and of less importance than visual elements. It is undeniable that this problem in describing sound signals often entails enormous difficulties for the development of brand sounds and audio brands. For example, it can complicate the communication between sound designer, clients, marketing or advertising experts etc. just as much as searching for a suitable sound in large digital sound libraries.

4. Relevance and effect of acoustic events

Analysis of the characteristics of acoustic perception shows that purposeful input of sound in brand communication is not only profitable but also absolutely essential for best possible effect. Below, the relevance of acoustic events, its transmission and possible effects are discussed.

4.1 Information content of acoustic events

As already stated, sound signals can never be comprehensible objects per se, but only the result of a preceding or maybe simultaneously occurring physical process. Acoustic event and process are therefore intrinsically tied to each other. Thus, sounds and noise always mirror the characteristics of these processes and of all objects involved. Hence, they possess an objectifiable information content which allows reference to the sound source, the sound stimulus and the space wherein the acoustic events was triggered. In many cases, material, size or shape of the sound source may be identified without any difficulty since location and movement of the sound source can be heard. Generally, state and size of space can also be perceived and speed, intensity, type and rhythm of the sound stimulus may be determined, at least approximately. For example, the sound of footsteps allows conclusions regarding type of shoe (e.g. spike heels, sandals, clogs etc.), floor surface (e.g. wood, tarmac or gravel), walking speed etc. Occasionally, the sensitivities of the walker may be identifiable. Usually, we can recognise from the sound of walking whether the walker is hurrying, strolling, stumbling, staggering, jumping around joyfully etc. Therefore, specific emotional undertones are not only represented by melodies and rhythms in music, but already dwell in each individual sound. It is important to note that the information content of acoustic events – in contrast to the visual level – is not limited to the surface of objects but may, via dynamic actions, give information on their physical and material state. The resulting acoustic event also always conveys the quality (Blutner, 2006) of the entire process, i.e. of the stimulus and all involved objects. This characteristic is successfully utilised, e.g., in the acoustic monitoring of mechanical processes. If an engine runs lumpy or components show signs of wear, this is immediately recognisable from the sound. Acoustic signals are also often revealing in material testing. The exterior of a cheap piece of furniture made from chipboard may appear solid, yet the actual quality of the object can be revealed quickly by the sound of simple tapping.

For acoustic brand communication, the information content is of major importance since it can transmit – potentially in the fraction of a second - the desired characteristics of products and the special quality of a brand without requiring particular attention or even rational performance from the consumer. For example, the often used clear, bell-like sound logos in mobile phone communication convey clarity, as a symbol for the quality of the respective provider so to speak.

4.2 Symbolic content of acoustic events

The symbolic content of acoustic events describes the fact that effect and relevance of a sound signal always depend not only on the context of the stimulus and the perceptive environment, but also on personal experience and the listener's current emotional state. Therefore, acoustic events can be perceived very differently even if signal theory analysis produces almost identical results. For example, the whooshing of a mountain torrent and the noise from a motorway, when perceived at some distance from the sound source, are technically almost indiscernible, while their effect and relevance are almost the opposite for most people. Here, attribution of a specific symbolic relevance can be based on association with personal, subjective memories as well as on cultural, historical and societal aspects. These findings have been utilised for many years in movie soundtracks, especially in combination with the descriptive technique or the mood technique.[8]

Hence, sound and noise not only represent the action that triggered them and the environment they can be heard in, but also their overriding relevance. A sound signal which can be technically described as broadband static may symbolise untouched nature - in the case of a mountain torrent - as well as modern, busy and noisy mobility – in the case of a motorway.

---

[8] For good introductions into soundtrack composition techniques see Schneider (1997) and Bullerjahn (2001).

Ultimately, the context plays a major role in the interpretation of the acoustic event. Therefore, sound and noise are often deemed ambiguous, confusing, not very meaningful and – compared to visual signals – insignificant. However, when considered within a holistic, intermodal concept, which naturally includes the context, sound signals have a mostly unambiguous implication. In this case, the symbolic content may be used to convey unique, product- or brand-inherent connotations. Again, no conscious perception is required for this. These acoustic messages are unconsciously perceived by the listeners.

4.3 Direct effects of sound signals

Undoubtedly, sound signals, apart from their information and symbolic content, can have quite direct and immediate effects on the human organism and subjective sensitivities. The mere thought of the sound of chalk scratching on a blackboard is unpleasant to many people. Cries of fear – regardless whether of human or animal origin – not only alarm us and force us to act, but may also literally "go right through" us. Specific acoustic wave patterns can cause physical reactions and influence pulse and breathing rate. Some of these direct effects of sound signals have biological, neuronal or psychological causes. Others may be explained by human phylogenetic development: the sense of hearing could be life saving in case of ambushing danger.

While in Far Eastern cultures, sound has traditionally been used in healing and pain relief[9], and the positive effects of music therapy are now also recognised in Western cultures, scientific review of these direct effective properties remains surprisingly incomplete to date. A growing interest in interdisciplinary research in the field of music effects has only been noted in recent years.[10] Regretfully, apart from numerous highly interesting professional publications, several dubious, highly contentious, popular science findings[11] have also been published. Especially the relevance of direct effects for acoustic media production and the resulting fields of application in sound design for film, TV or brand communication have as yet been only sparingly researched or systematically reviewed.

---

[9] *The esoteric wave of the 1990s introduced, inter alia, the sound bowl therapy to the West where it enjoys great popularity.*

[10] *A compilation of contributions to this topic can be accessed here: http://www.tomdoch.de/ (as of 30 August 2006). For popular science, yet readable introductions in neuronal effects see Spitzer (2005) and Jourdain (2001). In October 2006, the effects of music were the topic of a major international congress in Baden/Vienna http://www.mozart-science.at.*

[11] *The probably best known example in this context is he so-called "Mozart effect", whereby in an experiment performed in 1993 by Gordon Shaw und Frances Rauscher, listening for ten minutes to the music of Wolfgang Amadeus Mozart resulted in an improvement in mental abilities. Although the experiment of this study could not be reproduced in 1999 by Kenneth Steele at the Appalachian State University in Boone, North Carolina, it received enormous media attention and was profitably marketed. The American Don Campbell patented the term "Mozart effect" and uses it on http://www.mozarteffect.com.*

5. Classification and categorisation of timbre

The difficulties to sufficiently describe acoustic events and the resulting problems in acoustic media design have already been mentioned in section 3.5 above.

In contrast to volume and pitch, timbre is not a one-dimensional characteristic perceivable on a scale ranging from loud to quiet or high to low, but a complex and composed dimension. Technically, it can be compared to measurable parameters such as the spectrum and especially the formants.[12] However, the chronological progress may also play a decisive role. The technical parameters are important mostly to experts. While they are measurable and objectifiable and can also be specifically designed with digital signal processing methods, they nevertheless describe the actual human perception only insufficiently. Psychoacoustics, which attempt to combine perceived characteristics with technical measurands, essentially identify the following parameters for the description of timbre: Klanghaftigkeit, extent of fluctuation, roughness, volume and density, acuity and brightness. These terms are explained in detail elsewhere.[13]

However, a comprehensive theory for description, classification and categorisation of sound signals is still missing.[14] It should include significant aspects of timbre as well as different effect and relevance patterns linking to measurable signal characteristics in order to significantly improve the quality of acoustic media design.

The "AllThatSounds" research project[15], which ran until Mai 2008, tried to help solve this problem. Aiming to improve the search for suitable sounds in media productions, the following four approaches were examined and optimised:

1. More efficient and consistent description of sound signals via meta data by the creator.

2. Determination as to in what context and for what aim etc. a specific acoustic event is used in media production.

3. Mathematical or signal theoretical models for analysis of sound signals in line with technical parameters.

4. Semantic-associative categorisation to determine the relevance of sounds or their effects, respectively, for the recipient.

---

[12] Formants are maxima in the frequency spectrum of a sound signal which can be traced back to the specific resonance area of the sound sources. They are independent of basic frequency and thus characterise sound source and with it also its specific timbre.

[13] A general introduction into the aspects of acoustic perception in combination to important basics of psychoacoustic may be found in Raffaseder (2002), chapter 5. For a comprehensive review of this subject matter from a technical perspective see Terhardt (1998), for a comprehensive description of important psychoacoustic facts see Howard & Angus (2001).

[14] Trend-setting contributions in Truax (2001) and Leeuwen (1999).

[15] http://www.allthatsounds.net

6. Summary

In conclusion it can be stated that sound and noise, as inseparable raw material in acoustic communication, can contribute significantly to brand communication. In contrast to musical dimensions such as melody or rhythm, which are more often at the focus of attention and which may be mainly typified by pitch, volume and time structure, the significant characteristic of individual sounds and noises is first and foremost timbre. Rational evaluation is not absolutely necessary for the perception of acoustic events. Individual sounds can have significant effects already after a fraction of a second, transport a lot of information and express emotions, even when perceived only unconsciously. The information as well as the symbolic content inherent in every sound signal can be utilised in a variety of ways for acoustic brand communication. The same may apply to the comparably sparingly researched direct biological, neuronal or psychological effects. In any case, acoustic events must always be assessed and designed in the respective context. Hearing characteristics are multisensually merged in the complex interplay of the senses (Blutner, 2006). Therefore, in acoustic brand communication, only an intermodal concept will result in the desired effects. Visual and acoustic design elements must aim for joint transmission of the product or the brand, respectively, including its characteristics, specific quality and attributed emotions with as many interactive and supplementing cross-references as possible.

References

Blutner, F. (2006). *Klang ist Leben, unpublished manuscript of a lecture held at symposium ‚AllThatSounds – Die Tonspur in den Medien' at Museumsquartier Wien, 27th March 2006.*

Bullerjahn, C. (2001). *Grundlagen der Wirkung von Filmmusik. Wißner-Verlag: Augsburg.*

Howard, D., Angus, J. (2001). *Acoustics and Psychoacoustics. Focal Press: Oxford.*

Jackson, D. (2003). *Sonic Branding. Palgrave MacMillan: London.*

Raffaseder, H. (2002). *Audiodesign. Hanser Fachbuchverlag: Leipzig, Wien.*

Roth, S. (2005). *Akustische Reize als Instrument der Markenkommunikation. Deutscher Universitätsverlag, Gabler Edition Wissenschaft: Wiesbaden.*

Schafer, R. M. (1993). *The Soundscape: Our Sonic Environment and the Tuning of the World. Destiny Books.*

Schneider, N.J. (1997). *Komponieren für Film und Fernsehen. Schott: Mainz.*

Terhardt, E. (1998). *Akustische Kommunikation. Springer Verlag: Berlin, Heidelberg, New York.*

Truax, B. (2001). *Acoustic Communication. Ablex Publishing: Westport, USA.*

Van Leeuwen, T. (1999). *Speech, Music, Sound. MacMillan Press: London.*

The Process of Brand Sound

Rainer Hirt
Anemono; www.audio-branding.de, Konstanz

1. Introduction

When dealing with the development of an acoustic brand identity, it is advised to take a closer look at the planning, development and supervision of this often complex task beforehand to be able to create customized solutions.This article is meant to help gain insight as to how brand sound development can be operated and which methods are needed to approach the topic brand identity and sound. The article is to be seen as a process outline, based on the diploma thesis *Brand Sound Process. Methodology and Direction of Pattern of Acoustic Brand Profile Development* (german title *Der Markenklangprozess*) and on the author's practical experience.

It is also meant to help creators of audio and visual content approach this seemingly abstract topic. Furthermore, it aims to provide decision makers with insight into the concept of successful brand sound development and experts with inspiration to further develop their own methods.

2. Process Theory

The selected course of system conditions is called a process. It stems from the Latin word *procedere,* which means to proceed. In terms of [ISO 12207] a process is a set of interrelated means and actions that transform input into results. Processes are often separated into smaller processes.

2.1 Models of Process

Process models of brand development, as well as sufficiently used marketing plans, were observed and analyzed. Useful basics were also found in the stable process models of software or automotive development. The following approaches can be found when dealing with process definitions and models: First of all there are condition definitions. In determinate processes every condition is the result of a preceding condition. In stochastic processes there is a given chance that the condition of a system is a result of preceding conditions.

Chronological definitions can be found in so-called continuous processes such as power generation, and discontinuous processes such as agriculture. The words material (physical operations on actual objects) as well as informational (the exchange or handling of information) define the material-related processes.

For example: service processes can either be developed in a material or informational manner. The processes that contain the planning and control of aims and measures, as well as personnel management and organizational-structure arrangement are described as management processes.

Operative processes depict goods and services, the outcome of which can either be material or informational. The concept of core process (a derivation of core competence), or primary process, comes from the area of business administration. Core process or primary process consists of a combination of activities, decisions, information and material flow. Together these form the competitive edge of a business. Support Processes, on the other hand, support the core process.

2.2 Process Design
The basic pattern of a brand sound process is made up of the following stages:
Objective > Planning > Decision > Execution > Control

The design of the brand sound process is derived from this basic structure below:

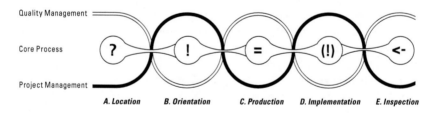

Figure 1. Basic structure of brand-sound process.

Core Process
A. Location
B. Orientation
C. Production
D. Implementation
E. Inspection

Support Processes
1. Project Management (PM)
2. Quality Management (QM)

2.3 Brand Sound Techniques
Based on the comprehension of brand identity, it is advised to develop individually adapted techniques.

Brand Sound Programmes
A. Modular Programme
  Coordinated sound system. Especially interesting for businesses and brands with a range of products, where brand sound elements can be put into effect. An example at this point would be the *Avira* (German manufacturer of anti-virus software) brand sound.
B. Modification Programme
  Development based upon an already existing sound space. Usually found in the shape of a brand song or audio logo. Example: *02* A song by the group *Leftfield* serves as a sound space. This either remains constant over time or is slightly modified.
C. Attribute Focused Programme
  A single music or sound attribute is focused upon and thus enables thematic variations. Example: *UPS*: Tango as an attribute. *Red Bull*: a voice as an attribute.

3. Core Process Content
One of the components of the brand sound core process is the stage that directly deals with development of an acoustic brand identity.

3.1 Core Process Stage 1: Locating Brand and Sound
The first stage is about identifying the current state of the market. This includes market and competition situation, business structures (employees, branches etc.), supply, the history and philosophy of a business. Furthermore an analysis of self image and public image should be made, to provide objective insight to the business.

Acoustic Competition
Acoustic competition describes sound events in the sensory environment of the application area. Within the brand sound development for a software manufacturer, for example, it is of great importance to analyze and evaluate the acoustic signals of a computer environment.

3.2 Core Process Stage 2: Brands and Sounds – First Orientation

Verbal Sensitization Part 1 – The Orientation Workshop
How do you bring participants in contact with the abstract topic of Sound Definition in a short and precise manner, without scaring them away or swamping them with seemingly scientific instruments, hence spoiling interest in the topic? You try to sensitize them. In doing so, it should be clear which sound rank the participants of an orientation workshop are in.

Unlike visual brand awareness, sound awareness is in a far more rudimentary condition. It is possible to provide a basis for sound and music understanding by means of conversation, description and lateral thinking methods, as well as discussion rounds on the topic of sound. Subsequently, methods of sound sensitization are described.

Sound Adjective Selection
The workshop participants are asked to write down all associations, ideas, application areas etc. they can come up with in connection with brand personality and sound, in a predetermined amount of time (between 5 and 10 minutes). The results of this brainstorming are then evaluated and documented together.

Lateral Thinking
This well-known creative technique is used to stimulate the participant's capacity for abstract thought. It also serves as a good training for the following workshop chapters.

Object Sound Description
Two objects are to be described in terms of sound impression based on their appearance. Sound Game: 'I hear with my little ear...' Two groups are formed to compete against each other in a sound game. Course of the game: One team member at a time listens to a well-known sound example through headphones (for example: raindrops). This team member then has to describe the sound to the other team members, but cannot be concrete, i.e. cannot use descriptions that create connotations.

Reflections Round
The problem that arises through subjective experiences and associations becomes clear quite quickly in the following conversation. By dealing with sound in general, its effect on individuals and the manifestation of subliminal influence, a basis is created upon which the acoustic methods of sensitization can be established.

Brand and Sound Sensitization (Part 2) – The Orientation Workshop
The second part of the workshop contains brand specific parameters like brand essence, brand values, goals, visions etc. Brainstorm techniques (mind-mapping etc.) help to create a shared understanding of brands.

Acoustic Sensitization
Talking about sound is one of the best ways to analyze and evaluate what is heard in a brand context. By means of quantitative and qualitative evaluation methods in the form of polarity profiles, brand sound preferences can be determined. In the next step these preferences lead to a relevant catalogue of requirements.

Orientation Conclusion

So far this exercise has shown that the separate sound query modules have to either be specifically customized, according to the respective projects, or they need to be redesigned completely in order to master the mass-market of sounds.

Brand Sound Moods

After sorting and documenting the brand and sound specifications in a catalogue of requirements, the composers, or rather the sound designers, can be briefed. The sound moods are to be seen as an impression of brand sound. All the elements of brand sound are to be derived from this. In other words, they are the foundation of brand sound. The sound moods are developed in collaboration with the sound designers and are then embedded in various formats.

Sound Moods And Their Formats

Moodtrack
A 10 – 30 second soundtrack.
Suitable for: Presentations (selection process).
Moodtrailer
An audio-visual production of separate moods. Suitable for: Presentations (selection process) and for AV relevant Brand sound programmes.
Sound-Mood Architecture
Core cells model. Also used in the final phase of the process.
Suitable for: Presentations (selection process).
Sound-Mood Set
Back-up model for derivations in presentations. This back-up model consists of a music track arranged in succession (sound element A > sound element A+B > sound element A+B+C etc.). Suitable for: Presentations (selection process). The Brand sound techniques matching the brand identities can be found in the catalogue of requirements.

Mood Conclusion

The display formats are suited for the customers and projects depending on their preferences. An integrated programme developed for a linen goods company, for example, needs a display format that that can show a scope of sound elements.

An entertainment company on the other hand, would pay more attention to sound quality and effect of the track (sound duration). Putting oneself in the position of the customer, at a point when insecurity arises and help is needed, is essential in combination with these display tools. In future more display forms will definitely be needed to cope with oncoming media etc.

Selection Of The Appropriate Mood

The selection of an ideal sound mood is something that should be done in collaboration with the decision makers. In doing so, it is important to use a conclusive evaluation and selection procedure. In the past, the following procedures have produced very good results:

Catalogue Of Requirements
The catalogue of requirements, based on the orientation results, is also used in another workshop. Suitable for: complex mood layers and decision makers with little affinity to sound.

Query Matrix
A preferred mood is chosen in a common dialogue according to notation. Suitable for: theme focused moods.

Scenario Evaluation
Assembly of a typical sound application surrounding for a qualitative evaluation. An everyday situation is simulated and the sound events are evaluated according to function, brand fit and effect. Suitable for: Brand sound designs related to their surroundings (Museums, exhibitions etc.).

3.3 Core Process Stage 3: Production Of The Elements

All the elements based on the selected brand sound moods can now be prepared. At this point it is advised to do one more test round in order to counteract the routine-deafness of the sound designers.

3.4 Core Process Stage 4: Implementation

Brand sound developments arise in situations such as upcoming advertising campaigns, commercial launches, redesigns, brand expansions and even a change of crew... As a person in charge of an acoustic brand management, it is important to stay in close contact with those responsible in order to act accordingly if technical problems or obscurities should arise. A sound style-guide is a useful tool when it comes to directing sound as an integrated part of brand communication. The sound style guide includes sound parameters, scores, application guidelines as well as technical descriptions and instructions.

3.5 Core Process Stage 5: Inspection

A target group's stylistic preferences and perception can change, therefore it is essential to constantly verify the brand sound and adjust it if necessary. There are no rules as to how often a check-up should be performed. However it is advised to react to social events or musical preferences.

3.6 Support Process: Project Management

An important part of successful brand sound development is project management. It consti-tutes the interface of the different areas and is a fundamental component of brand sound development.

3.7 Support Process: Quality Management

Efficient quality management is needed to ensure successful further development of existing models and methods. Sound brand creators should also be aware of their ethical responsibi-lity towards the environment. Keyword: sound ecology. For example the *Deutsche Telekom* reacts to current events by varying their audio logo (whistling, trumpeting, etc.).

Conclusion

The core of acoustic brand profiling is acting responsibly when dealing with customers and creative people. Regrettably brand sound seems to be creating a gold-digger-type mood of late. Many people see it as a way of making quick money. To that effect, many brands end up with more harmful than supporting results.

With the help of a plan, provided it is followed and not used for purposes other than intended, the wheat is separated from the chaff. When it comes to responsible dealings with brand sound in a social context, my appeal is: not everything that can be given a sound, needs one...

Responsibility sometimes means: silence takes courage!

References

Becker, J. (2002). *Process Management. Berlin: Springer Verlag.*

Esch, F.-R. (2005). *Strategie und Technik der Markenführung. München: Vahlen.*

Fichter J., Kunz R. (2004). *New Genus and Species of Chirotheroid Tracks in the Detfurth-Formation of Central Germany.*

Flückiger, B. (2001). *Sounddesign. Die virtuelle Klangwelt des Films.*

Helbig, R. (2003). *Prozessorientierte Unternehmensführung. Heidelberg: Physica Verlag.*

Hieronimus F. (2003). *Persönlichkeitsorientiertes Markenmanagement. Eine empirische Untersuchung zur Messung, Wahrnehmung und Wirkung der Markenpersönlichkeit. Frankfurt am Main.*

Kaplan, R. B., Murdock, L. (1991). *Core Process Redesign. In: The McKinsey Quarterly 2, pp. 27-43.*

Osterloh, M., Jetta, F. (2003). *Prozessmanagement als Kernkompetenz. Zürich: Gabler Verlag.*

Schmelzer, Sesselmann (2003). *Geschäftsprozessmanagement in der Praxis. München, Wien: Hanser Verlag.*

Acoustic Brand Management and the Digital Revolution

Lukas Bernays
audio relation - acoustic communication & corporate sound

1. The Digital Lifestyle Goes Audio

Nowadays, anyone who is out to capture hearts and mindshare communicates on multiple levels. A modulation of marketing instruments that appeal to identity, emotionality and trigger product differentiation is the mantra of every brand manager. It's a magic bag, and in the mix, information, entertainment and education define modern brand management.

And this is exactly the potential of digital media: As a stabile foundation for showcasing audiovisual brandexperiences, digitalization has given birth to a trend towards new, interactive communication forms. This trend, with its ubiquity and manifold psychological impact, will transform all businesses into media-makers whether they be middle-sized or multinational.

Sound design is a crucially emotional communication element that has ascended to being an image carry-all, an associative anchor and a source of product differentiation. As a result, the increased awareness regarding acoustic brand management is not a coincidence: analog to binary coding, sound is also a lingua franca, which in itself knows no cultural or linguistic limitations.

Music downloads, podcasts, Internet radio, audio guides and books, ringtones, etc. are all expressions of the new digital audio lifestyle. Their intense proliferation could lead us to think that our lives were somehow aurally barren before their advent. A flash in the pan? On the contrary: these (as of yet) subcultural manifestations can be expected to variegate and creep more and more into our collective awareness.

2. From Medium-Bound to a Boundless Medium

"It goes without saying, that people will soon regard the compact disc as being a cute anachronism hailing from the 20th century" (Moby 1)

The digital revolution in the recording industry began when the compact disk was launched in 1982. Initially the two seemed an odd couple. Based on continuous soundwaves impinging on the eardrum and air pressure swells, music could be said to be analog technology manifest. In contrast to previous recording techniques, in which sound was transmuted into physical analogies, the compact disc stored the acoustic waves in the form of binary codes.

The new silver platter, touted as the chosen and bringer of glass clear sound, garnered considerable criticism at the outset: "straight from the freezer", "shrill", "loud", "sterile", "devoid of charm", is how some hifi-critics once postured about the new sound. Still the CD has become the most successful music medium ever created. The digitalization of analog signals has changed our mindsets regarding the process forever. Today, a quarter of a century later, the CD has lost its sex appeal. Meanwhile, its reduction to being a pure data storage medium has become more popular.

The invention of the MP3 established the portability of music files for once and for all. As a fathomless source of virtual variation, they not only allow music consumers to do what they please with them, but also to choose any storage medium.

3. MP3 - The Birth of the Music Exchanges

MP3 (Moving Picture Expert Group Audio Layer 3) is a data compression algorithm, that was developed at the *Fraunhofer Institut* in 1995. At the beginning, the disruptive power of the format was not even apparent to its inventor *Karlheinz Brandenburg.* For him, it was merely a data compression algorithm, which could reduce the space required by digitalized music by 12 to 1.

The psycho-acoustic trick of the tale, secreted in MP3 and the formats[2] that followed, lies in the truncation of all the frequencies beyond the perception of the human ear. In other words, the MP3 algorithm should compress audio files without any noticeable loss of quality. These smaller data streams translate into shorter loading intervals and reduced storage requirements. The compression algorithms, so-called encoders, spread like wildfire and soon the generation and distribution of MP3s over the Internet became child's play. What followed afterwards has been described today as a classic example of media convergence.

---

[1] *The New Yorker Moby aka Richard Melville Hall represents a "new" kind of "notebook musician": Forged by the omnipresent digitalization, he produces everything alone on the computer.*
[2] *MP3 is, with certainty, the most popular but not necessarily the best quality format. The following potential format aspirants produce better sound and at a lower bit rate as well:*
1. AAC Plus 2. Ogg Vorbis 3. WMA 4. MP3Pro 5. AAC

Michael Robertson and *Shawn Fanning*, two young programming cracks recognized the revolutionary potential shadowing the discovery of the MP3. In particular, the appearance of *MP3.com* provoked rampant democratization: Newcomer bands without recording contracts used the portal as a platform to attract attention through free downloads. This talent-promotion model has since encouraged countless imitations.

But the real time bomb was the 18 year-old Shawn Fanning. *Napster*, his music exchange platform, which till this very day symbolizes the Internet music revolution, leveled the playing field. Orignally the student and music aficionado had planned to write a simple search program for songs because then supply was short on the Web. In the end, his program worked as follows: I swap my music files for yours and vice versa. The Web-networked computers became a gigantic jukebox. The Napster server surfed the harddrives of registered users and published updated lists throughout the Web to the same. Besides that, Napster was dead simple to use. Even fans that had no songs to offer were allowed to participate. As a result, Napster was able to nochalantly thumb its nose at the traditional music distribution constraints. Needless to say, a world came tumbling down for the music business. A new digital music lifestyle was born and at the turn of the century already some 40 million exchange participants were busy as bees.

4. Business strikes back

The recording industry believed that Napster's popularity, as well as that of others precipitated massive losses. However, to this day it has not been proven that the exchanges had any direct influence on the sequence of events. At any rate, Napster was a thorn in the side of the recording industry. In December 1999, the *RIAA* (Recording Industry Association of America) filed a suit, the charge being massive copyright infringement. The RIAA was successful and a court order took Napster offline. Still, the recording industry was forced to realize that they had been sleeping soundly.

On the heels of Napster's demise, countless new exchanges materialized: *Gnutella, Morpheus, Audiogalaxy, eDonkey, KaZaa, Grokster, Limewire* etc. which also allowed the trading of pictures, films, texts and programs. More suits made the rounds, but the second generation of exchanges had found a chink in the armor of the recording industry through a clever technical adaptation, which till today constitutes a precedence: The data streams no longer flow over a central server. Instead, the users send their jams directly to each other (peer2peer). As a result, constricting such data flows is difficult at best, while the exchanges themselves are no longer liable for the behavior of their clients. Trading programs that merely supply directories are not deemed illegal.

What still remains in the sights of the International Federation of the Phonographic Industry (IFPI) are the private users of illegal exchanges and here the jurisprudence per country can vary enormously. For example, while revised Swiss copyright law allows downloads for private use, Germany and Great Britain forbid the same from apparently illegal sources.

With the help of DRM (Digital Rights Management), part of the music industry hopes to win back control over amorphous music files. A veritable army of programmers is working on a new software architecture employing several protection schemes. The target is a legally binding copy protection as a basis for implementation on all hard and software systems.

Envisioned is an electronic management system accompanying licensing, usage regulations and invoicing. Detractors from the scheme speak of "Digital Restricted Management", a strategic, industry-driven machination, as an attempt to nip today's emancipated and democratic distribution system in the bud.

5. The Music Business and the Internet

In spite of the copyright gray zones and conundrums still trailing illegal exchanges; notably with *Apple Computer* in the midst of the fray, money hand over fist is still being made with music downloads. With their MP3-Player *iPod,* their software *iTunes* and a store bearing the same name, *Steve Jobs* and Co. tread in quasi-legal territory: Apple's iPod has become the standard bearer of the digital lifestyle and has simultaneously put Apple on the map as the uncontested authority in the digital download marketplace.

No one other than Steve Jobs himself had had the necessary clout to bring the music industry with its restrictive usage laws to its knees. His appeal to basically reconsider Digital Rights Management and to drop copy protection on downloads altogether not only found assent in the related media but also in the upper echelons of the major recording labels. With or without DRM, the 300 worldwide largest providers of music downloads, global players such as, *T-Online, Microsoft, Yahoo, Sony, AOL* and *Coca-Cola* now have something to crow about.

The trend continues to draw a steep upward progression. As an alternative to the above, there are countless talent and community portals[3] that also have little to complain about. Here service providers assume the role of promoters and a fecund hothouse for new music. Conveniently, the cooperating bands enjoy artistic freedom and an attractive platform for marketing themselves.

The music futurologists *Gerd Leonhard* and *David Kusek* are both convinced, that music in the digital age will become as banal as electricity or running water. Access to music should become as simple as using a faucet. Seductive as the vision is, there are a few hurdles, such as a successful implementation of Digital Rights Management. Codes would guarantee music consumers access to all of the DRM protected music files found on the Web. A flatrate fee similar to that required for radio and television reception rights could be charged.

---

[3] *garageband.com, besonic.com, peoplesound.com, mp3.de, uptrax.com, myownmusic.de, myspace.com, tonspion.de, micromusic.net, etc.*

6. Brands - Mediating between Producers and Consumers

The new generation of musicians is smart, agile and flexible. Still, the economic realities of supply and demand remain valid, even on the Web. Indeed, many sceptical experts consider musicians and small labels looking for simpler and cheaper access to publics via the Web to be naive. On the contrary, some fear that a music glut may make it more difficult than ever to become the next big thing. However, this situation strengthens the positions of the financially potent organizations – ones that can marshall the necessary marketing resources.

One thing is clear, the decoupling of music files from standard recording storage media nudged a key log resulting in a flood of promising marketing and branding interfaces. Companies and brands respectively, that offer music downloads as a cross-product and figure as go-betweens among producers and consumers, invigorate the legal music market on the Web and in the long run cannot be overlooked in the marketplace.

Coca-Cola has launched their own music platform called mycoke.com where you can collect points for each and every Coca-Cola bottle. The points can be traded in for download credits. Thanks to close cooperation with Apple's iTunes, Coca-Cola was not only able to expand their repertoire but also increasingly offers exclusive recordings and pre-releases. Joint promotions permit territorial expansion on both sides. A classic win-win situation with a clear message: Cooperation and sponsoring models present interesting variations for strategic brand marketing. Music consumers land at companies' doorsteps through the sponsored, exclusive recordings of their favorite artists.

The coffeehouse chain *Starbucks* has already made a name for itself for years as a music producer and media company: Music has always been part of coffeehouse culture. Important is also what it means for brand positioning: The satellite radio station "Starbucks Hear Music" brings Starbucks' particular sound, ranging from singer/songwriters to cool jazz into the coffeehouses. By using their in-house label *Hear Music* for compilations and choice (see article *Bands for Brands*), local attractions they can sell songs via iTunes' online music store, as well as over conventional channels. Hear Music also has a good reputation with the big names in the business. For example, *Paul McCartney* chose the coffeehouse chain to debut his newest compositions. He understands his agreement with Starbucks as a reaction to the changes in the music industry. "We are living in a new world. People are discovering new ways to communicate with each other. And this has always been my goal." With its expansion in the direction of digital music shop integration, Starbucks intends to offer its clients an opportunity to indulge their lives as digerati: Behind the java-jerking lifestyle, downloading music and CD ripping, customers in certain test shops are also allowed to make their own compilations. The Mixed Tapes assortment propagated by *Mercedes* is also worth mentioning (see also article *Jingle all the Way? Basics of Audio Branding*). Participative culture props up the concept: Mercedes lures musicians, regardless of their musical direction or age to submit songs. A team of music journalists chooses tracks appearing in eight week intervals on the Mercedes-Benz website, complete with artwork, which can be then downloaded individually or in compilations. The online platform is enhanced by editorial contributions, music videos, album tips and artist bios. The Mixed Tapes series, distinguished by respectable musical quality, has already morphed into a brand: After eleven issues, beginning in 2004, Mercedes can now boast 20 million downloads. That the platform is also the place to be for newcomers has been clearly demonstrated by the Swedish singer *Urzula Amen.* Her ditty, Push It to the Limit, crowned a Europe-wide advertising campaign for the *Mercedes B-Class.* An exclusive remix of the song appeared as a free download on the website as the campaign got off the ground. The company let it be known, that in the future more and more Mixed Tape artists would be featured in various areas of brand communication. The repertoire is not only made accessible to all marketing and communication heads but also recycled in Mercedes podcast library.

7. Podcasting - Personal Platforms Inspire PR-Instruments

The term Podcasting is derived from a blend of the words, broadcasting and Apple's iPod. Podcasting serves audio and audiovisual content in a new form and is obviously on its way to leapfrogging the radio standard. The contributions can be downloaded at any time from the Web and transferred as often as it pleases to PCs, notebooks, mobile phones or MP3-players. Thanks to Web subscriptions (Real Simple Syndication (RSS)-Feeds) podcasts are a push medium predestined for proactive communication with focus groups.

But what is it that makes podcasting so interesting for producers and consumers? It is the direct nature of the medium. Everyone can make a (long) statement – worldwide. All you need is a computer and a microphone. According to studies made by the renowned marketing research company, *Forrester,* the number of American households in which podcasts will be consumed in the future will climb considerably. Exponential growth can also be expected in Europe, whether it be in the form of financial analyses, reports, conferences or statements made by CEOs. Everything is fair game and can be broadcasted over the Web. Search machines and podcast portals in combination with content indexes make navigation possible. And their integration in existing websites is a piece of cake.

Reputable publishing houses are also fattening up their offerings with audio products. The German language publications *Die Zeit, Das Handelsblatt* and *Die Schweizer Weltwoche* have been able to spark considerable interest among their readership in this respect. The automobile manufacturers *Audi, BMW, Mercedes* & Co have also become tireless podcasters and have absorbed the new medium into their communication without much ado. Media and annual reports, new service and product presentations along with focus group tweaked audio features complete the branding-toolbox. Obviously the undiluted strength of the recordings provides intimacy, a psychological asset to be reckoned with in communication. And aside from getting the straight facts, preferred clients can also be sure to get their fill of culture and entertainment. For example, commuters can download music and audiobooks for longer commutes or in traffic jams and enjoy branded entertainment.

8. Streaming Audio - A Utility for the Future

Since the general discourse has been dominated by MP3, exchanges and podcasting, streaming technology has become something of a media wallflower. However, if we take a closer look at the distribution of audio and audiovisual content, it is an elephant in the room. Actually, a stream is nothing more than a constant data flux, delayed or in realtime. In contrast to downloads, the data does not land on the harddrive, a fact that simplifies copyright stipulations and simultaneously reduces load times and susceptibility to viruses.

This means, that streaming is basically the same as watching television or listening to the radio and thanks to DSL (Digital Subscriber Line) and other highspeed connections, it has been able to carve out an existence within a very short time. Audio streaming is so easy to use, that more expensive alternatives such as DAB (Digital Audio Broadcasting) have been out-maneuvered. The thousands of independent radio stations that have burst onto the scene worldwide attest to the popularity of the medium. Comparable to modern transistor radios, mature products such as the *Squeezebox* from *Logitech* have hit the market and by way of wireless reception over WLAN's (Wireless Local Area Networks), let users listen to radio programs directly on their own stereos leaving their PCs or notebooks out of the loop.

Predictions have been made that streaming also has great potential as a substitute for traditional marketing and PR instruments. In this way, new products and services can be emotionally charged and focused company information distributed on the fly. Against this backdrop, the medium Webradio as a branding tool or instrument is asserting itself more and more where points of sale can benefit from a customized musical experience. Additionally, since pictures and music can also be streamed to mobile phones, the media convergence now has the stuff to make dialog with focus groups a systematic process.

9. The Mobile as a Jukebox

The triumph of the ringtone and the related turnover billions that filled coffers came as a surprise to many. And from that point onward, as mobiles were not only empowered to beep, but also learned to reproduce authentic sounds (realtones), the turnover increased again. Soon businesses discovered the ringtone as a transport vehicle for identity.

More interesting, however, is the general upgrading of the mobile phone to a music machine. The mobile as a jukebox has all the features that a digital lifestyle has waited for. It can send, receive, play and save sounds. As far as convergence is concerned, the music features now top consumers' list of favorites. More and more telecoms offer music streams and downloads for mobiles. Although mobile music still has a way to go, the previous experiences with the ringtones could lead us to expect exorbitant growth developments.

And just when it was needed, another development from the *Fraunhofer Institut* appeared to speed the popularity of downloads on mobiles - Audio IDs now help with the identification of unknown songs. After connecting to an identification service, listeners first have to remain tuned in to the same source for some 20 seconds. Afterwards, in a databank consisting of millions of songs, the chosen song titles are searched for and immediately sent back to inquirers as a text message.

10. Game Audio Identity – New Game!

The video- and computer-game boom has led to new realizations among brand communicators. "In Game" advertising provides, aside from the product placement offerings, a platform for audio branding. For example, games created for brand campaigns are a natural for gamer-focussed campaigns. Since audio design has eminent status among gamers, giving each game its own identity breathes life into the individual game settings. In contrast to film soundtracks, this form of audio design does not progress linearly but is adaptive in nature. The sound adjusts to the ability of each player and changes following actions or locations.

The technical aspects of its production approach more and more that of the same for film. It is not a rarity, that a symphony orchester is engaged for a production and the soundtrack sales in the USA now exceed those of the standard film scores. Clearly, it is but a matter of time till businesses seize upon computer- and video games for branding purposes.

11. Web Acoustics for the Hitherto Unheard

Professionally designed audio for websites demand attention, increase the entertainment quotient and make the presentation an emotional experience. The increased inclusion of sound as a design element got its upswing from technical developments. Thanks to DSL and highspeed connections the loading time for websites, which was once the obstacle, is no more. Still, in respect to the actual sound design, the advances can be said to be in their infancy. Orchestrating Web-surfers' experiences without using a sledgehammer remains a balancing act. Often, attempts at Web-scoring overshoot their goal and only manage to get on surfers' nerves. If the reciprocal dynamics between users' reactions to sounds and the spoken texts are not correctly correlated, misunderstandings are sure to result. Besides, who wants to voluntarily subject themselves to obnoxiously saccharinated riffing when they are actually bent on surfing?

An integrated and coherent presentation requires organic points of reference between the texts, visuals and sounds. Sounds can subtly insinuate themselves into the depths of our unconscious. To achieve this to a positive end - applicability, Web acoustics must divorce itself from common conventions and assert itself as a separate and respectable design discipline.

12. In Dialog with Digital Technologies

"Initially the industrial society anonymized everything, now the process is being reversed. Objects are taking back their identity. Soon your cashmir sweater will complain because it has been neglected and washed too hot." (John Gage, Head of Research, Science Office of Sun Microsystems)

It is the time-honored wish of everyman and everywoman to have mobile and kitchen devices, home electronics and toys that can be used in the most intuitive and easiest manner possible. We are now quite accustomed to functional warnings, start and confirmation tones, be they from the water kettle, the mobile or an operating system. Few devices are not equipped with one. But while manufacturers for the longest time directed their attention to acoustic signals, today, differentiation and affect play an increasingly important role. And that operating instructions tend to disappear without being consulted is also common knowledge. What could be better than letting products explain themselves to users? For many, this may smack of science fiction but the fact is, the juggernaut of digitalization is letting this scenario appear less and less far-fetched. Chatty navigation systems are standard in most new cars. Mobile telephones read text messages out loud and on the computer Agnes, Victoria, Bruce or Junior stand ready to alert users that programs require their attention.

Ringing, squawking and speaking products as helpers and entertainers have slipped almost unnoticed into our daily lives. And if that were not enough, they are penetrating the mass market and have begun shape our purchasing decisions. Aside from text-to-speech software aimed at applications ranging from Web pages to mobile devices, speech synthesizer developers also offer custom corporate voice packages. If you think that computer generated voices all sound canned and like robots, you should hear them now; many of the new versions are amazingly rich in emotional nuance, some can even laugh. Since one-way communication can never replace dialog and products should also be able to listen, text-to-speech software specialists are also improving on voice recognition sytems. Already today PCs can carry out simple language commands. In the future, natural language command interfaces will make it possible, for example, to select a song from a databank or even use certain devices entirely. *Apple* and *Microsoft* both consider natural language recognition an important future trend. According to a patent application, Apple is working on an iPod that uses speech recognition software. Not a bad idea, since while jogging, driving or bike riding, it can be annoying to dangerous to try to change a sequence of songs on an MP3 by hand.

13. The Brand as Surround Sound

The vision of a house digital with access to digital content around the clock, anywhere and on any device is today not far off. In particular, the soft- and hardware industry is working overtime to perfect home and car entertainment. Surround sound has become the standard for home cinema. This spatial acoustic technology, known as *Dolby Surround* since 1975, popularized the cinematic phenomenon in which the audience acoustically has the impression that it is in the very midst of all the action. For example, those listening may perceive a helicopter approaching from behind, hear/feel its rotors moving overhead for fractions of a second, as well as its whirring from the front as it finally as it appears on the screen. Because of their inherent emotional effect, surround sound systems can be used for events, at fairs and for installations at points of sale.

Depending on the surround system chosen, and there are many to choose from, three to seven speakers are needed, each of which has a bass speaker and, are arranged in a half-circle facing or encircling listeners. Those less enchanted with the idea of having so many speakers in the living room will opt for a virtual surround sound configuration. This variation employs both stereo channels and simulates the room effect by using psycho-acoustic principles, that is, the surround effect is actually interpolated within the heads of the listeners. The MP3 surround format is quite similar: Using the principles of psycho-acoustics, the simulation is now for the first time reproducible with stereo headphones.

14. Harddrive Recording – Digital Music Production

Audio production processes have experienced a paradigmatic shift at the hands of the digital revolution. In the past, if the goal was high quality, it was necessary to book an expensive studio crammed full of assorted high-tech audio devices. Today, thanks to virtual simulations, good quality productions can be achieved for less. The digital revolution and democratization go hand in hand. In fact, using the proper hard and software, one can already achieve reasonable results on notebooks. All of which can transpire spontaneously, intuitively and independent of venues and time constraints. The same can be said of sound generation, modulation and effects. From the recording to the arranging to mixing and mastering, everything can be done in real time. Once the sound sources have been digitalized, endless permutations can be propagated and reassembled into new contexts. Ever greater storage and memory capacities guarantee almost unlimited access to instrument and sound libraries, all of which can be loaded within seconds. What does this mean for the producer? The technical infrastructure dwindles in importance as the audio concept begins to take precedence. The production process has become much more flexible and now starts much earlier than the trip to the expensive recording studio. Producers can also constantly stay informed about the production stagings and related events. Lastly, sound files can also be sent around the world within minutes for approval.

References

Boeing, N. (2000). Bürgerkrieg des Rock 'n' Roll. KM21.0.

Gross, T. (2004). Digitale Revolution, Teil II. Die Zeit-Feuilleton.

Kusek, D. & Leonhard, G. (2005). The Future of Music - Manifesto for the Digital Music Revolution. Berklee Press.

Moby aka Richard Melville Hall (2001). Wir werden alle digitale Musiker - Der Laptop-Performer ist die Zukunft der Musikindustrie. Das Magazin.

Schneider, Reto U. (2002). Eine Revolution aus 0 und 1 - Über die grosse Karriere der kleinsten Informationseinheit. NZZ Folio.

Sieben, U. (2003). Ein vegetarischer Hund, Essay im Rahmen der Ausstellung "adonnaM.mp3" - Filesharing, die versteckte Revolution im Internet. Museum für angewandte Kunst, Frankfurt.

Bands for Brands – How much do they really have to fit?

Cornelius Ringe
Consultant for Audio Branding and Brand-Artist-Partnership, Hamburg

1. What you want is some bombastic ...

In 1995, in a commercial for *Levi's* "Double Stitched" jeans that was shown in cinemas world-wide, a song was used that transformed its singer into a reggae pop megastar. The story of the commercial and the music fit perfectly: In a clay animation, the ultra cool Mr. Bombastic wearing his indestructible Levi's jeans rescues a helpless woman from the flames of a burning skyscraper. The song "Mr Bombastic" and the charismatic deep voice of the singer are as ultra cool as the heroic protagonist of the commercial. Right at the beginning, the stage name of the singer can be heard briefly: *Shaggy*! Jamaican artist *Orvill Richard Burrell* was already a successful international musician, but it was the massive attention the Levi's commercial attracted that resulted for him in a comeback and international success culminating in a Grammy award in 1996. Both sides profited from this cooperation, Levi's as a commercial brand and Shaggy as an international artist.

The following article deals with the subject of brand artist partnership, which is becoming increasingly relevant, and introduces a model for determination of a definitive fit between brand and artist.

2. Status quo in the advertising and the music industry

For several years, an exciting constellation has developed in the advertising and music industry, both of which are undergoing a fundamental paradigm shifts. Most affected is the
music industry, where after a short-lived boom after the launch of the compact disc in 1983
a serious crisis has set in following the total digitalization of the music supply. This concerns
mainly the sound carrier market, which is still at the hub of the music industry. In the centre
of this paradigm shift in the music industry are new income-creating potentials for artists
and the discourse on future function and relevance of music businesses. While proponents
of the distribution perspective cling to the current model of market cultivation of the music
industry and call for a rapid adaptation for the digital music market, the proponents of the
content perspective question all traditional process of the music industry. The latter have
recognized the extent of change and are developing concepts for new sources of revenue.
The disintegration of the dogmatic separation between principal and ancillary rights in music
utilization is possibly a significant step towards new concepts in music marketing. Essentially, principal rights of music utilization include marketing of rights of use of composition
and production of music. To date, these are observed mainly by music labels, publishers and
collecting companies. All other rights of use are termed ancillary rights and belong directly
to the artist or his/her management. These primarily include live performances and use of
artist images in merchandising/licensing, advertising contracts and other forms of cooperation with brands.

While up to now, principal rights of music utilization are at the fore of commercial use,
the economic focus is increasingly shifting towards the commercialization of ancillary rights.
Already, the majority of revenue in the music market is not generated from the sale of music
per se, but from the commercialization of the relevant ancillary rights. Most attractive for
the artist is the commercialization of his/her image as it requires not too much additional
work and expense. Thus, a distinct change can be observed in the attitude towards the
advertising industry.

While in 1968, *Jim Morrison* deemed the potential use of the song "Light My Fire" in a
commercial for the car manufacturer *Buick* to be in league with the devil, it is today almost
taken for granted that *Lenny Kravitz* (obviously motivated by an appropriate remuneration)
was inspired by the market values of the Vodka brand *Absolut* when he wrote his song
"Breathe" exclusively for this company. In 2006, Absolut communicated this fact with its
"Absolut Kravitz" campaign including an own web site with free downloads of the song and
various remixes. By now, cooperation with brand producers, i.e. brand artist partnership, has
become a constant factor in the marketing of a pop star. The advertising industry, just as
the music industry, albeit not quite as dramatically, is also experiencing a period of change.
The reasons are mainly the increasing information overload and consumers with marketing
experience, who respond to advertising far more knowingly and deliberate. Here also, the
effects of digitalization can be noted which offer increasing opportunities to avoid adver-

tising (e.g. through video on demand, pay TV, HDD recorder, TV commercial filter etc.) and for individual consuming (e.g. via *youtube.com*). While above-the-line advertising continues to claim most of the communication budget, a trend towards below-the-line advertising is becoming apparent. The separation between above- and below-the-line is increasingly discarded by advertisers. Instead, individual advertising features are linked and integrated in holistic communication strategies.

3. Branded entertainment and brand artist partnership
While in the 1950s and 1960s, commercials resembled consumer information, the advertising of today must first of all be emotional, captivating and entertaining. It has to offer the consumer more than simple product information or it runs the risk of not being accepted resulting in ineffectiveness or negative impact. Therefore, brands are increasingly including their advertising message into their own or other tailor-made entertainment. Branded entertainment may be defined as the convergence of the advertising and the entertainment industry attempting to reasonably and authentically combine the advertising message with a relevant entertainment content which would not exist without the input of the brand. It is mainly found in the area of pull marketing, while push media may also be employed. Thus, brand entertainment comprises an almost unlimited variety of manifestations.

In the area of TV and radio, there is the advertiser funded programming (AFP) comprising not only classic program sponsoring but also provision of complete sections or entire shows by a brand. The idea to sponsor the content of radio and TV shows or to actually produce them is almost as old as radio itself. For example, between 1923 and 1933, NBC stations broadcast the popular weekly music show "The Cliquot Club Eskimos" sponsored by the US American drinks manufacturer *Clicquot Club Company.* In 1924, the *Washburn Crosby Company* bought an entire radio station (WLAG) to broadcast the "Betty Crocker Cooking School". In 1932, *General Mills*, as the successor of the Washburn Crosby Company launched the first real soap opera "Betty and Bob".

Today, several brands have their own TV station on the internet, often including extensive music offers (e.g. the Mercedes Mixed Tape music magazine at mercedes-benz.tv or Tommy TV at tommytv.com). Other online forms of branded entertainment are, for example, corporate pod- or vodcasts, brand's own web radio players or free music downloads. In the area of live entertainment, mainly sports, music, comedy and theatre are involved. All of these can be termed events. Initiation of an event from outside for the purpose of brand communication is generally considered sponsoring. If the event is organized from within, this is called event marketing or sales promotion. In the long run, all types of branded entertainment have one thing in common: They communicate on an emotional level and offer the recipient added benefits resulting in significantly stronger brand bonding than through conventional advertising.

Music is the perfect content for branded entertainment. It can be easily (digitally) distributed and integrated in almost all communication channels. Pop music (in the broadest sense also rock, metal, punk etc.) also offers the advantage of the global music culture. Music provides intercultural and meaningful semiotics and optimum opportunities for differentiation with its almost unlimited and constantly changing reservoir of genre. And finally, the compactness of musical items is a significant aspect for new distribution methods. A free download of a pop song in mp3 format or a music video on youtube is a completely different affair than the download of a *Wagner* opera. One characteristic of pop music is the fact that often (but certainly not always) the artist and not the music is the main attraction. As the long-time rock artists of the band *Survivor* sing in "It's the singer not the song!":

"When there's magic in the music
It's the singer not the song
When it's comin' from the heart
All the people sing along
It's the man behind the music
It's the singer not the song"

Hence, branded entertainment with pop music only makes sense when the respective artist is incorporated in a brand artist partnership. This cooperation can be designed in many ways and offers uncountable links for cross promotion. Thus, target groups which have been difficult to reach with conventional advertising can now be focused on with branded entertainment. Its protagonists, the pop stars, are idolized by their fans and have enormous power as opinion leaders. Mostly, they have a clear-cut profile with a distinctive image. Their music videos are often like commercials for an entire life style and thus for a complete range of products. Their music moves people and often expresses what cannot be put into words. And the lyrics of their songs (especially those from critical and politically active artists) can impart messages which normally may not find the same level of attention. Manufacturers who promote their produce with the assistance of *John Lennon, Jimi Hendrix, Kurt Cobain, U2, Ozzy Osbourne, Madonna* or *above* can (!) issue a strong statement about their brand that reaches far beyond the respective piece of music. Therefore, pop stars are most attractive as advertisers for many brands and are increasingly integrated into brand communication with far reaching cooperation. The artist's perception of the advertising industry has also changed along with the above mentioned paradigm shift. Advertising is no longer considered to be incompatible with artistic aspirations, but rather an opportunity for the realization of productive synergies. For many a newcomer, cooperation with a brand offers considerable promotional support, such as for the newcomer band *The Subways* whose song "Rock 'n' roll queen" from their debut album was used in 2006 as background music in the advertising campaign "Your fragrance, your rules, your song?" for the *Hugo Boss* perfume "Hugo". The band attracted extra attention because the audience of the first TV spot was asked to vote on the Hugo web site for their favorite from a choice of three more of the band's songs for the upcoming TV commercial. Artists who are already megastars are not only delighted about the financial aspects of brand communication. In 2004, *Christina Aguilera* composed her song "Hello" exclusively for the world premier of the second generation *Mercedes* A-class. She performed the song live at the launch which was simultaneously used as background music in the advertising campaign. She profited from worldwide media presence, while at the same time, improving her image towards more integrity.[1] The fact that the song could be downloaded for free exclusively and for a limited period only from the *Mercedes-Benz* web site attracted an even bigger media echo. One example for the strong trend that is currently evolving in brand artist partnerships is the brand-owned music label "Green Label Sound" which was founded in 2008 by *Mountain Dew*. This is a program especially aimed at promotion of newcomers through free music downloads on greenlabelsound.com. However, closer inspection reveals that it is simply another form of free music download, comparable to the Mercedes Mixed (mercedes-benz.tv/mixedtape).

The only real and at the same time successful music label managed be a non-music company as branded entertainment is the label "Hear Music" which was founded in 2007 by *Starbucks*. It resulted from the cooperation with *Concord Music Group* and was the outcome of a music compilation program by the same name from Starbucks, which had been in existence since 1999. It profited mostly from the direct chain of distribution via Starbucks branches worldwide. Most CD sales were probably impulse purchases giving in to the temptation to buy from the invitingly presented music on offer while waiting for the ordered coffee. The multisensory and thematic fit between brand and coffee experience plays a key role here: everything fits, the smell of coffee, the taste of coffee, the look and feel of the branch interior, the music from the loudspeakers and, finally, the choice offer of music CDs at the cash register. Artists who have published under this label include megastars such as *Paul McCartney, Alanis Morissette, John Mellencamp* or *Joni Mitchell*. As already mentioned, Starbucks is an isolated case profiting from established distribution channels and relying on a professional music label. The competence to build up pop stars continues to remain with actual music companies, labels and publishers. Another innovative and unconventional example for successful branded entertainment with music is the label "DEF Mini Records" which was set up in 2007 by the agencies *BBDO Germany, .start* and *Interone Worldwide*. This is an obvious advertising campaign of the *Mini* motor car presenting a fantasy label with plenty of wit and irony that satirizes common clichés of the music industry. In contrast to Green Label Sound and Hear Music, the audience clearly realizes that this is simply an advertising campaign dealing in a sympathetic way with a serious issue.

---

[1] *Of note, regular image change used to be a distinct characteristic of this artist.*

The especially cast bands are all named after the most important safety features of the Mini which also appear in the lyrics. For example, the Country singer *Runflat* sings in his song "Another 100 Miles": "50 Miles an hour, a nail stuck in the tyre, a little light is warning me ... but I shift one gear higher". Another example are the punk rockers *The Disc Breaks* with their hit single "Save me": "One road one curve the perfect blend, the ABS won't let me end" (defminirecords.com).

4. Image transfer from pop star to brand

Partnerships between brands and pop stars are usually intended to increase brand popularity or to cultivate an image. Below, the aim of image cultivation will be discussed which may be divided into three subcategories:

- Image creation: Due to the novelty value when a brand is launched, its image has not yet become consolidated with its target groups. In this case, brand artists partnership offers the opportunity to build a unique brand image.
- Image modification: If the existing brand image does not represent the intended image, brand artist partnership can be used to move the brand image in the desired direction with target groups. Radical changes should be avoided here.
- Image stabilization: Even an already existing and well positioned brand image requires continuous attention. Brand artists partnerships can help to support the brand image through associations with the artist.

Although self evident, the essential importance of decisive target definition for every communication campaign cannot be stressed often enough. Despite the fact that target definition always stands at the beginning of every process model it is often marginalized due to time pressure or aimless actionism. Once a campaign has been decided on the first creative ideas will bubble forth before the direction of the campaign has become clear. Thus, image transfer and maximum fit between artist and brand will soon be discussed despite the fact these are per se mutually exclusive as will be shown below. A preconceived target definition, however, is based on careful actual-theoretical analysis of the brand image which will determine whether an image must be built, modified or stabilized. In order to establish a purposeful and definitive amount of image fit between artist and brand, a model can be used which is essentially based on the congruency theory by *Osgood* and *Tannenbaum*. With this model, direction, extent and distribution of a possible image transfer can be decided on. According to Osgood and Tannenbaum: „[…] changes in evaluation are always in the direction of increased congruity with the existing frame of reference" (Osgood & Tannenbaum, 1955, p. 43).

This model is based on triadic relationship structures between recipient, artist and brand. In the initial situation, the recipient has already formed his/her personal opinion of the artist and the brand, which may be located on a continuum between the positive and the negative pole. If the recipient notices a positive relationship between artist and brand, he/she will unconsciously and automatically attempt to conciliate his/her present opinion of the artist and the brand. In advertising psychology, this is referred to as congruence through cognitive reorganization. Usually, it implies that both opinions are moving towards each other. If, for example, an attitude towards a brand was not as good as the attitude towards the artist, the artist will lose some of his esteem, while the brand will gain some. The actual extent depends on the degree of the relevant polarization, i.e. how negative or positive the attitude had been. Here, firmer attitudes are more resistant to change than weaker ones, i.e. in case of incongruence; firmer attitudes will be changed less than weaker ones. If the aim of communication is an image transfer from artist to brand (image creation or image modification), the artist should be positively polarized by the respective target group significantly more than the brand. This ensures that the brand image and not the artist image are influenced. On the other hand, for the artist, the congruence theory implies that his/her image may be affected more or less through cooperation with a brand depending on incongruence and polarity constellation. From the point of view of the artist, careful examination of the potential partner's image is highly recommended. However, in practice, this is rarely done sufficiently.

Another important aspect of the model is the credibility of the partnership between artist and brand since with increasing incredibility a brand's image effect decreases and it could, in the worst case scenario, reverse to a negative one. The general aim of image cultivation implies that the artists contributes at least the same if not even more positive image values to the partnership than the brand.

Based on a given brand image, the interplay of congruence pressure (dependent on artist image) and incredibility in relation to image affect of the brand can be demonstrated in a diagram. For this see figure 1. Here, the best areas for image aims, creation, modification and stabilization can be deducted.

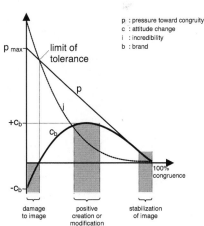

Figure 1.
Areas of image effect
in brand artist partnerships.

As shown, depending on the target of communication, a different degree of congruence (fit) should be aimed for. Hence, to create or modify a positive brand image, a degree of congruence with maximum transfer potential (+cb max) should be selected. This corresponds with a moderate incongruence where the partnership between brand and artist is still considered credible. For stabilization of the brand image, on the other hand, maximum congruence should be aimed for. In case of extreme incongruence, a high level of incredibility can additionally damage the brand image resulting in the so-called "boomerang effect" where the exact opposite from the desired effect occurs. The critical point between positive and negative image effect is i = p representing the individual limit of tolerance of recipients.

Regarding credibility of a brand artist partnership, this model not only allows prognoses on direction, extent and distribution of an image transfer, but also simultaneous assessment of potential risks for the cooperation partners.

5. How to find the right artist for partnerships

To ensure selection of the right artist for a partnership two additional factors apart from the image fit must be considered in a filtering process. These relate to sound identity and the respective target group (see figure 2). Obviously, pop stars have a distinct sound identity determined by the music they produce. This comprises, e.g., genre, instrumentation, general emotional appearance, timbre and the singer's voice. The fact that brands have sound identity should be apparent after reading of this book. In a first step in strategic planning for cooperation with pop stars, it must be determined what sound profile the artists in question should have to achieve the desired fit.

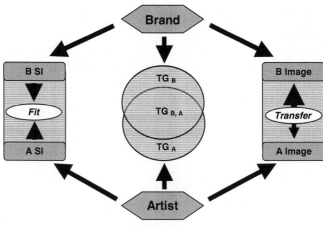

Figure 2.
Three factor model
of artist selection.　　　B: Brand　　A: Artist　　TG: Target Group　　SI: Sound Identity

Next, the target group of the relevant artists must be compared with the brand's target group. For this, a variety of tools for target group segmentation is available whereby the choice of tool depends on the requirements of the brand. Once these two filtering processes are completed, only a small selection of potentially suitable artists should remain. Finally, in the last and most elaborate step, the relevant artist images must be compared with the brand image to achieve the desired fit.

6. Conclusion

The image of advertising has changed. Advertising no longer has to be pesky or allege things which are untrue or misleading. Instead, advertising can be authentic, cool and entertaining. Here, exclusive partnerships with pop stars offer brands a high potential for distinction. And a complete fit of artist image and brand image is not mandatory. Indeed, a moderate measure of positive incongruence offers the highest potential for the image effect of an advertising campaign. A too distinct misfit, however, may result in image damages. Therefore, the following points should be preferably considered when planning brand artist partnerships:

- What is the image aim? Should the image be created, modified or stabilized?
- Depending on the aim, the anticipated measure of congruence must be determined between artist image and brand image.
- The credibility of the partnership must be considered as moderating variable. Hence, brand image modification can only be performed in small steps in the medium or long term. Too dramatic "image jumps" may be seen as not credible by recipients and result in reactance.

References

Osgood, E. C. & Tannenbaum, P. H. (1955). *The principle of congruity in the prediction of attitude change. In: Psychological Review. Vol. 62, No. 1, pp. 42-55.*

Silence of Brands

Cornelius Ringe, Kai Bronner, Rainer Hirt

The pause is an important element of music. Silence is a basic need of the human organism. Hence silence is also an essential element of acoustic brand management.
Acoustic brand management cannot be reduced to the application of music and sound.
In fact it is about the conscious acoustic design of a brand. The crucial elements of what we finally hear, or think we hear, are capacity, quality, aesthetics and effect.

Audio Branding consists of two components:
Audio: I hear
Branding: to label something

Perhaps the term Audio Branding does not quite suffice. The Branding component automatically implies an audible feature, for example the audio logo.
But we are also capable of hearing silence. Can silence be an acoustic feature?
The term 'akustische Markenführung' has established itself in the German language.
In English: acoustic brand management. For brands this leads to a more revised understanding of how to deal with sound.
Now it is not only about the acoustic feature, but rather the integral management of an acoustic brand. And so, it is also about the effective and efficient application of acoustic stimuli and the silence between.

Producing silence effectively and elegantly,
where it belongs,
where it is pleasant and not oppressive,
where it brings peace and quiet,
where it stands for virtues such as purity, quality and exclusiveness,
where it gives an acoustic brand range and structure,
is perhaps one of the biggest challenges of acoustic brand management in our time.

Silence is ambivalent.

It can be perceived as pleasant or as unpleasant.

Squashed between complete strangers in a tiny elevator, we perceive silence as oppressive.

It generates fear, aggression or tension.

George O. Squier realized this and consequently invented elevator music.

After a noisy hard day's work on the other hand, silence is welcome and provides relaxation.

Thus, silence is not just silence.

The general understanding of silence is a subjective, situation dependant sensation.

The effect of silence depends largely upon the context.

Just try it. Read the following four pages, once privately in silence and then publicly in front of a large audience:

E.
Multi-sensory Design

Acoustics as Resonant Element of Multi-sensory Brand Communication

Karsten Kilian
University of St. Gallen, Markenlexikon.com, Würzburg

1. Communication Makes Sense

While branded offers are always perceived in a multi-sensory way, brand managers are mainly focused on one or two sensory channels: sight and sound. In contrast to this, touch, taste, and smell almost always remain unmanaged. This does not mean, however, that these channels are silent. The opposite is true. Information is delivered in some way via all sensory channels, mostly however, not in favor of the brand and its identity.

Thus, enormous potentials to stand out in the flood of brands are wasted: opportunities to be different, one, if not the goal of branding! Therefore, *Franz-Peter Falke*, president of the German *Markenverband* (brand association) stresses the relevance of multi-sensory branding: "Customers want to be addressed via their five senses" (Engeser, 2006, p. 83). Similarly, *MetaDesign* manager *Jens-Ole Kracht* points out that "the future belongs to multi-sensory branding" (2006). For brand managers one of their key challenges therefore is "to break the two-dimensional advertising impasse" (Lindstrom, 2005a, p. 9). The multi-sensory design and communication of branded products and services has become the precondition for singular brand experiences, which in turn positively affect customers' willingness to pay, and stay.

1.1 Multi-sensory Perception

While the argument for multi-sensory branding seems more than logical, one could, at first view, argue that approaching customers purely visually and acoustically is sufficient, since 83% of our sensory impressions are gathered by our visual nerves and an additional 11% by our acoustic nerves, while only 3.5% are perceived by our sense of smell, 1.5% haptically, and 1% by our sense of taste as can be seen in table 1 (Braem, 2004, p. 192).

Sensory Receptors	Perception	(in %)	Sensations (Examples)
Eyes	visual	83,0	bright/dark, coloured
Ears	acoustically	11,0	quiet/loud, near/far
Nose	olfactory	3,5	fruity, aromatic
Skin/Movement	tactile/kinesthetic	1,5	warm/cold, plain/rough
Tongue	gustatory	1,0	sweet/bitter, salty, sour

Table 1. Systematization of sensory perceptions and sensations.

At second view, however, this audio-visual dominance quickly becomes relative as 99% of all brand communication take place via these two senses (Lindstrom, 2005b, p. 85). Besides, the alleged dominance of the optic nerves can be qualified, as a current study by *Millward Brown* and *Lindstrom* reveals. When asked for the importance of the five senses for their purchase decisions, 58% of the respondents named, on average, the sense of sight, closely followed by the sense of smell with 45% and the sense of hearing with 41%. In addition, the sense of taste with 31% and the sense of touch with 25% where also frequently mentioned when evaluating brands (Lindstrom, 2005a, p. 69).

Product Category	Sight	Sound	Touch	Taste	Smell
Sportswear	86.6	10.2	82.3	8.4	12.5
Home Entertainment	85.6	81.6	11.6	10.7	10.8
Automobiles	78.2	43.8	49.1	10.6	18.4
Phones	68.9	70.2	43.9	8.0	8.9
Soap	36.0	6.7	61.5	5.6	90.2
Ice Cream	34.9	6.8	21.7	89.6	47.0
Soft Drinks	29.6	13.2	15.1	86.3	56.1
Fast Food	26.3	12.0	10.4	82.2	69.2

Comment: See above the percentage shares of the two highest importance levels on a five point Likert scale (from "most important" to "least important")

Table 2. Relative importance of the five senses in eight product categories.

As can be seen from table 2, the importance ratings of the five senses vary significantly as a function of the product category. While sight, sound, and touch have the strongest influence on the evaluation of car and phone brands, soap is predominantly evaluated by our sense of smell. For ice cream, soft drinks, and fast food, in turn, our sense of taste dominates the decision-making (Kilian, 2007a, p. 326). Although at least one quarter of the respondents attributed high importance to sight in all eight product categories, four of which even reach shares clearly beyond 50%, reality clearly shows that in highly contested and saturated market with increasingly homogenous products, the visual channel is increasingly "overcrowded". This is the case for about 85% of all products as they are evaluated at least as "good" by independent research institutes (Scheier/Held, 2006, p. 17). For brands it therefore becomes more and more difficult to be seen and noticed by customers.

1.2 Unconscious, Cumulative Sensory Impact

While *Kroeber-Riel* still assumed that less than 2% of all information in the mass media reaches our consciousness (Kroeber-Riel/Weinberg, 1999, p. 90), *Häusel* estimates – based on data by *Norretranders* – that only 0.0004% of all stimuli from the outside world reach our consciousness (Häusel, 2008, p. 70; Scheier/Held, 2006, p. 47 and p. 61). This does not mean, however, that the remaining 99,99% of all stimuli remain ineffective. They are just experienced and processed subconsciously. As subliminal stimuli they are nevertheless effective as they directly affect our behavior without consciousness intervening (Scheier/Held, 2006, p. 49 and p. 54ff.). We often act without knowing why and/or find appropriate arguments for our behavior as soon as we become aware of the results. Thus, these indirect, subtle "backstage" processes are quite relevant, as they affect our "live performance" strongly, without us noticing. It is therefore not surprising that, according to current estimations, 70-80% of all decisions are made unconsciously (Häusel, 2008, p. 70). Similarly, *Zaltman* estimates that 95% of our cognition (as preliminary stage of our decision-making) takes place unconsciously (2002, p. 26). One reason for this is that our explicit visual perception only covers a radius of 5 grades while our peripheral perception implicitly handles up to 120 grades. An outcome of this is that our implicit knowledge about a brand is up to four times as vast as our explicit brand knowledge (Scheier/Held, 2007a, p. 168 and p. 205).

An example shall illustrate the impact implicit knowledge has on our behavior. British researchers tested the effect of different images on contributions to an honesty box they used as a device to collect money for drinks in an unsupervised university coffee room. When they replaced a flower image on the payment instruction notice with an image of a pair of eyes directly looking at the observer, people paid, on average, 2.76 times more. Interestingly, participants did not notice the image changes, at least not consciously. Subconsciously they obviously did (Bateson/Nettle/Roberts, 2006, p. 412f.).

What is even more important is that our multi-sensory perceptions make our nerve cells in the brain send out impulses that are 10 to 12 times stronger as compared to mono-sensory perceptions. However, this is only the case as long as the sensory impressions are consistent (Scheier/Held, 2006, p. 82; Salzmann, 2007, p. 93). As a consequence, desired associations are not only activated with higher probability but also with more accuracy. With respect to print ads, a recent meta analysis has revealed, that, on average, 48% of all announcements are wrongly assigned or not assigned to a brand at all when the name and logo are covered (Scheier/Held, 2007b, S. 90). This is largely due to the fact that the average viewing time of a print ad is less than two seconds (Kroeber-Riel/Esch, 2004, p. 17). Thus, linkages to a brand are mainly established through dominant key visuals or prominent design elements while exchangeable ad images and layouts are, at best, being recognized as an advertising for the product segment, but not for a particular brand. Cosmetics, perfumes, and fashion are classical examples of this ineffective advertising approach. A recent study in which fashion ads of familiar brands like *Bogner, Boss,* and *Betty Barclay* were tested showed that there is, till this day, a strong need for the establishment of unique brand elements and their effective usage. On average, 92% of all ads tested were assigned to the wrong brand with *D&G* showing the weakest results. 98% of the respondents assigned D&G ads to another brand. 20% thought it was an *H&M* advertisement and 13% linked it to the fashion label *Cinque* (Serviceplan/ Facit, 2007, p. 50). With less exchangeable key visuals and layouts, a purposeful application of unique brand elements, and possibly some coherent tactile ad characteristics, e.g. more significant and thicker paper or embossed printing, results would have been significantly better!

2. Linkages between the Five Senses

A reason for this is that different sensory modalities are oftentimes strongly interlinked. In rare cases this might take the form of synesthesia, a neurological phenomenon in which the stimulation of one sensory modality leads to automatic experiences in a second sensory modality (see article *Synesthetic Design – Building Multi-sensory Arrangements*). A synesthete might, for example, perceive letters or numbers as inherently colored while not actually seeing the numbers in these colors. This kind of grapheme-color synesthesia might lead a synesthete to involuntarily associate certain numbers and letters with particular colors. The number 1 might be associated with blue, 2 with red, 3 with yellow etc. Similarly, for people with sound-color synesthesia certain musical stimuli, e.g. timbre or key, might elicit specific color experiences. A certain note might always elicit red or a harp might trigger the experience of seeing yellow (Kroeber-Riel/Weinberg, 1999, p. 12; Knoblich/Scharf/Schubert, 2003, p. 49).

Color	Sound	Touch	Temperature	Weight	Taste
yellow	screaming, major	even, bright, soft (when reddish)	warm, hot (when reddish)	light (brighter = lighter)	sour (when greenish), sweet (when redish)
red	loud, trumpet	firm, very rough (when dark-red)	warm, hot	heavy (varying with brightness)	sweet, beefy, spicy, crisp, biting
pink	tender, gentle	tender/fine, very soft	skin temperature	light	sweet, mild
green	acute (when deep), curbed (when blunt)	flush up to damp	fresh, cool	light (varying with brightness)	sour-salty, bitter, salty
blue	remote, flute till violin	flush up to not palable, firm (dark-blue), soft (pale-blue)	cool, fresh up to very cold	relative light (varying with brightness)	almost neutral

Table 3. Color-dependent sensory associations.

While synesthesia describes a stimulus transfer from one sensory modality to another, irradiation refers to the associative transfer of an assessment of one characteristic onto another. With regard to brands, the subjective mental linkage of perceptions causes the evaluation of a particular brand characteristic to affect another characteristic of the same brand. The color of margarine, for example, impairs our evaluation of its fat content (Kroeber-Riel/Weinberg, 1999, p. 123 and p. 304; Linxweiler, 2004, p. 68). Table 3 provides an overview of color-dependent sensory associations (Behrens, 1982, p. 223).

The color yellow, for example, is typically associated with a screaming major tone, considered bright and soft, linked to warmth, perceived as lightweight, and, depending on its shade, associated with a sweet or sour taste. The described linkages between the five sense, in particular the addressed irradiation effects, provide various possibilities to make a brand desirable and distinctive via multi-sensory design and communication.

3. Options for Multi-sensory Communication

During the perception process the spatially separated sensory organs initially gather information via largely independent sensory channels. Subsequently, the gained sensory impressions are consolidated to a holistic mental image. When buying a peach, for example, one might not only consider color, form, and size, but also the smell, hardness, and felt surface texture of it. The relevant stimuli for a targeted sensory appeal are listed in table 4 (Kilian, 2007b, p. 220).

Product Category	Sight	Sound	Touch	Taste	Smell
Material (Substance)	√	(√)	√	(√)	(√)
Shape	√		√		
Color (Light)	√		(√)		
Scent (Gas)	(√)			(√)	√
Flavor				√	√
Sound (Tone)	(√)	√	(√)		
Movement	√	(√)	(√)		
Temperature	(√)		√	√	(√)
Speciality	√	(√)	√		
Legend: √ = applies (almost) always (directly perceivable) (√) = applies only seldom (indirectly perceivable)					

Table 4. Brand elements and their sensory appeal.

Sensory stimuli enable design – defined as the sensuously perceptible composition of an environment – to express the brand identity in a truly multi-sensory way. According to *Weinberg* design generally covers "the entire sensuously perceptible configuration via form and color, smell, taste, and noise" (1992, p. 7). Similarly, product design contains "the entire range of design elements of a product perceptible via the different senses, e.g. color, surface, form, smell, taste, noises" (Meyer, 2001, p. 5). However, multi-sensory brand signals are not limited to products and their packaging (see article *From Brand Identity to Audio Branding*, especially figure 5). The arrangement of services and their surroundings, e.g. the multi-sensory design of showrooms, and the multi-sensory combination of brand elements in the media, e.g. print ads that can also be smelt or felt, are also viable means of multi-sensory branding. In the same way, people linked to the brand can, and always should be, part of multi-sensory brand experience. They should be dressed in accordance with the brand, use key differentiators of the brand in their verbal communication and provide various non-verbal cues, e.g. a friendly welcome smile or a firm handshake. In the airline industry, the onboard staff oftentimes even uses a particular perfume. At *Air France*, for example, *Chanel No. 5* is being used (Kilian/Brexendorf, 2005, p. 14) while *Singapore Airlines* provides its staff with *Stefan Floridian Waters* (Munzinger/Musiol, 2008, p. 71 and p. 79). However, not all brand signals can – for technical or cost-reasons – in all cases make use of all sensory channels as table 5 illustrates.

Brand Signals	Examples	Sight	Sound	Touch	Taste	Smell
Products	e.g. packaging	√	√	√	(√)	√
Media	TV	√	√	(√)		(√)
	Radio		√	(√)		
	Cinema	√	√	(√)		(√)
	CD/DVD/Internet	√	√	(√)		
	Telephone		√			
People	e.g. sales staff	√	√	√		√
Surroundings	Buildings	√	√	√		√
	Shops/POS	√	√	√	√	√
	Events	√	√	√	√	√
	Fairs	√	√	√	√	√
Legend:	√ = applies (almost) always (directly perceivable) (√) = applies only seldom (indirectly perceivable)					

Table 5. Brand signals and their sensory appeal.

While products and surroundings almost always allow for the application of all five senses, media and people are typically restricted to the use of two to four sensory channels. With regard to TV commercials, the direct transfer of brand signals is only feasible visually and acoustically. However, in certain situations brand signals might also be conveyed indirectly via touch and smell. This is not meant to take place literally, but figuratively, for example by showing us a rough surface and/or by making us hear the vibrations of someone streaking over it. Similarly, we might see the vapor of a hot tomato soup or hear someone who enjoys eating it and expresses his pleasure by saying "delicious, just like fresh tomatoes". In contrast to this, shops, events, and fairs typically have all five senses at hand. Whether they are purposefully managed by a brand or not, the customer will perceive and evaluate a brand presence taking all sensory stimuli into consideration. Three examples shall highlight how this can be managed sensibly.

The brand value "naturalness", for example, could be conveyed visually by the color green or the image of a meadow, acoustically by a birdsong, haptically by the roughness of certain elements of the surroundings, olfactorily by the smell of fresh flowers, and gustatorily by providing customers with a homespun dish prepared according to "grandma's recipe". In similar ways, the brand values "Caribbean" and "freshness" could be experienced in a multi-sensory way, as table 6 illustrates (Kilian, 2007b, p. 221).

Elements	Value "Caribbean"	Value "Freshness"
Images	Palm trees, parrots, a beach, tropical plants, the sea, dark-skinned, happy people	Flowers, spring/water scenery, young people with a refreshing facial expression
Colors	blue and yellow, green, red	green and yellow, light blue
Words	Caribbean, palm trees, South Seas island, sun, the rushing sea, tropical paradise, endless beaches	The wild freshness of limes, April freshness, juvenile vigor
Tones	bright, clear (major), cheerful melody, steel-band music	bright, clear (major), cheerful melody, rush of a mountain creek
Feel	wooden, fibered surfaces, e.g. coconut paring	chilly materials, glossy surfaces, e.g. glass, metal, or wood
Smell	tropical fruits or a salty ocean	Citric or apple, grassy-green
Taste	coconut, rum, mango	menthol, peppermint, lemon

Table 6. Multi-sensory combination of brand elements to form brand signals.

The brand value "Caribbean", for example, could be represented figuratively by palm trees and/or using bluish green or red colors, by means of a bright, clear, and cheerful melody, by applying wooden, fibered surfaces, dispersing the smell of tropical fruits, and by offering a coconut snack or drink.

3.1 Current Multi-sensory Research Findings

Except for a few examples of brand communication, the effects of three to four sensory channels are still, in most cases, left to chance (MetaDesign/diffferent, 2005, p. 1). As current research by *Millward Brown* and *Lindstrom* implies, approximately 40% of the Fortune 500 enterprises are intending to integrate a multi-sensory brand strategy into their marketing plans (Lindstrom, 2005a, p. 7).

A reason for this might be, that both, brand value and brand loyalty, can be significantly increased by means of multi-sensory brand communication. According to their research, the number of sensuously activated memories increases with each additional sensory channel being purposefully used. As a consequence of this, more sensory memories can be activated, which in turn increase the linkage between the customer and the brand (Lindstrom, 2005a, p. 69). The research findings for a wide range of global brands showed, that consumers, who only mentioned one relevant sensory channel when recapitulating their own experiences with a particular brand, only in 28% of all cases selected the highest score "first choice" on a six-point Likert scale. This share rose to 43% when two to three sensory channels were considered relevant, and up to 59%, when four to five sensory channels were classified relevant. The research results also stressed, that the number of senses, which are addressed by a brand, strongly correlate with the perceived quality of a brand. The perceived brand quality, in turn, exerts strong influence on the value of a brand and thus on the price readiness of the consumers (Lindstrom, 2005a, p. 70 and p. 140).

A research project by *MetaDesign* and *diffferent* came up with similar results. According to the two agencies, brand commitment increases on a diminishing scale with each sensory channel that is additionally addressed: "The more strongly the consumer is supposed to immerse into the experience world of the brand, the more senses must be addressed consistently" (MetaDesign/diffferent, 2005, p. 2). The results of the study lead to the construction of a so-called "5-sense-branding-box". As a starting point, characteristic images, tones, materials, smells, and tastes were assigned to a set of 10 archetypical values. The value categories encompassed vitality, power, security, achievement, freedom, benevolence, tradition, tension, fair balance, and norm. In 75% of all cases, for example, the image of a bar code was assigned to the value "norm" and a 440-Hz tone with 58% likelihood. Table 7 provides exemplary results for the first two value dimensions vitality and power.

Sense	Value "Vitality"	Value "Power"
Sight	multicolored, deep colors, sunny, childlike; e.g. children playing, strawberry ice cream	dark, significant colors, distant picture language, solid forms, powerful; e.g. judgment, stretch limousine
Sound	humane, expressive; e.g. sounds of children, jubilation	loud, pervasive, specific rhythms; e.g. march, fanfare, lion
Touch	playful, airy, warm, flexible; e.g. artificial turf	cold, smooth, hard, heavy, high-class, leathery; e.g. gold leaf
Smell	fresh and fruity, stimulatory; e.g. Haribo gummy bears	ground-covering, heavy; e.g. incense
Taste	sweet and fruity; e.g. strawberries, Nutella spread	bitter, spicy, hot; e.g. whiskey, nutmeg, dark chocolate with chili

Table 7. Exemplary allocation to two value dimensions.

While "vitality" can be best characterized by self gratification, pleasure, desire, lust, and amusement, the value dimension "power" contains aspects like reputation, importance, and authority. For the multi-sensory communication of "vitality" a combination of multiple deep colors, sounds of children, warm and flexible surfaces, fresh and fruity smells, and a sweet and fruity taste would be most appropriate (MetaDesign/diffferent, 2006, p. 2ff.).

3.2 Framework for Multi-sensory Communication

As we have seen, various options for the multi-sensory communication of brand values towards the customer exist. They address the prevalent information overload of mass media and a further increasing media fragmentation which both lead to a continued decrease in media efficiency and effectiveness. In addition, an increased exchangeability of images used for advertising can be observed as the research results in the introductory part of this text highlighted. This has, in recent years, lead to shift from classical communication channels like TV, radio, and print towards below-the-line communication channels. Among them are direct marketing and sales promotions, sponsoring and events, fairs and exhibitions as well as public relations, guerilla marketing, viral marketing, and word-of-mouth. Most below-the-line "media" share one common characteristic: They enable brand communication via more than two senses. At the same time, they allow not only for a physical approximation, but also for a psychological rapprochement of consumer and brand. Hereby, tactile and gustatory perceptions in particular, require an active perception by the consumer that is volitional, whereas olfactory, acoustic, and visual perceptions most often take place in a passive way and more or less involuntarily. Figure 1 provides a systematization of the five senses with regard to range, perception, and communication type.

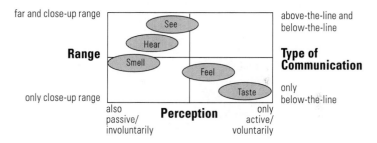

Figure 1. Systematization of the Five Senses.

Taste, feel, and smell are also referred to as "close-up senses". Their range is limited. Therefore, their implementation requires a direct exposure of the customer with the sensory stimuli of the product or service and/or the branded environment. The following two examples shall highlight this.

3.3 Examples of Multi-sensory Communication

The German carmaker *Daimler* has already recognized the importance of multi-sensory product design as platform for multi-sensory brand communication years ago. Daimler CEO *Dieter Zetsche* points out that "we can only differentiate ourselves, if we do not only activate the grey cells but also get the endorphins aboil" (Hillebrand/Schneider, 2006, p. 43). For this reason Daimler focuses its efforts on "the feeling of holding a steering wheel in one's hand, the sound of a closing door, the latching of a switch, or the smell of leather" (Hillebrand/ Schneider, 2006, p. 43). To accomplish this, Daimler has set up a Customer Research Center (CRC) in Berlin in 2002 where 17 psychologists and computer scientists research the emotional life of more than 1,000 car drivers annually. Among other things, the sensory impressions of the customers are systematically evaluated by measuring pupil movement and skin resistance. The results are then factored in when developing new operation and display systems. With the help of haptic tests, leather, paint, and metal surfaces are optimized through systematic changes and in the sound laboratory engine, airstream, and switch noises are being evaluated by customers (Maillart, 2005, p. 45f.). The results are directly incorporated into the vehicle development. By doing so, the company ensures that a *Mercedes-Benz* remains a Mercedes-Benz throughout all sensory experiences a customer might have.

The largest European travel firm *TUI* has even gone a step further. TUI has opened their first "travel experience center" in Berlin a few years ago. The travel offers at "World of TUI Berlin" are presented by showing short films, playing country-specific music, and dispersing scene-adequate scent. In addition, country-specific beverages and snacks are being offered at the in-house bar which help customers join in on the vacation (Schubert/Hehn, 2004, p. 1259). The multi-sensory offer turns the purchase act into an experience itself. At the point-of-purchase already, the customer anticipates the holiday experience that lies ahead of him and experiences the offer in extracts with all his senses prior to the actual vacation.

4. The Future of Communication is Multi-sensory

Multi-sensory brand communication increasingly receives attention by brand managers. This is not only due to the fact that the pressure for differentiation increases further, but also because more and more brand managers recognize the impact all five senses have on our purchase behavior. People, at any time and wherever they are, observe their environment with all five senses and form their decisions based on their multi-sensory impressions, no matter whether they are processed consciously or subconsciously. The multi-facetted input leads to a more or less rich set of associations. It also addresses varying values within the receptor which, in turn, trigger a purchase and guide the decision for one brand or another.

Profoundly defining a brand's identity, therefore, becomes a prevalent task for brand managers. For one, employees need to understand the brand values and how they impact their daily duties and responsibilities. As brand ambassadors, employees "live the brand" on a daily basis. They are, next to the product, the media, and the surroundings, providers of brand signals. Besides, all four types of brand signals (see article *From Brand Identity to Audio Branding*) need to incorporate, step by step, further multi-sensory brand elements and managers need to work hard on an ongoing basis to supervise and refine their utilization.

Three consecutive steps need to be undertaken to reach multi-sensory brand excellence. In a first step, visual differentiation needs to be established. As we have learned from research findings in the fashion industry, this is not yet the case in all industries. While the brand name and/or the claim should always incorporate the brand idea, other visual brand elements should at least establish a clear and fast connection with the brand. The beer brand *Beck's*, for example, uses the training ship *Alexander von Humboldt* with its green sails in most of its TV and print advertisements. The color scheme is further enhanced through the typical green Beck's beer bottle. As a consequence, customers link Beck's print ads with 66.8% likelihood to the brand when name and logo are covered. Similarly, the German brewery *Krombacher* has established the key visual "island" as a strong brand trigger. 77.3% of all subjects could link the island with Krombacher. Print ads of the *Deutsche Telekom* made anonymous, in turn, are correctly attributed to the brand with 85,8% likelihood just by using the color magenta and the typical Telekom "dots" (small grey squares) (Brandmeyer et al., 2008, p. 179ff.).

Once visual differentiation has been established and its continued utilization is anchored in the organization, additional senses should be used. Typically, the focus for the arrangement of "brand" elements at this stage is on the assumed liking of certain attributes by the target group, e.g. a particular style of music that is being used as background music at a brand outlet or at a trade fair. While this typically leads to an agreeable atmosphere, it is typically not linked to the brand as it cannot be used exclusively by the company. As a consequence, the atmosphere created is everything but brand-specific. If possible, companies should leap the second stage and move directly towards the third stages. In reality, however, many companies are currently trapped just there.

In order to reach the third stage, a company should not only address as many of the five senses as possible, ideally all five, but it should also make sure that the sensory stimuli all lead to the same kind of experience, a true brand experience. To accomplish this, all sensory brand elements should strengthen each other and result in uniform, brand-specific experiences. The link to the brand needs to be appropriate and direct. Once all brand signals are in line with the brand identity, brand excellence is almost inevitable as the brand offering is perceived by customers as strong, favorable, and unique. It will be preferred, not only once but again and again.

The prerequisite for this singularity is the definition of a durable brand identity, the establishment of singular brand elements derived thereof, their brand-specific combination to brand signals, and their implementation throughout the company and beyond, which is typically a complex task. Altogether, this makes me-too approaches by competitors difficult. In combination with a wide range of possibilities for their legal protection, imitations of brand-specific experiences can be avoided altogether. When properly executed, these multi-sensory brand experiences will enhance brand royalty and loyalty!

References

Bateson, M., Nettle, D. & Roberts, G. (2006). Cues of being watched enhance cooperation in a real-world setting. In: Biology Letters, vol. 2, no. 3 (September) , pp. 412-414.

Behrens, G. (1982). Das Wahrnehmungsverhalten der Konsumenten. Frankfurt: Harri Deutsch.

Braem, H. (2004). Die Macht der Farben. 6. edition. Munich: Langen Müller/Herbig.

Brandmeyer, K., Pirck, P., Pogoda, A. & Prill, C. (2008). Marken stark machen. Weinheim: Wiley.

Engeser, M. (2006). Kick im Kopf. In: WirtschaftsWoche, no. 7 (February 9), pp. 81-83.

Häusel, H.-G. (2008). Brain View, 2. edition. Freiburg im Breisgau: Haufe.

Hillebrand, W. & Schneider, M.C. (2006). Politur vom Chef. In: Capital, no. 18, pp. 42-43.

Kilian, K. & Brexendorf, T.O. (2005). Multisensuale Markenführung als Differenzierungs- und Erfolgsgröße. In: Campus 02 Business Report, no. 2 (June), pp. 12-15.

Kilian, K. (2007a). Multisensuales Markendesign als Basis ganzheitlicher Markenkommunikation, in: Florack, A., Scarabis, M. & Primosch, E. (eds.), Psychologie der Markenführung, pp. 323-356. Munich: Vahlen.

Kilian, K. (2007b). Akustik als klangvolles Element multisensualer Markenkommunikation. In: Bronner, K. & Hirt, R. (eds.), Audio Branding, pp. 214-227. Munich: Verlag Reinhard Fischer.

Knoblich, H., Scharf, A. & Schubert, B. (2003). Marketing mit Duft, 4. edition. Munich: Oldenbourg.

Kroeber-Riel, W. & Esch, F.-R. (2004). Strategie und Technik der Werbung, 6. edition. Munich: Vahlen.

Kroeber-Riel, W. & Weinberg, P. (1999). Konsumentenverhalten, 7. edition. Munich: Vahlen.

Lindstrom, M. (2005a). Brand Sense. New York: Free Press.

Lindstrom, M. (2005b). Broad sensory branding. In: Journal of Product & Brand Management, vol. 14, no. 2, pp. 84-87.

Linxweiler, R. (2004). Marken-Design, 2. edition. Wiesbaden: Gabler.

Maillart, M. (2005). Wie es Euch gefällt. In: Mercedesmagazin, no. 3, pp. 44-48.

MetaDesign & diffferent (2005). 5-Sense-Branding-Box. Unpublished empirical research findings.

MetaDesign & diffferent (2006). 5-Sense-Branding, Multisensorische Markenführung mit der 5-Sense-Branding-Box. Corporate Brochure, March.

MetaDesign (2006). Klingende, schmeckende, riechende Marken. http://www.metadesign.de/html/de/1875_p.html, 31.01. 2006

Meyer, S. (2001). Produkthaptik. Wiesbaden: Gabler.

Munzinger, U. & Musiol, K.G. (2008). Markenkommunikation. Munich: mi-Fachverlag.

Salzmann, R. (2007). Multimodale Erlebnisvermittlung am Point of Sale. Wiesbaden: DUV.

Scheier, C. & Held, D. (2006). Wie Werbung wirkt. Freiburg et al.: Haufe.

Scheier, C. & Held, D. (2007a). Was Marken erfolgreich macht. Freiburg et al.: Haufe.

Scheier, C. & Held, D. (2007b). Die Neuro-Logik erfolgreicher Markenkommunikation. In: Häusel, H.-G. (ed.), Neuromarketing, pp. 87-124. Freiburg et al.: Haufe.

Schubert, B. & Hehn, P. (2004). Markengestaltung mit Duft. In: Bruhn, M. (ed.), Handbuch Markenführung, 2. edition, pp. 1243-1267. Wiesbaden: Gabler.

Serviceplan & Facit (2007). *Modemarken bleiben in der Werbung ohne Profil. In: Horizont, no. 43 (October 25), p. 50.*

Weinberg, P. (1992). *Erlebnismarketing. Munich: Vahlen.*

Zaltman, G. (2002). *Hidden Minds. In: Harvard Business Manager, June, pp. 26-27.*

Synesthetic Design – Building Multi-sensory Arrangements

Dr. Michael Haverkamp
Ford-Werke GmbH, Köln

Introduction: Why Synesthetic Brand Design?

During the last decades it has been realized that corporate design gains crucial value if it provides activation of various senses. Synesthetic brand design means an optimization of a brand image and its symbols by using various references to multi-sensory perception. This design process implies synesthetic principles which are based on common properties of human perception (Haverkamp, 2008). The wording follows an extensive definition of synesthetics (Filk, 2004). All types of processes of cross-sensory coupling within the perceptual system are covered by this approach. Beside common ways of interaction between the senses, the generic concept additionally refers to individual phenomena like genuine synesthesia, which are currently the subject of various scientific studies. Synesthetic design can also be applied to product development and refinement of living environments.

The human perceptual system is designed to process multi-sensory data. We know from daily experience that we can use each sensory space separately: we can listen, and only listen, see, and only see, smell, taste etc. This experience makes us believe that sensory processing is split up into different spaces, strictly separated between each other. But in fact the phenomenon of separated senses is a result of a focus of attention on a specific sensory space. In contrary, when we are using sensory information intuitively during daily life, there is no separation of the senses, while nearly all stimuli are referred to multi-sensory objects.

First, on a physiological basis, our senses are specific. We always can clearly distinguish audible sensations from visual sensations from tactile sensations from smell … etc. Stimuli are processed via very different sense organs and through specific neuronal networks, finally projected upon specific areas of the brain (primary fields). Secondly, within brain structures of higher level, perception tends to match the data to provide a clear description of objects we are dealing with. For daily life activities and behaviours it does not make sense to handle data of different sensory spaces separately, but to identify objects with multi-sensory properties. A bell is not defined by only its shape, but by a variety of visual, tactile, auditory, olfactory and other features. Only the combination of all is what we describe as the "bell". While not all sensory data are available at one time – the bell may only be heard from a distance – memory helps to add the missing features from previous experience. Only the combination of multi-sensory features allows us to identify the object. Therefore the perceptual system always tries to relate even single stimuli to a multi-sensory model. Thus, with view on design tasks it can be concluded that multi-sensory references must be taken into account even if design is limited to one sensory space. It must clearly be understood that even a purely graphical logo can have multi-sensory references which strongly can influence its perception and subjective assessment, although it only stimulates vision as a single sensory channel.

Perceptual Objects

In general, the perceptual system tends to provide multi-sensory models of physical objects. These models are needed by the individual to interpret his environment and to coordinate his actions, while it is surrounded with objects whose physical nature cannot be accessed directly. As a result of perception and cross-sensory integration, an image occurs in consciousness. This image can show aspects of vision, audition or of any other sensory channel. In contrast to the physical object, which provides the stimuli, these subjective representations are here named perceptual objects. A sensory channel will further on be described as a modality. Within this context, image means a multi-sensory, not only visual representation. Here, a physical object is anything that provides specific stimuli. It is not necessarily a solid structure, but can be a liquid, a gas, a human being, an animal – or can be characterized by lack of material, like a hole.

A subjective representation of a physical object is based on a sensory hypothesis, generating a perceptual object that in some ways correlates to its physical source. While physical objects always provide various stimuli, perceptual objects usually appear to be multi-sensory, i. e. they contain auditory, visual, tactile and other data. Only if stimuli of a single sensory channel are presented which are unknown to the individual, a first approach is made by generating perceptual objects of this single modality, e.g. auditory or visual. It therefore can be stated that - in case of known stimuli - perceived auditory, visual or tactile data are always related to multi-sensory perceptual objects.

Sensory information which is not perceived at a moment is supplemented by data stored in memory, which is a result of previous experience (figure 1). If no mnemonic data has been stored, the whole features must be taken from instantaneous perception. In this case more time is needed for a multi-sensory observation of the object. The combination of actual stimuli and data from memory is an effective way of generating multi-sensory perceptual objects.

The quality of a perceptual object is only experienced by the perceiving subject itself. The various qualitative aspects inherent to a specific perceptional object are named qualia.

Process of perception

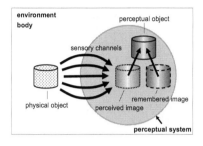 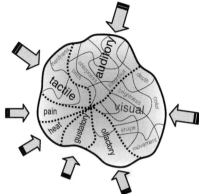

Figure 1. A multi-sensory perceptual object is a mo-del of a physical object. It is generated from instan-taneous sensory input and data from memory.

Figure 2. Contributions of various modalities shape a multi-sensory perceptual object.

The function of the perceptual system is aimed at identification of physical objects by gene-rating multi-sensory perceptual objects (figure 2). Those perceptual objects accumulate data from the various sensory spaces, each including a specific set of features, like color, pitch, loudness, hardness and many others. If this object is known and represented in memory, its cross-sensory features can be recalled by stimulation of only one single modality. Learning to handle the physical objects of daily life initially requires testing of all sensory properties, like vision, audition, smell, taste, surface structure, hardness and many others. The learning process can easily be observed while a baby is handling a toy. It looks at the object, immedi-ately grasps it, hits it towards another object to experience its sound, puts it into its mouth, etc. After a while, it has learned that a specific sound indicates a hard or a soft surface, a heavy or lightweight object, etc. The baby then is enabled to remind the perceptual object of a toy by hearing the sound, and this recalls all cross-sensory properties which have been experienced before. From these observations it must be concluded that design of brand sym-bols as well as of products must be based on analysis of possible references to multi-sensory perceptual objects, even if only stimuli in single sensory spaces are presented.

Parallel processing is a basic feature of the brain (see e.g. Campenhausen, 1993). It can be found on all levels of neuronal activity, from the interaction of single neurons with its inhibitions and amplifications up to the binding activity of complete cortical domains.

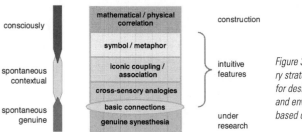

Figure 3. Model of cross sensory strategies. Most important for design of products, brands and environments are strategies based on intuitive features.

Coupling Strategies

A multi-sensory perceptual object can be understood as a cluster of perceptual objects of single modalities. The data of different modalities can be coupled by various strategies (Haverkamp 2004, 2007a). Those strategies are methods which are applied by the human perceptual and cognitive system to couple different sensory spaces. On the other hand, these strategies can be understood as basis of design procedures, which closely refer to the cognitive and intuitive capabilities of the customer. Figure 3 provides an overview. The main intuitive strategies are:

analogies = correlations of single features/attributes
iconic coupling (concrete association) = identification of sources of stimuli
symbolic connections = semantic correlations by analysis of meaning

Each main intuitive strategy splits into a variety of mechanisms, e.g. analogies can be made up between basic attributes, like brightness or roughness, or can consider movement, shape, emotion and many other aspects.

Some of the main strategies of interaction as listed above are interpreted intuitively and do not need conscious analysis: symbolic and iconic coupling, cross-sensory analogies and basic connections. Therefore these strategies are of main impact on multi-sensory design. Other correlations can be constructed with reference to known physical properties or mathematical rules, e.g. the frequency of color light can be related to pitch frequency of a given pure tone by means of appropriate calculations. Common ways to provide constructions can easily be found by programming specific algorithms, as used by audio-visual media players and automated light-shows. If the perceiving subject, however, cannot find any correlations by use of the above mentioned intuitive strategies, it will not be able to find any match of data provided by different senses. A minority of subjects additionally experiences sensations in sensory channels which are not instantaneously stimulated. In those cases tones can have a color, or taste can cause audible sound. Any kind of sensation can subsequently appear in connection to a primary, stimulated sensory feature, but each subject has its very individual, fixed connection. Although rare and strictly individual, such phenomena of genuine synesthesia are assumed to be im-

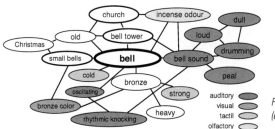

Figure 4. Multi-modal network
(extract) – Example: "bell".

portant to understand the multi-sensory capabilities of the brain. Various research projects are directed towards these specific ways of synesthetic perception (Harrison, 2001; Cytowic, 2002; Day, 2005; Robertson, 2005). In contrary to genuine synesthesia, basic multi-sensory connections are evident in each individual. They enable performance of generic tasks like body movement, which requires perception of muscle forces, tension and displacement, visual orientation in space, vestibular information, haptic feedback and others. Cross-sensory data are integrated without specific attention of consciousness. Merging of taste and smell is another common example of basic connections.

It is evident that the listed main strategies of interaction are acting in-parallel, showing mechanisms that initially are independent of each other. Therefore, during the first step of perception the data processing is separately done according to these strategies. The next step then integrates the results of all strategies to provide a map of correlations which is consistent, with contradictions reduced to a minimum. Shaping of perceptual objects from a variety of data requires integration of all perceived elements. This includes various mechanisms of grouping and segregation. First approaches which are also valid today have been provided by Gestalt-psychology (Werner, 1966). Recently, theories of scene analysis have added essential insight into integration processes (Bregman, 1999). The model presented in figure 3 is suitable for classification of all multi-sensory phenomena.

Each strategy contains various processes of cross-sensory interaction with references to single features of each sensory space. As mentioned above, main strategies which are intuitively processed within every subject are cross-sensory analogies, iconic and symbolic coupling. Those strategies depend on the context of perceived features. Therefore analysis of contextual relations is part of each strategy during cognitive processing, and must be considered by any design process. The analysis of all single elements and attributes of an object or a complex sensory environment can be understood by means of a multi-modal network, as sketched in figure 4. This network can contain both iconic (concrete associative) and symbolic elements. The iconic elements are stored in memory as shapes/images of sensory perception, i.e. as visual image, sound, odor etc. The number and grade of cross-linking of elements is determined by the level of experience (number and intensity of perceptual events) and by the mental und emotional involvement of the perceiving subject.

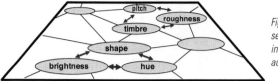

Figure 5. Correlation of cross-sensory analogies, exemplified in case of perceived visual and auditory attributes.

With reference to the aforementioned perceptual objects, they can be understood as connected clusters of attributes, for which a certain probability exists that they belong to a specific physical object (or term/item). If such a cluster is intuitively integrated within a single modality, it defines a perceptual object of one sensory channel. Attributes of single modalities can be connected via analogies, i.e. correlation functions. Complete perceptual objects of single modalities can be coupled via iconic or symbolic coupling.

The described strategies are performed in-parallel. This principle of parallel processing is in accordance to recent findings of brain functionality. It also refers to daily experience that – e.g. during perception of music – it is possible to experience a concrete association at one time with a sensation of brightness and with conscious analysis of the musical structure.

If activated, each strategy gains an independent result that can be contradictory to other strategies. In this case, perceptual conflicts (cognitive dissonances) can occur which can cause uneasy feelings or negative rating of perceptions. On the other hand, perceptual conflicts can attract attention. An example is the colouring of colour terms in contrary to their meaning, like "green" is displayed with red letters.

While strategies are acting independently, the in-parallel activity can provide similar results and thus amplify coupling of specific senses. This redundancy supports reliability of multi-sensory perceptual objects, e.g. multi-sensory brand symbols.

Attention can consciously be focused on a specific strategy. During daily life, however, all available methods of cross-sensory coupling contribute to multi-sensory perception. Therefore an isolated, focused experimental environment can cause artificial results with limited relevance to common perception.

Cross-sensory Analogies

Cross-sensory analogies refer to the capability of the perceptional system to detect correlations of specific attributes and to analyze them for identification of physical objects and atmospheric features (figure 5, see also Haverkamp 2004, 2007b). The analysis of analogies can refer to:
– generic attributes (intensity, sharpness, brightness ...)
– motion (straight, rotational, irregular, expanding ...)
– body perception (tense, relaxed, floating ...)
– emotion (calm, troubled, angry ...)

■ ■ ■ T Deutsche Telekom

Figure 6. Visual logo of Deutsche Telekom AG, as used until August 2007.

A series of generic attributes is valid for correlation of each sensory channel. *Werner* explicitly named intensity, brightness, volume, density und roughness (*Werner,* 1966). Correlations of generic attributes have been comprehensively discussed by *Stevens* (Stevens 1961, 1966). For the aspects of motion as a visual and auditory attribute see (Shove, 1995) and (Eitan, 2004).

The capability to detect cross-sensory correlations as well as correlations of various attributes within one sensory space is an essential feature of the perceptual system. Without the ability of evaluating analogies, perception would not be possible because the build-up of perceptual objects would not be enabled. A jingling bell can only be recognized if the jingling noise (auditory space) is connected to the image of the bell (visual space). If the necessary integration process fails, only a noise with unknown source is detected in-parallel to a moving visual object that cannot be determined as sounding or not sounding. Identification of physical objects and analysis of the complex environment which surrounds the individual is not possible without determining correlations.

Analogies are capable of consolidating unknown or unexpected perceptual objects by correlating the perceived attributes. A sound source localized in a specific angle and distance will be coupled to a physical object seen near its location. A connection will also be presumed in case of different location, but with accurate temporal correlation (synchronicity; Kohlrausch, 2005). Therefore spatial and temporal correlations must primarily be considered. In example, a heard speech can be allocated to a specific person via synchronic sound and motion of the mouth, additionally supported by correlated visual and auditory localization.

The correlation of the visual and auditory logo of *Deutsche Telekom* provides a good example of cross-sensory coupling via the generic attributes visual height and tone pitch (figure 6). The signet consists of 4 dots and one "T". The sound logo consists of five single tones related to the five visual objects, with the one tone related to "T" increased in pitch. Like a system of musical notation, tone pitch is correlated to the height of these objects, with time scaled from left to right-hand-side. Additionally, prosody of the term "Deutsche Telekom" with its five syllables correlates to jingle and image (see also article *From Brand Identity to Audio Branding*). Cross-sensory analogies are a main topic of recent psycho-physical research on multi-sensory relations (Calvet, 2004). Beside coupling of auditory and visual stimuli, analogies are also suitable to include tactile, olfactory and gustatory features into any multi-sensory design concept.

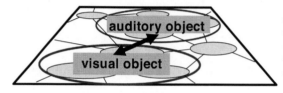

Figure 7. Perceptual objects of single modalities, grouped from the visual and auditory attributes of figure 5 as base of iconic coupling.

Iconic coupling

This strategy to establish cross-modal connections is based on associations suitable to identify a known physical object (figure 7). A single stimulus can refer to a multi-modal perceptual object stored in memory. Thus a specific sound stimulus can evoke imagination of the sound source with all of its cross-sensory attributes, if the variety of properties was experienced before. In example, the sound of the siren of an ambulance refers to the image of emergency light and of the whole vehicle. The sound of a bell refers to its visual image as well as its tactile feeling. Iconic coupling is therefore processed via an identification of the source of stimuli. In case of audition, *Chion* uses the term causal listening, while *Flückiger* refers to it as semantics of first order (Chion, 1994; Flückiger, 2002). The term concrete association underlines the fact that this strategy is based on assignment of perceived features to known objects (Haverkamp, 2004).

Listening to music often evokes imagination of landscapes or interiors which fit to the associative content of the music or a comparable atmosphere. More directly, images of musical instruments can be recalled. Onomatopoeia in speech and music is also a common application of iconic features, while the imitation of natural sound generates an intuitive connection to multi-sensory objects or to the atmosphere of an environment. While iconic coupling refers to objects in memory, it is based on learning and experience of the subject. It therefore depends on living environment and cultural background of an individual. Design of multi-sensory objects must always refer to the perceptual context and experience of the recipient (customer/user).

In the case of the visual logo of the manufacturer of milk products *Milch-Union Hocheifel eG*, the German onomatopoetic expression of the cows moo ("Muh") is used instead of a sound logo (figure 8). Thus, the sound logo is included by visual means, beside the image of a cow. Therefore the high degree of sympathy for the cow as the initial producer of the milk is utilized for brand identity.

Iconic coupling is the main strategy of correlating gustatory and olfactory stimuli to multi-sensory perceptual objects. Therefore most terms used for description of smell and taste refer to physical objects which are identified as the source (e.g. "citrus flavour"). In rare cases, however, cross-sensory analogies are used (e.g. "sharp odour").

Figure 8. Visual logo of Milch-Union Hocheifel eG, including the visual image and the onomatopoetic represented sound of a cow.

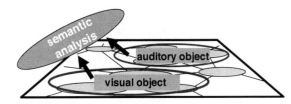

Figure 9. Additional relations of sensory objects are established using a semantic analysis, enabling multi-sensory grouping by correlations of meaning as base of symbolic coupling.

Semantic relations / symbolic coupling

Stimuli of a specific modality can also refer to semantic codes (figure 9), which e.g. are given in the visual modality by established signals and logos, sometimes based on aspects of ancient heraldry. Those symbols can only be understood if sender and recipient of a message are based on the same context. Therefore the functionality of signs and symbols is limited to specific aspects of culture and era. Semiotics provides the basic understanding of decoding meaning (Jekosch, 2005). Flückiger describes symbolic coupling as semantics of higher order (Flückiger, 2002). Synesthetic terms as a special kind of metaphor are an important element of literature, especially of lyrics. Synesthetic metaphors are also applied for description of sensations during psycho-physical experiments. For example, a sound can be described as warm, bright or heavy. Those terms are primarily conscious constructions, but need the recipient's capability of imagination via cross-sensory analogy or association. Semantic relations refer to a known content of meaning, while the source of stimuli may be unidentified. Speech that is understood includes semantic information, but usually iconic features are added, which are suitable to identify the source, e.g. a person. Speech of a language unknown to a subject, however, only refers to iconic coupling as well as cross-modal correlations. In this case, a speaker can still be identified and onomatopoetic and emotional information can be interpreted via associations, but meaning cannot be decoded. A popular example of symbolic coupling of auditory and visual symbols is given by the sound logo and visual symbol of *Eurovision*, a joint venture of the *European Broadcasting Union*, which started 1954. It initially included a visual image which was combined from the star banner of the European Union with floodlights, providing the impression of a brilliant festival event (figure 10). The sound logo was taken from the Ouverture of *Marc-Antoine Charpentier's* "Te Deum" in D-major, which has been composed around 1690 (see article *Audio Branding – all new?*). This colourful sacred music includes musical symbols to honour the King, whereby God and the Sun King Ludwig XIV are put on the same level. It also shows martial aspects, while it was possibly performed to celebrate the French victory in the battle of Steinkerque (1692). The Eurovision sound logo keeps the original mood of festivity, but removes references to military (no drum roll at the beginning) and to the King (reduced dotted rhythms).

Figure 10. First visual logo of the Eurovision, established 1954. The visual logo has been updated, while the sound logo as popular "Eurovision-Hymn" is still in use.

The coupling strategies genuine synesthesia and mathematical/physical correlation are of minor importance for multi-sensory brand design, but shall be included to complete this comprehensive overview.

Genuine Synesthesia

In contrast to analogies as well as iconic and semantic coupling, genuine synesthesia is not a common cross-sensory process. It is very individual. Only relatively few people report this way of perception. It is induced by a primary, common perception in one sensory channel. This excites perception in a secondary channel without need of a specific stimulus. The correlation is fixed (absolute) and is neither influenced by the perceptual context nor by learning or experience. Every subject has its own schema of correlation, which remains constant for a lifetime. This definition of genuine synesthesia was first described by *Cytowic* (Cytowic, 2002). Many reports and earlier investigations throughout the last century show that genuine synesthesia is widely independent from the cultural, scientific and historical context (see e.g. Bleuler, 1881; Anschütz, 1927; Mahling, 1927; Baron-Cohen, 1997; Emrich, 2001; Robertson, 2005). The most common phenomena of genuine synesthesia as coupling between two senses are visual phenomena induced by auditory events (colour hearing). Additionally, correlations of visual features, e.g. colour, to visual shapes are often reported, especially graphemes can appear in perception with synesthetic colours added. Those phenomena are often, but not always related to the semantic content of stimuli. In this manner, series of numbers or terms can show specific shapes (number forms). In principle, all types of stimuli can induce all types of secondary features. In fact, most secondary perceptions show visual features (Day, 2005).

Although the scientific interest to genuine synesthesia is actually high, it is difficult to draw conclusions which are relevant for common multi-sensory perception. Some preliminary results:

– All parts of the brain can couple sensory information back to specific perceptual areas, especially to visual fields. It does not seem to matter whether the areas are adjacent or not. A variety of feedback loops transfers results of high cognitive processing back to primary fields of perception.

– Basic shapes play an important role in processing of sensory data. Lists of elementary visual shapes have been collected by various authors (e.g. Horowitz, 1970). For design purposes it seems reasonable to search for elementary shapes within all sensory spaces which serve as "atoms" from which perceptual objects are composed.

– Ideal, generic combinations of sensory features may exist, e.g. of visual shape and colour, timbre and tactile surface features, etc.

– Semantic relations can be transformed to visual shapes.

In the near future, research on synesthesia will definitely improve knowledge of cross-sensory connections and thus offer further approaches on multi-sensory design.

Conscious Construction (Mathematical and physical Correlation)

Beside the intuitive ways of cross-modal coupling, concepts can be made up by conscious construction to correlate attributes of different sensory spaces. Many of those concepts have been discussed during the past, using mathematical expressions and/or references to physical facts, like relations of frequencies of coloured light to pitch of audible tones. It was often assumed that a physical relation as an objective fact will have specific relevance for human perception. On the contrary, however, there are deviations: The intuitive way to choose a colour scale is to sort colours by brightness, not by frequency. Therefore, all mathematical or physical relations used for design of multi-sensory objects have to be proven for intuitive validity.

Today, computational tools offer a large variety of algorithms to correlate stimuli of various modalities with each other. Media-players use simple expressions to generate visualisations of music, using correlations of visual features to auditory attributes. The spectator/listener, however, will only feel an alignment of vision and sound if the result includes at least one of the intuitive correlations described above. If cross-modal correlations are technically used which cannot be perceived, the mathematical/physical coupling will remain abstract and will not show any alignment to subjective observations.

The physical analysis of auditory and visual stimuli shows some common characteristics. In both cases energy is transported to the sense organs via physical waves, which are of mechanical (sound) or electro-magnetic (light) nature. A main difference is given by frequency (sound: 16-16000 Hz; visible light: 390-790 THz).

Several trials have been made to directly relate frequencies (or wavelengths) of light to those of sound in order to construct light events similar to audible music. A musical system based on various octaves, however, cannot be established with visible light. The relative bandwidth of audible sound is more than 12 octaves, whereas visible light covers less than one octave (!).

Another discrepancy is given by different resolution of auditory and visual perception: auditory resolution of frequency and time is high compared to vision, whereas spatial resolution of the eye is much higher than that of the ear. A complex spectrum of sound can simultaneously lead to various perceptions like several tones with pitch and timbre independent from each other, while every light spectrum only induces sensation of one single colour.

Therefore a polyphonic structure cannot simply be transferred from sound to vision by use of spectral properties, but must include transformation from the spectral domain to spatial properties. *Jewanski* gives a detailed analysis of theories and trials up to the beginning of the 19th century (Jewanski, 1999). Many further trials were made: Among others, *Rimington* wrote the first comprehensive book regarding correlations of music and colours, followed by *László* and *Klein* (Rimington, 1911; László, 1925; Klein, 1926). All three authors have built up colour organs that were successfully presented to the public. Technical progress during the 20th century improved availability of lighting systems and computational tools (Sidler, 2006). The interest in theoretical approaches in colour music, however, de-creased after a euphoric phase within the first half of the century, and changed to more creative and free use of capabilities provided by light show, movie and video clip.

Combinations

The perceptual system collects information of all modalities and performs sophisticated integration processes to merge the naturally incomplete data into a multi-sensory image of the world. The individual's world includes exterior as well as interior body perception. The aim of the integration processes is to generate subjective representations of objects which are free of contradictions and gaps. An optimized design must take into account various processes of multi-sensory integration.

The perceptual system is able to analyze analogies, iconic and semantic strategies of cross-modal coupling in-parallel. Therefore, with view on a multi-sensory design process, it appears to be reasonable to focus on a structure with 3 layers for multi-sensory alignment of object features, as shown in figure 11. In the first step, it implies that characteristic attributes of perceptual objects are clearly perceived and segregated from each other. On the level of analogy, correlations of single properties are evaluated. The features with the best capability for a given task must be selected and optimized. For example, correlations of visual shape of a logo can be aligned to dynamic features of a melody.

As the next step, the analysis of iconic content identifies and connects attributes which are recognized as elements of known perceptual objects (causal listening). Even a rudimentary stimulus within one modality is capable of initiating the reconstruction of a complex multi-sensory perceptual object by adding all features stored in memory. The main problem of a design process is that a variety of features has to be considered which are only available in the memory of the perceiving individual. The set of subjective qualities (qualia) related to a stimulus also depends on past experience and external context. Within a known cultural and environmental context, however, experience and learned symbols can be evaluated. Especially global brand design is a challenge due to a large variety of cultural expectation and perceptual experience of the customers in various regions of the world.

On the semantic level, perceptual objects are coupled according to additional information which is learned separately, like e.g. language, traffic signs, philosophical, political or religious interpretation and thinking. The meaning of symbols can be very different within various cultures – therefore a global design approach must be based on comprehensive, cross-cultural studies. A basic hierarchy of the three strategies shown in figure 11 can be stated: Within the recipient's perceptual system, unknown objects can be loaded with information about the physical source and meaning by correlating their cross-sensory features. Well known objects are already defined by iconic coupling during presentation of single features. Meaning can be added by observation of known objects and by learning of additional, abstract information.

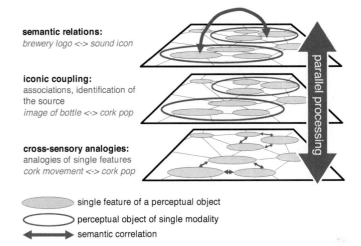

semantic relations:
brewery logo <-> sound icon

iconic coupling:
associations, identification of
the source
image of bottle <-> cork pop

cross-sensory analogies:
analogies of single features
cork movement <-> cork pop

single feature of a perceptual object
perceptual object of single modality
semantic correlation

Figure 11. Three-layer model of in-parallel processing of cross-modal analogies, iconic coupling and semantic correlations. Examples for audio-visual features of a brewery's brand image are added.

The parallel processing of various strategies gains independent results which can be contradictory or similar. Friendly sentences e.g. can be vocalized with aggressive facial expression, or aggressive sentences can be supported by slight body movement and gentle voice. Different strategies are used by the perceptional system to eliminate those contradictions. If visual and auditory signals contain different data, the result can be dominated by one sensory channel, while the other is inhibited. Ventriloquists make use of the dominance of the visual modality: the mimic action of their doll indicates that the source for its speech is at its mouth, while information about the location of the true sound source is suppressed. Another possibility is that contradictory sensory information is merged to shape a different result. This has been exemplified by means of the *McGurk-effect*, where the mimic action of a speaker modifies the perceived sound of syllables (McGurk, 1976). If contradictions of data provided by different modalities cannot be matched, this can cause negative feelings like indisposition or cognitive dissonance. The fact that this attracts specific attention of the subject is nowadays well known and used in print and screen advertising. Cognitive dissonance can also be used for brand design, but shall be carefully proven to avoid negative feelings induced to the customer. For example, a visual logo can use aggressive colours, but the sound logo supports a peaceful and calm feelings. The general approach, however, should prefer an appropriate alignment of several strategies, e. g. a similar direction of cross-sensory correlations, associations (iconic content) and meaning.

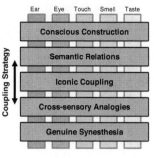

Figure 12. Synesthetic design compared to conventional process of multi-sensory design.

Conclusion: Ways to Synesthetic Brand Design

A conventional process to include more than one sense into brand design is based on single modalities (figure 12, left hand side): auditory elements are usually designed separately from other sensory spaces. Only during a late phase, some features may be correlated to each other. In contrary, the synesthetic design is targeted to cross-sensory alignment in an early phase of the development process (figure 12, right hand side; Haverkamp, 2008). At first, the intuitive coupling strategies analogies, iconic coupling and semantic relations are considered. Then, appropriate attributes (like pitch, auditory dynamics, colour, symbol shape, associative elements, symbols) are chosen to fulfil the alignment of these strategies. In the last step, the chosen attributes have to be adjusted to provide an optimized integration of the selected features. Final integration must be based on the relevance of each coupling strategy and each attribute. It should include processes for minimization of contradictions, to avoid negative emotions induced by cognitive dissonances. First steps have been taken to find cross-sensory design of brand elements – but much more is possible if all opportunities are addressed by a systematic approach to synesthetic design.

Michael Haverkamp

References

Anschütz, Georg (1927). Farbe-Ton-Forschungen. Bd.1. Leipzig: Akademische Verlagsgesellschaft.

Bleuler, Eugen and Lehmann, Karl (1881). Zwangsmässige Lichtempfindungen durch Schall und verwandte Erscheinungen auf dem Gebiete der anderen Sinnesempfindungen. Leipzig: Reisland.

Baron-Cohen, Simon and John E. Harrison (1997). Synaesthesia. Classic and Contemporary Readings. Oxford und Cambridge: Blackwell Publishers.

Bregman, Albert S. (1999). Auditory scene analysis. The perceptual organization of sound (2nd edition). Cambridge, Massachusetts: The MIT press.

Calvert, Gemma A, Spence, Charles and Stein, Barry E. (2004). The handbook of multisensory processing. Cambridge (MA): The MIT press.

Campenhausen, Christoph von (1993). Die Sinne des Menschen (2nd edition). Stuttgart: Thieme.

Chion, Michel (1994). Audio-vision. Sound on screen. New York: Columbia University Press.

Cytowic, Richard E. (2002). Synesthesia, a union of the senses (2nd edition). New York: Springer Verlag.

Day, Sean A. (2005). Some demographic and socio-cultural aspects of synesthesia. In: Lynn C. Robertson & Noam Sagiv (ed.): Synesthesia. Perspectives from cognitive neuroscience. Oxford: Oxford University Press.

Eitan, Zohar and Granot, Roni E. (2004). Musical parameters and images of motion. In: R. Parncutt. et al. (eds.), Proceedings of the conference on interdisciplinary musicology. Graz.

Emrich, Hinderk M; Schneider, Udo and Zedler, Markus (2001). Welche Farbe hat der Montag? Synästhesie: das Leben mit verknüpften Sinnen. Leipzig: Hirzel.

Filk, Christian; Lommel, Michael and Sandbothe, Mike (2004). Media Synaesthetics. Konturen einer physiologischen Medienästhetik. Köln: Herbert von Halem Verlag.

Flückiger, Barbara (2002). Sound Design. Die virtuelle Klangwelt des Films (2nd edition). Marburg: Schüren.

Harrison, John (2001). Synaesthesia. The strangest thing. Oxford: University Press.

Haverkamp, Michael (2004). Audio-visual Coupling and Perception of Sound-Scapes. Oldenburg: DEGA, p. 365-366.

Haverkamp, Michael (2007a). Percezione sinestesica e design del rumore. Progetto Graphico, Anno 5, Numero 10. Roma: Aiap, p. 162-169.

Haverkamp, Michael (2007b). Essentials for description of cross-sensory interaction during perception of a complex environment. Proc. of Inter-Noise 2007. Istanbul: Turkish Acoustical Society.

Haverkamp, Michael (2008). Synästhetisches Design – kreative Produktgestaltung für alle Sinne. München: Carl-Hanser Verlag.

Horowitz, Mardi Jon (1970). Image Formation and Cognition. London: Butterworths.

Jekosch, Ute (2005). Assigning meaning to sound - Semiotics in the context of product-sound design. In: Jens Blauert (ed.): Communication acoustics. Berlin: Springer, p. 193-221.

Jewanski, Jörg (1999). Ist C = Rot? Eine Kultur- und Wissenschaftsgeschichte zum Problem der wechselseitigen Beziehung zwischen Ton und Farbe. Sinzig: Studio, Verlag Schewe.

Klein, Adrian Bernard (1926). Colour-Music. London: The Technical Press Ltd.

Kohlrausch, Armin and van de Par, Steven (2005). Audio-visual interaction in the context of multimedia applications. In: Jens Blauert (ed.): Communication acoustics. Berlin: Springer, p. 109-138.

177

László, Alexander (1925). *Die Farblichtmusik. Leipzig: Breitkopf & Härtel.*

Mahling, Friedrich (1927). *Das Problem der "Audition coloreé". In: Georg Anschütz (ed.): Farbe-Ton-Forschungen. Bd.1. Leipzig: Akademische Verlagsgesellschaft.*

McGurk, H. and MacDonald, J. (1976). *Hearing lips and seeing voices. Nature 264, p. 746-748.*

Rimington, Alexander Wallace (1911). *Colour-Music. The art of mobile colour. London: Hutchinson.*

Robertson, Lynn C. and Sagiv, Noam (2005). *Synesthesia. Perspectives from cognitive Neuroscience. Oxford: Oxford University Press.*

Shove, Patrick and Repp, Bruno H. (1995). *Musical motion and performance. In: J. Rink (ed.): The practice of performance. Cambridge: University Press.*

Sidler, Natalia and Jewanski, Jörg (2006). *Farbe-Licht-Musik. Synästhesie und Farblichtmusik. Bern: Peter Lang.*

Stevens, Stanley Smith (1961). *The psychophysics of sensory function. In: W. A. Rosenbith (ed.): Sensory communication. Cambridge: M.I.T. Press.*

Stevens, Stanley Smith (1966). *Matching functions between loudness and ten other continua. Perception & Psychophysics I, (I) 5-8.*

Werner, Heinz (1966). *Intermodale Qualitäten. In: Handbuch der Psychologie, Bd. 1. Göttingen: Hogrefe, p. 278-303.*

"In acoustic brand communication, only an intermodal concept will result in the desired effects. Visual and acoustic design elements must aim for joint transmission of the product or the brand, respectively, including its characteristics, specific quality and attributed emotions with as many interactive and supplementing cross-references as possible."

(Hannes Raffaseder, 2009)

"First steps have been taken to find cross-sensory design of brand elements — but much more is possible if all opportunities are addressed by a systematic approach to synesthetic design."

(Michael Haverkamp, 2009)

F.
Legal Aspects of Audio Branding

Intellectual Property in the Context of Acoustic Branding

Jasmin Junge
Consultant / audio consulting group

1. Introduction

When looking into the subject of acoustic branding, it is essential to deal with intellectual property as well as with every other issue. In this regard many different aspects have to be considered.

First of all the term intellectual property (IP) needs to be clearly defined. People often use the term intellectual property although they actually refer to a smaller or larger category (Stallman, 2006). Copyrights, patents and trademarks are often summarized under the notion of intellectual property. In fact, the term includes different kinds of laws. Besides that, several countries define some of these terms in different ways. As a consequence a clear definition is indispensable in order to avoid a mix-up. The figure below shows all terms and illustrates their relationship to each other.

In the context of acoustic branding trademarks are as important as copyrights. Regarding copyrights, collecting societies and publishers are the relevant institutions to deal with. Collecting societies exercise the author's rights and have the authority to license works and collect royalties. The publisher on the other hand establishes a connection between the composer or songwriter and the music merchandising as e.g. management companies, advertising companies or film producers.

Figure 1. Legal terms in context of acoustic branding strategy.

All these issues have to be considered in order to develop a well-defined intellectual property strategy. Not only optimal protection (trade mark registration) or clarifications of music usage rights are relevant for an effective IP strategy, but also flexibility, sustainability and easy administration procedures, as well as clear financial frameworks.

It is important to look into these subjects right at the beginning of the conception of a holistic acoustic branding strategy, since the IP strategy has to be adapted to the requirements of the acoustic branding strategy (touch points, respective media applications, relevant countries etc.).

2. Importance of copyright in the context of acoustic branding

As implied before, intellectual property right protects immaterial things like expressed ideas (copyright) and ideas, typified in a practical implementation (patents). Intellectual property thus includes copyrights, trademarks and patents (Miller & Davis, 1990). In the context of the acoustic branding strategy especially copyrights and trademarks are relevant. Copyright refers to creative pieces of work like literature, painting and music. It makes sure the author holds exclusive rights to his work. This means that the author has the legal right to publish, reproduce or change his work. In fact he is the only one entitled to use his work, as long as he does not approve usage by others.

Even though almost every country has different copyright laws, each author, regardless of his country of origin, has rights to his work in any kind of way. Especially in a commercial context it is important for the author to set limits for the usage of his creation, e.g. to decide in which situation his work should be used (Berndorff et al., 2004). In consequence of the copyright, companies which want to include music in their internal and external communications have to pay license fees in order to get the usage rights to the music. Copyright is a time-limited right, i.e. it loses its validation a certain time after the author's death. The validity period differs from country to country. In most countries the copyright is valid for 70 years after the author's death (Berndorff et al., 2004; Hertin, 2003). In few countries an author's work is protected 25, 50 or 100 years by copyright. After this retention period the creation is placed in the public domain where it is not protected by copyright any longer. From that time on everybody can use these pieces of work without official consent and without paying license fees (Berndorff et al., 2004; Movsessian & Seifert, 1995). For companies that do not want to pay license fees for their acoustic branding strategy, this aspect is very interesting. The cell phone producer *Nokia*, for example, successfully implemented the classical guitar title *Gran Vals* by *Francisco Tárrega* (died 1909) in its corporate communications. In doing so Nokia succeeded in establishing an associative link between this title and their company. One reason for having taken exactly that title might have been that it had already entered the public domain and does not generate recurrent payments. Unfortunately the advantages and disadvantages of using a public domain title in the corporate communications cannot be discussed here since this would go beyond the scope of this article.

2.1 International copyright protection

For companies that want to implement an acoustic identity on international level as part of their corporate communications it is helpful to know about the main issues of the international copyright. Although it turned out that copyright protection should not end at a country's borders, there is no such thing as an "international copyright" that automatically protects an author's work all over the world. Basis for the copyright is the principle of territoriality. This principle implies that the copyright law of that country is relevant where illegal use has been perpetrated in. Thus, the protection of the work depends on the particular national copyright law. The title of a French composer for example is protected in the United States as well, but, in this case, by US copyright law (US Copyright Office, 2006; Hertin, 2003).

The protection of intellectual property is arranged in two principal international copyright conventions, namely the *Paris Convention for the Protection of Industrial Property* of 1883 and the *Berne Convention for the Protection of Literary and Artistic work*, signed on September 9th 1886. Both agreements are conducted by the *World Intellectual Property Organization* (WIPO, 2008). An author who is citizen of a country that takes part in these agreements may claim protection for his work. The application of these rights is not bound to formal aspects to be abided by the author (Rentsch et al., 2007).

2.2 Exploitation right

The exploitation right is an exclusive right that authorizes the author to duplicate and publish his work. Normally the author is anxious for the exploitation of his work in an economical way since he generates money from the application (Movsessian & Seifert, 1995). Due to the diversity of possible exploitations of his work, the author would neither be able to look after the compliance of his rights, nor after the merchandising of his work. Hence the collecting societies as well as the publisher are incorporated into this process.

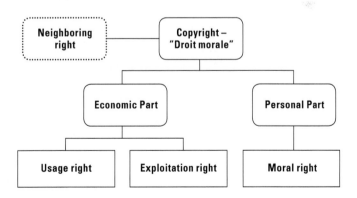

Figure 2. Copyright – "Droit morale". Source: Own work, 2008.

2.3 Usage right

The equivalent to the author's exploitation right is the user's usage right. If anybody intends to use an author's creation, first of all the author's approval is required. In the majority of cases the rights owner will agree to the request. According to this, the author has the possibility of transferring his exploitation rights in terms of usage rights to another person or company.

Assuming that a composer was requested by a company to create a jingle for their acoustic branding project, the composer per se would hold the exploitation rights to that jingle and the company would pay a license fee for the relevant applications, e.g. television and internet. If the company decides to use the jingle for another application, the license will have to be extended.

2.4 Moral right - Droit morale

As described before many countries have various kinds of copyright laws. Actually there exist two main types of copyright laws: one that includes so-called moral rights (mainly in Continental-Europe) and another one that excludes moral rights (mainly in Anglo-America) (Rigamonti, 2006).

Moral rights are personal rights and exist in addition to the exploitation right. These are rights that are directly related to the person of the author and cannot be assigned to another person or company. This right legitimates the author to oppose any use of his work. That way he is able to object to changes of the name to his work, radical changes to his work or other aspects. Hereby the author is given the right to control the final fate of his work. The idea of the moral rights is based on the relation between the author and his creation. In fact moral rights are primarily destined to protect the author's reputation rather than to secure financial aspects.

If the moral right is adapted to the particular copyright law, it mainly depends on the legal system of the country. In general moral rights occur in countries where the legal system is based on civil law - the lack of moral rights is confined to legal systems based on common law (Rigamonti, 2006; Rosenblatt, 1998).

As indicated before generally in Continental-Europe the moral right comes under the copyright law, whereas according to e.g. American Law moral rights can only obtain protection through judicial interpretation (Rosenblatt, 1998).

2.5 Neighboring right

To complete the explanations of the rights in the context of IP, the neighboring rights should also be mentioned here in a few words. The neighboring right is related to the author's work but protects the work of the performers, manufacturers of records and broadcasters with the authors' work (Acheson & Maule, 1994). In the context of acoustic branding this aspect normally is subordinated to the above mentioned issues.

The following issues should be taken into account for an acoustic branding strategy:
– extension of transferred copyrights
– transferal of neighboring rights
– coping with collecting societies.

To implement these requirements, the company has not only to know about the copyrights as mentioned before, but also about how collecting societies work.

3. Collecting societies

A collecting society protects the author's rights to his work and ensures that he receives remuneration. In fact a collecting society serves as an intersection between the author on the one hand and the music users like record labels, concert promoters and broadcasters on the other hand (Berndorff et al., 2004).

Normally it is advantageous for a composer to be a member of a collecting society, since his clearing is taken care of by the collecting society. Only in some cases could it be beneficial for the author to license his creations on his own, e.g. in order to negotiate higher fees.

Collecting societies dispose of many different applications like inter alia performances, playbacks, broadcasting or music in the internet etc. Especially advertising, radio as well as TV, music for premises or telephone on-hold are relevant applications in the context of acoustic branding. If a company wants to use a certain music title for its acoustic branding strategy, the company has to register it at the collecting society.

Almost every country has its own collecting society. On the international level there exist agreements between the collecting societies that ensure the exercise of a foreign author's rights in the particular country as well (GEMA, 2007).

When using music in different countries in the context of acoustic branding, the music has to be registered with a collecting society in each country.

4. Trademark rights

As seen before, in addition to copyrights, trademarks are the other important part of intellectual property that has to be considered in the framework of acoustic branding. Whereas copyrights are rights regarding the author of e.g. music, trademarks concern the rights of the company owning the trademark.

Strong brands receive a great value share of a company's total value (Meffert, 2000). That is the reason why companies want to protect their brands as a trademark. Competitors should not benefit from their brand value. By the inclusion of audio branding in the whole brand management process, the audible elements become part of the brand, so that the acoustic components contribute to the value of the brand as well. Hence, from the company's point of view, it is consistent to register the acoustic trademark, too. The Trademark rights as well as the registration process of a sound mark are disparate from country to country. The requirements to register a sound mark on national and international level have been described in detail by *Ralf Sieckmann* (see article *Sound Trade and Service Marks - Legal Aspects*).

5. Context between trademark right and intellectual property right – Case study "For Elise"

With the adjudication of November 27th 2003, the *European Court of Justice* decided that tone sequences and melodies could be registered as sound marks if this proved to be conducive to distinguishing goods or services from others. This case study serves as a good example for the interaction between copyrights and trademarks.

In this case the famous composition "For Elise", composed by *Beethoven*, is affected by protection as a sound mark. The Dutch company *Shield Mark* is the owner of 14 different trademarks for diverse goods and services, registered at the Benelux Trade mark office. Eleven of these trademarks consist of the nine first tones of Beethoven's famous opus. Two of these trademarks are explicitly registered as Sound marks. Regardless of the fact that Beethoven's "For Elise" is in the public domain[1], the European Court of Justice agreed to register it as a sound mark. The justification implies that the registration process considers all relevant parameters that were assumed for a successful registration as a sound mark (ECJ, C-283/01, 2003).

Irrespective of moral aspects like the question whether one should use famous classical creations for marketing aims, it is doubtful whether it makes sense to integrate these kinds of melodies or tone sequences in the framework of a holistic audio branding strategy.

However, a positive example for a successful exploitation of a public domain title in the context of an acoustic branding strategy is *Nokia* (see above). A further discussion of using that kind of music for acoustic branding would be interesting but cannot be part of this article.

Nevertheless, a significant reason why companies are fond of taking classical and famous old titles in their corporate communication is the fact that no fees for any collecting society will occur (Movsessian & Seifert 1995).

---

[1] *Since Beethoven died more than 70 years ago, all his creations passed into the public domain.*

References

Acheson, K., Maule, C. (1994). Copyright and Related Rights: The International Dimension. Canadian Journal of Communication, 19 (3) from the Canadian Journal of Communication Web site: http://www. cjc-online.ca/viewarticle.php?id=250.

Berndorff, G., Berndorff, B., Eigler, K. (2004). Musikrecht. Die häufigsten Fragen des Musikgeschäfts. Die Antworten, Bergkirchen: PPV Presse Project Verlags GmbH.

European Court of Justice (ECJ). C-283/01, Shield Mark BV ./. Joost Kist h.o.d.n. Memex Decision of 27 November 2003. Retrieved May 23, 2008 from the Office For Harmonization In The Internal Market Web site: http://oami.europa.eu/en/mark/aspects/pdf/JJ010283.pdf

Gesellschaft für musikalische Aufführungs- und mechanische Vervielfältigungsrechte (GEMA). Musik für alle. Retrieved 2007, from http://www.gema.de. Path: Presse; Publikationen; Kundenbroschüre; Musik für alle.

Hertin, P.W. (2003). Grundlagen des Musikurheberrechts. In R. Moser & A. Scheuermann (Ed.), Handbuch der Musikwirtschaft, pp. 771-803. Starnberg, München: Musikmarkt.

Meffert, H. (2000). Marketing. Grundlagen marktorientierter Unternehmensführung. Konzepte – Instrumente – Praxisbeispiele, Wiesbaden: Gabler Verlag.

Miller, A.R., Davis, M.H. (1990). Intellectual Property: Patents, Trademarks, and Copyrights in a Nutshell. 2nd ed., St. Paul, Minn.: West Publishing.

Movsessian, V., Seifert, F. (1995). Einführung in das Urheberrecht der Musik. Wilhelmshaven: Noetzel.

Rentsch, R. et al. (2007). Der Werksschutz endet nicht an den Landesgrenzen. Retrieved September 10, 2007, from the copright.ch Web site: http://www.copyright.ch/?id=75&leng=0

Rigamonti, C.P. (2006). Deconstructing Moral Rights. In: Harvard International Law Journal; 47 (2), pp. 344-412, from: http://www.harvardilj.org/print/58?sn=0

Rosenblatt, B. (1998). Moral Rights Basics. Harvard Law School, Retrieved March 1998, from http://cyber.law.harvard.edu/property/library/moralprimer.html

Stallman, R.M. (2006). Did you say Intellectual property? It's a seductive mirage. Retrieved December 15, 2007, from: http://www.gnu.org/philosophy/not-ipr.html

US Copyright Office (2006). International Copyright. Retrieved July 2006 from the United States Copyright Office Web site: http://www.copyright.gov/fls/fl100.html

World Intellectual Property Organization (WIPO) (2008). Understanding copright and related rights, from: http://www.wipo.int/freepublications/en/intproperty/909/wipo_pub_909.pdf

Sound Trade and Service Marks - Legal Aspects

Dr. Ralf Sieckmann
European Patent, Trade Mark & Design Attorney

1. Introduction

A trademark is a distinctive sign or indicator which is used by an enterprise or an individual to identify uniquely the origin of its products and / or services to consumers and to distinguish its products or services from those of other entities. Typically, it is a word, name, phrase, logo, design, image or a combination of these elements registered either in black and white or in specific colours. These types of conventional trademarks cover about 99 % of the trademark registrations all over the world.

There is also a range of non-conventional trademarks which may be either visible signs, e.g. shapes, moving images, holograms, colours, positions or non-visible signs, e.g. textures, sounds, scents and aromas which are available for registration in some parts of the world subject to the requirements laid down (Arden, 2000; Sandri, 2003; Lunell, 2007).

Normally, trademark registration must be made country by country wherever trademark protection is desired. However, as an exception to this rule the *Office for Harmonisation in the Internal Market* (OHIM) registers trademarks for all of the presently 27 member countries of the European Community. Likewise, an international registration can be made for more than 80 member states forming the Madrid System at the International Bureau of *World Intellectual Property Office* (WIPO), provided the first application / registration, referred to as home registration, was performed in a country and by a party being a member of the *Madrid Agreement* or of the *Madrid Protocol*. Such an international application will be registered as an International Registration on the basis of the home registration with the representation or description of the mark used by the applicant. After registration the patent offices of the member states have the possibility to check the application for formal and substantive grounds within the 12 or 18 months term set by the Madrid System. So they examine if this type of trademark is available under the national trademark act or if the representation used by the international trademark owner fits to the requirement set by the jurisdiction or should be supplemented prior to allowance.

2. What are the preconditions for registering Sound Marks?

2.1 The graphical representation approach in the European Community and related countries

In the *European Community* "any signs capable of being represented graphically" can be registered provided that such signs are capable of distinguishing the goods or services of one undertaking from those of other undertakings (Sandri 2003; Sieckmann, 2001, 2002).

The *European Court of Justice* (ECJ) has established clear precedents, and not merely guidance, as to what conditions a representation of a mark must fulfil. A trade mark may consist of a sign which is not in itself capable of being perceived visually, provided that it can be represented graphically, particularly by means of images, lines or characters and that its representation is clear, precise, self-contained, easily accessible, intelligible, durable and objective (ECJ, Judgment of 12 December 2002 in Case C-/00, 'Sieckmann', paragraph 55).

In the case of sound marks, those requirements are not satisfied when the sign is represented graphically by means of a description using the written language, such as an indication that the sign consists of the notes of a musical work, or the indication that it is the cry of an animal, or by means of a simple onomatopoeia, without anything else, or by means of a sequence of musical notes, by itself. On the other hand, those requirements are satisfied where the sign is represented by a stave divided into measures and showing, in particular, a clef, musical notes and rests whose form indicates the relative value and, where necessary, accidentals (ECJ, Judgment of 27 November 2003, C-283/01, 'Shield mark', paragraph 64). In the 'Shield mark' case, the Court did not expressly consider sonograms or sound files (ECJ, 'Shield mark', paragraph 54) but the representation must in any case comply with the SIECKMANN Criteria that it be clear, precise, self-contained, easily accessible, intelligible, durable and objective.

According to the case-law of the European Court of Justice, the requirements concerning a graphic representation of the mark serve a dual purpose, namely on the one hand to define the precise subject-matter of protection granted to the trade mark proprietor (and the Board adds that this ought not be confused with the scope of protection) and on the other hand that entry of the mark in the public Register makes it accessible to the competent authorities and the public, particularly to third parties who must be able to ascertain what is protected by their competitors (ECJ, Judgment of 12 December 2002 in Case C-/00, 'Sieckmann', paragraphs 47 – 51).

If the sound mark involves music in the traditional sense of the word, there is an obvious way to represent it graphically, namely by representing the theme or composition to be registered as a sound mark by standard musical notation, i.e. on or between the lines of a stave, giving the clef, bars, key and, if applicable, the tempo.

On the other hand, the situation is different when it is not music in the traditional sense of the word, which is to be registered as a sound mark, but human or animal noises such as the roaring or yelling or even completely different noises such as rolling thunder in a storm. Here, representation by musical notation regularly fails to work. Attempts have been made to describe sound marks, in particular using verbal description (cf. Decision R 1/1998-2 Déclic of the Second Board of Appeal of 7 October 1998), onomatopoeic description (cf. 'Shield mark') of the relevant sounds or even sonograms (cf. Decision R 781/1999-4 Roar of a Lion of the Fourth Board of Appeal of 25 August 2003, Decision R0708/2006-4 Tarzan Yell of the forth Board of Appeal dated 27 September 2007) but owing to a lack of precision and objectivity, these attempts have been regarded as inadequate by the jurisdiction. This approach is also followed by Hong Kong, Norway, Singapore and in Switzerland.

At OHIM there are two possibilities to register a sound mark:
Sound marks must be filed either in the form of a graphical representation or, if filed electronically, in the form of a graphic representation plus a sound file representing the sound itself in MP3 format with a file size maximum of 1 MB (about 1 minute of play). Presently, *OHIM* accepts a graphic representation which is sufficient in particular to comply with the criterion of the ECJ judgement "Shield mark", only traditional musical notations, not frequency oscillograms or sonograms.

However, after a change of the implementing rules of the *Community Trademark Regulation* (CTR) in July 2005 OHIM accepts non traditional (non musical) sounds if the graphic representation by means of an oscillogram or sonogram is accompanied by the sound file, through electronic filing (OHIM, 2007, item 7.6.1).

2.2 The descriptive representation approach in the United States and related countries

Under the open definition of § 1127 of the *Lanham Act of the United States* [a] trademark "includes any word, name, symbol, or device, or any combination thereof" that identifies and distinguishes the goods or services of one person from those of another and indicates their source.

This definition also applies to non-traditional trademarks such as sound marks "as long as it performs as an indicator of source and otherwise complies with statutory requirements, trademark protection should be granted" (In re General Electric Broadcasting Co. (1978)). Further, since human beings might use as a 'symbol' or 'device' almost anything at that is capable of carrying meaning, this language, read literally, is not restrictive (Qualitex Co. v. Jacobson Prods. Co. (1995)). So, trademark protection is available not only for a series of tones or musical notes, with or without words, a wording accompanied by music but also for animal or human noises and other noises occurring in nature or elsewhere (Gilson, 2005, p. 802; McCormick, 2006, p. 1106).

As stated in the *General Electric Broadcasting* decision "only unique and fanciful signs may be registered so that sounds that are commonplace will be rejected and refused, unless evidence of acquired distinctiveness could be shown". Sounds that may fail to be registered are the emergency sirens of police, fire brigade or ambulance.

Since sounds can not be represented graphically the requirement for a drawing does not apply to sound marks in the U.S. (see chapter 3, below, TMEP §807.09 (USPTO, 2007), §1202.15 (USPTO, 2007a). Instead, a description of the sound in the application is required such as onomatopoeia, listed musical notes or even declaratory phrases or lyrics (see chapter 4, below). "[W]hen registration of a sound mark is sought, the sound itself is not on the copy of the drawing sheet that is placed in the index of pending applications; nor will the sound be on the registration certificate that may eventually issue. Thus, the description of the sound is the only means for presenting, in any printed record, the essence of the mark" (Kawasaki Motors Corp. v. H-D Michigan, Inc., 1997). So sound marks coming to the US from abroad as cases under the *Madrid Protocol* or as *Paris Convention* cases must transform their appearance from musical notation to description.

For paper filing, audiotapes, compact discs, DVDs and videotapes may be accepted as specimens for sound marks to be filed with the description. To show that the sound mark actually identifies and distinguishes the services and indicates their source, the specimen should contain a sufficient portion of the audio content to indicate the nature of the services. If the mark comprises music or words set to music, the applicant may also submit the musical score as a specimen (USPTO (2007a, §1202.15)).

Allianz SE AG, Munich
Insurance, Finance Services

The sound mark consists of a sequence of five notes:
Tone 1 (H), 987,767 Hz; Tone 2 (A), 880,000 Hz; Tone 3 (H), 987,767 Hz; Tone 4 (C#),
1108,731 Hz; and Tone 5 (E), 659,255 Hz. The total duration of the sound mark is 3.8 seconds.

Figure 1. IR 881,231 (EC format - musical notation) and US 3,302,754 (US format - description of sound).

When filing through *Trademark Electronic Application System* (TEAS), a musical score must be submitted in an electronic file in .wav, .mp3, .mpg or .avi format. However, TEAS does not permit direct attachment of these types of electronic files. Therefore, the electronic reproduction must be send after the application is filed, as an attachment to an e-mail message directed to TEAS@uspto.gov, with clear instructions that the .wav file should be associated with "the application filed under Serial No. <specify> as a supplement to the mark description"(USPTO (2007a, §1202.15)). In South and Middle America trademark registration is possible and applications have been performed in Argentina, Brazil, Chile, Cuba, Ecuador and Paraguay.

2.3 The approach using representation and description
The Intellectual Property Offices of Australia und New Zealand require the submission of both graphical representation and description with the filing of sound trade and service marks (WIPO, 2007; AIPPI, 2002).

The representation of the trade mark may consist of a written description of sounds if the sign is not a musical-type sound. For example the graphical representation of the trade mark might be the words "CLIP, CLOP, MOO" and a concise and accurate description of the trade mark might be along the lines "The trade mark consists of the sound of a cow taking two steps on pavement, followed by the sound of a cow mooing as recorded on the compact disc accompanying the application form". A sign consisting of a musical sound might be most appropriately represented in the form of musical notation; however, this will depend on the trade mark *Australian Trademark Examination Manual* (ATEM) (2007, 3.3 sound trade marks).

2.4 Countries which did not allow registration of sound trade and service marks
At the moment national trademark legislation does not allow registration of sound marks in parts of Asia, namely in Belarus, Cambodia, China, Indonesia, Japan, Kirgizstan, Laos, Malaysia, Mongolia, Myanmar, Nepal, North-Korea, Philippines, South Korea, Sri-Lanka, Thailand, Turkmenistan and Vietnam, but registration is possible in Brunei, Hong Kong, India, Malaysia, Pakistan, Singapore, Taiwan, Turkey, and in the former Soviet Union states Kazakhstan, Moldavia, Russia, Tajikistan, Ukraine and Uzbekistan (WIPO, 2007). No registration is possible in most parts of the Arabian, Near East and North African countries except Morocco and Tunisia.

The same is true with respect to many countries in West Africa forming the Members of the *African Intellectual Property Organisation* (OAPI) whereas the countries of the *East African Regional Industrial Property Organisation* (ARIPO) in the Banjul Protocol allows audible signs (McCormick, 2006, p. 1116).

3. Clearance of sound trade and service marks

Searching for sound marks in the official online data bases is always difficult. It mainly depends on the search facilities of the official online trademark data bases not including national common law rights i.e. those sound marks which are only used in commerce without being ever registered.

Convenient search masks including a separate search for "sounds" are available at *Australian Trade Mark On-line Search System* (ATMOSS) (status always as per 01/03/2008: 36 registrations, 6 applications), at the official data base *DPMApublikationen*, Beginner's Search, in Germany (183 registrations, applications are not shown), at *New Zealand Patent Office* (23 registrations, 4 applications), at *SARG IPD* in Hong Kong (if you know the owner, more than 10 registrations) and at *CTM-online* at OHIM (53 registrations, 23 applications).

Searching trademarks in the United States is not easy although the search mask of the *Trademark Electronic Search System* (TESS) seems to offer many other choices. This data base does not offer a quick separate search for "sound" so you may choose one of the following routes. Click on "Structured Form search [Boolean]" under "Search Term" add "sound", under "Field" choose "Description of Mark" select "AND" under "Operator" and in the second line complete "Live" under "Search Term" before selecting "Live/Dead indicator" under "Field". You will get 361 living marks. However, if you go through the listing you'll also find word marks and figurative marks having the word sound in it which makes this search invalid.

So it is more convenient to do the following clearance: Click on "Structured Form search [Boolean]" under "Search Term" add "6", under "Field" choose "Mark Drawing Code" select "AND" as "Operator" and in the second line complete "Live" under "Search Term" before selecting "Live/Dead indicator". You will get 194 records for "situation for which no drawing is possible". In the next step go through the hits by clicking number by number and exclude those hits which refer to scent marks or motions marks, a total of 22.

What remains are 60 trademark applications and 116 trade and service mark registrations covering sounds, the first of which being registered in 1971 for broadcasting services. It should be noted that these searches are never 100 % complete since the data bases include wrong classifications of the trademark type, so that the relevancy of the results must be checked by hand.

A good overview on the sound trademarks worldwide, although never complete, but showing the application / registration by number, the drawing / description, the Nice Classification classes, the owner and the registration / refusal date is provided by Sieckmann (2003 – 2007, 2007 – 2009).

4. Example (attempted) registration of Tarzan yell in the US, Hong Kong and at OHIM by Edgar Rice Burroughs, Inc.

The mark is a yell consisting of a series of approximately ten sounds, alternating between the chest and falsetto registers of the voice, as follow –

1) a semi-long sound in the chest register,
2) a short sound up an interval of one octave plus a fifth from the preceding sound,
3) a short sound down a Major 3rd from the preceding sound,
4) a short sound up a Major 3rd from the preceding sound,
5) a long sound down one octave plus a Major 3rd from the preceding sound,
6) a short sound up one octave from the preceding sound,
7) a short sound up a Major 3rd from the preceding sound,
8) a short sound down a Major 3rd from the preceding sound,
9) a short sound up a Major 3rd from the preceding sound,
10) a long sound down an octave plus a fifth from the preceding sound.

Figure 2. US Trademark 2,210,506 registered for toy action figures 1998.

The same description is further registered in Hong Kong under 300,087,679 for software, electronic devices, games, toys, entertainment in 2004. Furthermore, this description is as well used in the trademark applied for under USSN 76,670,441 for slot machines in 2006 which will shortly pass to. registration.

Figure 3. Community Trademark (CTM) application 736 826, rejected by OHIM, 2003.

Figure 4. CTM application 1807 080, rejected by OHIM, 2000.

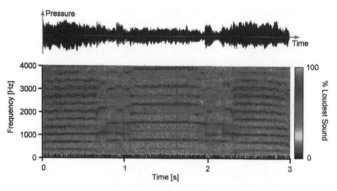

Figure 5. CTM application 3 661 329, rejected by OHIM, Board of Appeal, 2007.

Figure 6. CTM registration 3 673 308, registered for software, hardware, printed matter, stationary and entertainment, 2005.

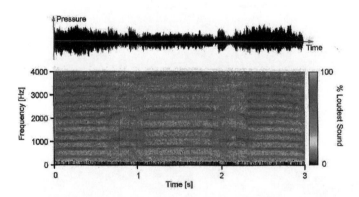

Figure 7. CTM registration 5 090 055 applied for together with a 5 second MP3 sound file sample in June 2006, registered for software, hardware, printed matter, stationary, clothing, footwear, (electronic games), toys, advertising, retailing services, telecommunication, entertainment, computer services and provision of food and drinks, 2008.

Ralf Sieckmann

References

AIPPI Reports Question Q 181 (2002). Conditions for registration and scope of protection of non conventional marks, Zurich, Association Internationale pour la Protection de la Propriété Intellectuelle, available for download at http://www.aippi.org/reports/q181/gr_q181_index.htm.

Arden, T. P. (2000). Protection of Nontraditional Marks – Trademark Rights in Sounds, Scents, Colors, Motions and Product Designs in the U.S., New York, International Trademark Association see http://www.inta.org/-index.php?option=com_catalogshop&Itemid=55&func=detail&getcontent=1&id=18.

ATEM (2007). Examination Manual for Trade Marks, Part 10(3) available for download at http://www.ipaustralia.gov.au/resources/manuals_trademarks.shtml.

ECJ, Judgment of 12 December 2002 in Case C-/00, Sieckmann v DPMA, [Full Court Decision] , available for download at http://oami.europa.eu/en/mark/aspects/pdf/JJ000273.pdf.

ECJ, Judgment of 27 November 2003 in Case C-283/01, Shield Mark BV v Joost Kist [Decision of 5th Chamber], available for download at http://oami.europa.eu/en/mark/aspects/pdf/JJ020100.pdf.

In re General Electric Broadcasting Co.; Inc, 199 U.S.P.Q. 560 (T.T.A.B., 1978).

Gilson, J. & Gilson, LaLonde, A. (2005). Cinnamon Buns, Marching Ducks and Cherry-Scented Racecar Exhaust: Protecting Nontraditional Trademarks, Trademark Reporter (TMR) 95 , p. 773 – 824, 801 – 806 available for download at http://www.usebrinks.com/docs/publications/ 141.pdf.

Kawasaki Motors Corp. v. H.D. Michigan, Inc. (1997). 43 U.S.P.Q.2d 1521 (T.T.A.B. 1997).

McCormick, K. K.(2006). "Ding" You are now free to register that Sound, TMR 96 , 1101 – 1121 available for download at http://home.comcast. net/~jlw28129/07McCormick.pdf.

Lunell, E. (2007). Okonveltionella Varumärken - Form, Färg, Doft, Ljud, 189 – 207, Stockholm, Norstedts Juridik summary available for download at http://www.prv.se/upload/dokument/Biblioteket/nyforvarv/2007_juli_oktober/pdf/okonv_varum.pdf.

Office for the Harmonisation in the Internal Market (OHIM), (2007). Examination Guidelines, available for download at http://oami.europa.eu/en/mark/marque/pdf/Examination-EN-12-12-2007.pdf.

Qualitex Co. v. Jacobson Prods. Co. (1995). 514 U.S. 159, 165, available for download at http://caselaw.lp.findlaw.com/scripts/getcase.pl?navby=-CASE&court=US&vol=514&page=159.

R 0001/1998-2 – Déclic (SOUND) Decision of 7 October 1998, available for download at http://oami.europa.eu/LegalDocs/BoA/1998/fr/R0001_1998-2.pdf.

R 0781/1999-4 – roar of a lion (SOUND) Decision of 25. August 2003, available for download at http://oami.europa.eu/LegalDocs/BoA/1999/en/R0781_1999-4.pdf.

R 0708/2006-4 – TARZAN YELL (SOUND) Decision of 27. September 2007, available for download at http://oami.europa.eu/LegalDocs/BoA/2006/en/R0708_2006-4.pdf.

Sandri, S. & Rizzo, S. (2003). Non-Conventional Trade Marks and Community Law, Thurmaston, Marques, summary available for download at http://www.copat.de/markenformen/lit_sandri.pdf.

Sieckmann, R. (2001). Die Eintragungspraxis und –möglichkeiten von nicht-traditionellen Marken innerhalb und außerhalb der EU, MarkenR 2001, p. 236 – 266, [Reasons for appeal of ECJ Case C-/00] available for download at http://www.copat.de/markenformen/si-markenr2001.pdf.

Sieckmann, R. (2002). Zum Begriff der graphischen Darstellbarkeit des Art. 2 Markenrechtsrichtlinie, eine Erwiderung, WRP 2002, 491 available for download at http://www.copat.de/markenformen/Si-WRP2002.pdf.

Sieckmann, R. (2003 – 2007). The Non-Traditional Trade Mark Archives, available for download at http://www.copat.de/markenformen/mne_markenformen.htm.

199

Sieckmann, R. (2007-2009). *The Non-Traditional Trade Marks Archives, available for download at http:// www.brainguide.us/ralf-sieckmann, see under publications: Hörmarken – Sound Trade and Service Marks Germany 2007-2009, Hörmarken – Sound Trade and Service Marks Abroad 2007-2009.*

USPTO (2007). *Trademark Manual of Examination Procedure, 5th Ed., available for download at http:// tess2.uspto.gov/tmdb/tmep/pdf/0800.pdf.*

USPTO (2007a). *Trademark Manual of Examination Procedure, 5th Ed., available for download at http:// tess2.uspto.gov/tmdb/tmep/pdf/1200.pdf.*

World Intellectual Property Office (WIPO) (2007). *Seventeenth Session, Geneva, May 7 to 11, 2007: SCT/17/2 Methods of Representation and Description of New Types of Marks, Geneva, WIPO available for down-load at http://www.wipo.int/meetings/en/details.jsp?meeting_id=12643.*

WIPO (2007a) SCT/17/3. *Relation of Established Trademark Principles to New Types of Marks, Geneva, WIPO, available for download at http://www.wipo.int/edocs/mdocs/sct/en/sct_17/sct_17_4.pdf.*

"Strong brands receive a great value share of a company's total value. That is the reason why companies want to protect their brands as a trademark. Competitors should not benefit from their brand value. By the inclusion of audio branding in the whole brand management process, the audible elements become part of the brand, so that the acoustic components contribute to the value of the brand as well."

[Jasmin Junge, 2009]

G.
Case Studies

The Narrative Ear - Realities in Creating Sound, Story and Emotion for Brands

James Bull
Executive Creative Director and founder of Moving Brands

Introduction

When I was asked to contribute a chapter to this book, it was to offer my experience of creating sonic assets as part of a comprehensive branding project at my company, *Moving Brands*. At Moving Brands we combine the knowledge of sonic specialists with our experience of creating brands. We have been pioneering and developing this approach and methodology on our own over the last ten years and are still pretty much unique in the world of branding. There have been times, however, when being unique has meant we've had to fight a pretty lonely ideological battle on two fronts: partly to bring our peers within the creative industry around to our way of thinking; secondly, and perhaps more importantly, to convince clients of the benefits, importance and power of sound as part of a brand, as much as logo, colour, typeface and photography.

Our determination has paid off. We are just completing work on our largest and most comprehensive re-branding project for Swiss telecom company, *Swisscom*. Unlike many branding exercises where sound is often an after-thought, for Swisscom, the sonic assets have been a consideration from the start. As a result, sound has been one of the building blocks across the strategic, identity and expression phases of the project. It is large scale projects like Swisscom which encourage me to keep pushing the importance of sound for brands. Today I feel as positive and enthusiastic for the future of sound design as a branding discipline as I have ever felt.

Multi-sensorial branding

To fully understand where sound fits within the branding spectrum, we need to look at the overall challenges that brands are facing today. We now live in a world where media changes so rapidly that a brand must be able to communicate across all types of media, including sound, in order to get its message across to people in the most engaging way possible.

The world doesn't stand still. It is always moving, so brands themselves need to move, in every sense of the word: they need motion, they need to be able to adapt, and they need to convey emotion. They need to be multi-sensorial and work across all media, and to tell strong, consistent stories. It is our responsibility to make this happen for our clients. Whenever we create a brand's identity, we must consider the many different ways in which its story can be told, and create assets that enable this communication across multiple platforms.

The story at the heart of a brand should inform its every manifestation – from stationery, livery, signage and print campaigns, to animations, mnemonics, transitions, movies, websites, TV ad campaigns, and to wikis, blogs, environments, architecture, and products and services. Everything the brand does should have its story stamped through it: no matter how fine you slice it, it should be there, in every cell of its being, ensuring that as the brand grows it can evolve, respond and adapt to the world around it. It is narrative, as opposed to static logos and sundry brand 'assets', that gives life to a brand and provides consumers with the fullest sense of interaction. This is why storytelling is at the very heart of what we do. Sound is perhaps the strongest media for conveying narrative in an emotional way and adding a feeling of life. Sound can affect us in ways that other media cannot – it can make us feel happy, sad or angry, and can inspire us in a number of ways. Moreover, our reactions are often physical: sound makes us get up and dance, increases our heart rates or, conversely, makes us feel relaxed and at ease. We intuitively understand the story and emotion of sound. This is why it's so important for us to understand the potential for sound in a branding context, and why sound design should be considered to be as equally important as other brand touchpoints. Sonic assets such as ringtones, call-waiting and *Sonic Mnemonic®* can have an enormous impact on the way in which a brand is received. Despite sound's obvious ability to convey mood and message, it is rarely adopted or recognized as part of a branding process by the traditional branding industry. I suspect this is due to the intangibility of sound – when a client comes to us for branding work they want to know what the brand will look like, what colours, fonts and forms it will take, and possibly how it will move. You never get a client coming to you itching to know what their new brand is going to sound like. Whilst this might be regrettable, it is also understandable, particularly if branding agencies don't understand sound themselves.

One of the key things about sound is that whilst it can be the part of the brand that smacks an audience in the face and grabs their attention, it is also most frequently the element that an audience takes away with them and which gets filed away in their memory. *Intel* is the obvious example – if I asked you to draw the Intel logo, how accurate do you think you'd be? If, however, I asked you to hum or sing it to me, I bet (despite the embarrassment you might feel!) you'd be able to pretty much get it right.

Interesting, isn't it? You can hum the sonic identity for a company that is the world's largest manufacturer of microprocessors, but you can't draw their logo? And, more importantly

– when you hear the word "Intel" it is the sound that jumps into your head before anything visual… surely this should tell us something about the power of sound as a brand asset?

Intel's reign as one of the world's most recognized sonic identities is partly due to their commitment to it as an organisation. Intel's long-standing corporate commitment to the power of sound and relentless usage means that it now has global recognition. What's even more ingenious is that most TV and radio ads that feature it are actually advertising another manufacturer's product which just happens to contain an Intel chip - therefore it's not even a part of Intel's ad spend. Once those four simple notes (actually five – but I'll come back to that later) get into your head, they will never come out, ever to be lodged in your mind and associated with their brand.

This is what I find so exciting about sound and what makes me so passionate about its value. Its impact on us is innate on so many levels that we almost take it for granted. We revel in the textures and complexities of sound when we listen to music. We accept sound as a source of inspiration and experiential depth when it is delivered on a compact disc, through our *iPod* or the radio… and yet, when it comes to identity design, sound is frequently tackled as an afterthought, if at all. That's the mindset I've been battling against for the last ten years – but at last, it feels like we might be getting somewhere in that fight.

The importance of an intro

When I started Moving Brands with some like minded contemporaries back in 1998, we always knew we wanted sound to be an integral part of our creative process for brand identity. We therefore spent more time and money than was probably healthy researching, conceptualising and theorising how to create a sound that is perfect for a brand, whilst also ensuring its effectiveness in creating an attachment between customer and the brand.

One of the products we created was the '*Sonic Mnemonic®*', our name (with a unique process behind it) for creating a short sequence of sound that could be used across various media to aid brand recognition – a sonic version of the moving logo. The word Mnemonic comes from the ancient Greek word mnemonikos ("of memory"), and is related to Mnemosyne ("remembrance"), the name of the goddess of memory in Greek mythology.

By 2005 we had gained enough industry clout to convince people that a Sonic Mnemonic was a truly viable and worthy asset, and for large brands to commit to engaging us to create them. *Vodafone* could see how beneficial it would be for their global business to have a sound that could be recognised in any region and to aid consistency across the brand. The eventual brief we were given was to create a sonic identifier that would be heard on start-up of mobile phones, and would also have the potential to be used across above-the-line TV and radio advertising. On top of this Vodafone wanted a set of branded ringtones and user-interface sound design that would be part of the default set of sounds pre-installed on all their mobile phones. The *Vodafone Sonic Mnemonic®* was designed to evoke the brand name in a simple musical form: Vo-Da-Fone. I refer to this type of Sonic Mnemonic® as phonetic – by that

I mean the construction of the sound follows the same phonetic structure that we hear through spoken word. So, Vo-Da-Fone became three recognisable notes... Or so I thought. You remember earlier when I talked about the Intel sonic identity being five notes and not four, well working on this Vodafone job is how I discovered a simple, yet very powerful, rule of sound. Here is how...

We created a whole host of three-noted versions for Vodafone and eventually thinned it down to a favourite. At this point we decided to do a series of user testing to find out more about how people really reacted. We wanted to find out things like "what kind of company does this sound like", "where do you think this company is from", "what feeling does it give you" – and all the feedback was absolutely in-line with what we had been trying to com-municate – "a technology company", "something to do with communication", "global" and "exciting". But when we asked people to sing it back to us (something we call a recall test), every single person sung back two notes, not three – they were in effect only remembering the Da-Fone part. This had me stumped and somewhat irked – how could this be the case?

I went back to my research to try and find an answer, reading up on studies in recall. I also listened to existing examples, played them to people, and asked them what they had just heard. Still I couldn't figure out what was going on.

Eventually, in a client meeting, I was talking about the importance of sound design and I asked the client to hum me the Intel sonic identity as a way of demonstrating how effective it is. They sang four notes back to me (not five) and I realised what had been going on. The brain seems to need a trigger (much like the intro to a song) to tell it to start listening, and therefore remembering. So, when you get short bursts of notes as you do in a Sonic Mnemo-nic®, this is accentuated even more, and three notes become two. The Intel sonic has a main melody of four notes but there is actually an extra fifth note at the beginning – an intro if you like.. We then re-made the Vodafone Sonic Mnemonic® with an intro note before the three notes of Vo-Da-Fone, thus making it V-O-Da-Fone and suddenly, in the second round of user testing, everyone tested recalled 3 notes.

Once we had nailed the Vodafone ringtones and user-interface sound design came eas-ily, as everything was made from the instrumentation and structure found within the Sonic Mnemonic® itself. We ended up producing two ringtones based around the sonic, one that was more technical sounding and complex and one that was warmer sounding and simpler. Through grafting and learning we created something very effective, something based on logic and reason.

The Sound that never was

Once you have created a Sonic Mnemonic® that the client likes, and that resona-tes with customers, you could be forgiven for thinking you had achieved the desired end result and that the job is done. Unfortunately, this isn't always the case. One of the biggest challenges facing the effectiveness and success of a sonic identity is client commitment and crucially, a well thought out usage and implementation strategy. Put simply, this is guidance on how, when, and where to use sonic assets. In 2004 (a year earlier than the Vodafone work) we created a Sonic Mnemonic® for *British Telecom*. It took 4 months of strategic thinking, developing multiple routes and meetings with many people from within the organisation. It was an intense job and we created a result that was fantastic, which had been developed so that it could be used across all media. But it was never used.

Why? Well, the team from within BT who commissioned the work were visionary and ahead of the rest of the organisation. But, despite this, they hadn't worked out an effective way of getting the rest of that organisation to use, commit to and understand what they had produced. It wasn't just internally that this team ran up against roll-out issues. An even bigger obstacle for the Sonic Mnemonic® can be summed up in three simple words: "The Advertising Agency". They didn't want to use it, of course, and why would they? They hadn't created it, it used up valuable on-air time (so their ads had to end a particular way in the last 3 seconds), and all of this meant that they couldn't charge for those last moments - a reason I suspect was the main driver for this discord.

So there we were with a great piece of work, having created BT's first Sonic Mnemonic® that could be used on all appropriate media including TV advertising, radio advertising, PowerPoint presentations, internal and external videos, call waiting and product sonification. We had worked closely with the brand and marketing teams within BT but it was never going to see the light of day. This was a massively frustrating experience, but also an eye opener. Now when we make sonic assets for a client we work with them to make sure it is sold into the organisation in the right way from the outset and has clear guidance for usage – and we even help the client brief the advertising agencies so that everyone involved in asset creation understands the power and consistency sonic media can deliver.

A well-known global mobile manufacturer

Sound for brands can take many guises and it certainly isn't just about Sonic Mnemonic®. A hugely interesting job in the evolution of sonic development as part of a branding process, and in particular as part of the Moving Brands approach, was one we completed as part of a entire brand re-fresh program for one of the largest mobile phone manufacturers in the world (sorry but, as much as I'd love to, I'm not allowed to mention their name).

We needed to help them communicate a recent re-categorisation of their products, as well as their global web offer, whilst injecting personality across different media, touchpoints, and to different audiences. The sonic work had to have a consistency, whilst at the same time conveying differentiation. Consequently a strategy for sonic was created that could help them align sound across all media. They needed a range of communications with different emotional qualities, from the completely human, to the entirely technological. This meant that the approach to sound needed to be flexible, whilst staying recognisable. At the human end of the spectrum you would find sounds that were created by a closeness to humans. A voice, handclaps, finger-clicking were appropriate, as were instruments that had direct contact between a person and the surface that made the sound; for example a plucked acoustic guitar was appropriate, whereas an acoustic guitar played using a plectrum was inappropriate as the player was one step removed.

As you moved along the human/technology spectrum you would find gradually more technology between the person and the surface and/or way the sound was made. At the human end of the spectrum you would have a drum, or an acoustic guitar. Moving along the spectrum you would then have a piano, then an electric guitar, before finally, at the technical end of the spectrum you would hear electronic sounds and newer forms of sound making being used in new and surprising ways. This scale of human-to-technology created a palette of sonic brand 'colours' that were directly applicable to, and used within, the communications across the various product categories.

This meant that there was plenty of creative flexibility for the client and external agencies. They could find or create the best music for a communication, but were always aligned to the kinds of instrumentation, arrangement and tempo needed to express the essence of each product category. This is a particularly good approach and system for large global companies that have to deal with consistency and flexibility across many local regions, all of whom have their own slightly different spin on the brand. The balance between consistency and expressiveness is a constant struggle for a brand. With flexible systems that embrace creativity and expressiveness in place, this balance can be embedded in the hearts and minds of everyone working within it. This ability to change, whilst also accommodating, people's mindsets within a business can really make an impact on that company's success. Brands that allow for this requirement by adopting a flexible approach to identity can truly open up a their ability to communicate in more powerful and memorable ways.

Changing a national icon

This brings us to now, 2009, eleven years on, and we are in a place where our processes for creating meaningful sonic assets for clients are very well developed and successful. Our latest complete brand re-design for Swisscom had sound as an important part of its output – we needed to create a logo that would work in static, moving, responsive and sonic applications. With the many Swisscom businesses aligning under one service spanning from telecoms to media and entertainment, the brand needed a broader and more aligned meaning, or story. We needed to make the brand more about people's lives rather than technological products. The identity system therefore needed to be simple and flexible: the identity we developed evolves around one central axis, as does the business. Take the new photographic style as an example: Swisscom has its own media portal and now understands the value of embracing user-generated photography, rather than contriving it. This is a new approach to brand identity.

Swisscom already had a sonic device that had been in place for a number of years, a sound that people in Switzerland recognised in the same way that the rest of the world recognises the Intel sound. The existing sonic was recognisable and successful, but it needed to change in line with the rest of the brand. It was clear that this unique melody should stay – the challenge was: how do we re-fresh this melody to reflect the new brand story and identity? For those of you who don't know, the Swisscom sonic is a string of six notes, and the version they were using was successful but felt technical, with a sense of closeness and simplicity missing. So, what should Swisscom sound like? How can closeness and simplicity be communicated without falling into obvious clichés? How would that be interpreted by the Swiss? And, would that be a different interpretation to the rest of the world? It was going to be tricky. A massive process of research ensued. Importantly, this was part of the overall branding process and not carried out in isolation, meaning that sound was able to affect the final outcome of the way the brand looked as well as sounded.

We gradually gained an insight as to how to start blending the human aspects of the brand, which we did by working heavily with voice. By having the six notes of the sonic sung as opposed to being played we were able to create a very open and approachable sounding brand. The specifics of the voice were very important. But what makes a singing voice sound right for Swisscom? We needed it to feel close and simple – but also compelling and reassuring. So we developed a style of singing that fell somewhere between being sung and spoken, a breathy intimate sounding voice, much like the way a trusted friend might reassure you. This technique would also allow the Swiss accent to come across more subtly than it might with a more powerfully belted out or classically sung voice.

After a lot of testing and re-recording we eventually ended up with a female voice that delivered on the sense of friendliness and reassurance. It was also found (through user-testing) to be taken more seriously than a male voice. When a male voice sang in the style we had developed, it was often felt to confuse the listener, feeling ironic or jokey. It seems as though, as much as we like to be open to masculine/feminine roles in society, our ears are as traditional and closed as they ever have been. However, I have heard anecdotally that one of the reasons we are so in-tune with sound is that it is actually the first sense to develop in the womb, much earlier than we start to develop sight. In addition, when we are born, it is our hearing that initially allows us to distinguish between our mother and father – and even this difference between the two is somehow pre-programmed to as a survival mechanism – so it's hardly surprising then that female tonality makes us feel more open, friendly and warm. On some primal level they take us back to the womb. The next major aspect of the development was instrumentation. The voice wasn't going to be heard on its own, it was going to be accompanied by a series of instruments and structures that could counterbalance the feeling the voice created and give us even more information about the brand. Again, our research revealed that the sound of an acoustic guitar was deemed to be very accessible, especially if strummed or plucked gently. This is, I believe, due to the accessibility of the instrument itself.

It's very easy to play and is also very common in people's lives. It is an instrument that you hold against your body, rather than sit at (like a piano) so it feels more like a part of us, less apart, and playing it feels natural, intuitive almost. Even people with no musical talent feel at ease doing so. This gave us a link to folk music and the idea of people around a camp-fire became a motivator for the use of guitar. Also, the tones that are created by an acoustic guitar are very akin to the voice itself – they inhabit a very similar acoustic range and tonality, which in turn is why the human voice and acoustic guitar compliment each other so well, and why so many emotive songs use this simple combination. Finally, a warm synthetic sound was used in the background as a reminder of the technological aspect of the brand's product offer, contributing a sense of modernity and innovation. The end result is a very finely balanced and understated Sonic Mnemonic® that feels much more in line with the brand and communicates the right feeling and story. This Sonic Mnemonic® is not yet quite reaching the consumer, but it will gradually roll-out during the remainder of 2008, along with a ringtone that will be pre-installed on all Swisscom mobile phones. We are eventually hoping to create a full-palette of user-interface sonic elements to be used across all touchpoints.

And so…

I'm hoping this has been worth the read. Talking about sound is difficult enough, but at least with talking you can gesticulate and use an array of squeaks, bleeps and gesture-type sounds using your mouth to get your point across. Writing about sound sometimes feels a bit like describing colours to a blind person. So I hope the most of this article has at least made some sense. Ultimately, sound is a creative and emotive medium, one that we all intuitively and subconsciously understand in a very detailed and confident way. When writing about sound it is hard not to feel that one is stating the obvious, let alone saying anything revolutionary. However, I have found over the last 10 years that the effect sound can have on a business really can be revolutionary. The eye-opening that a brand experiences once it starts to take sound seriously is phenomenal – even though it is often hard to quantify and prove. I liken it to some of the eye-opening experiences in life – love, art, great literature, great music – they are all hard to pin down, but incredibly powerful motivators for change.

With that, if you're willing, I will leave you with one last thought (well, more of a task really). Spend the next minute with your eyes closed and listen to the environment you have around you. Try to listen as far into the distance and as close to you as you can – and in doing that, think about how is it possible for your brain to be able to sort all those sounds out - especially when you're not concentrating on them. Finally, think about how those sounds affect the way you relate to the environment you're in right now… if you can do that, and create an understanding of it you're already halfway to being able to use sound in an effective way for brands. You could even set up your own agency doing just that – but please don't be surprised if it takes at least ten years for people to hear you.

"The eye-opening that a brand experiences once it starts to take sound seriously is phenomenal – even though it is often hard to quantify and prove. I liken it to some of the eye-opening experiences in life – love, art, great literature, great music – they are all hard to pin down, but incredibly powerful motivators for change."

(James Bull, 2009)

The Samsung Global Sound Project: Cross-culture Innovation

Aaron Day
Receive-Transmit, Berlin

1. Introduction

In this world, the eyeball is king. We have huge vocabularies dedicated to the description of information we receive via the visual channel. Not so with sound. It is difficult to talk about sound with individuals who are unfamiliar with, or in some cases, scared of the subject. It is too often the case that decision makers consider sound as either A: Music and music only or B: That annoying part of the project that you do after everything else is done.

Baldly stated: all music contains sound but not all sound is music (John Cage et al. not withstanding). Understanding this distinction by the client is vital for any AUI (audio user interface) or sound branding project to develop successfully.

Now, consider this issue compounded by working across a significantly different culture (than one's own) and language. This brief case study will illuminate some of these issues and provide some insights into how they were navigated in the context of a six month strategy, design and research project. The *Global Sound Project* (GSP) represented *Samsung's* first major attempt to develop a sound design and brand strategy for North America and Europe. By the end of the project we delivered a strategy for the creation and use of audio user interface (AUI) elements as well as branded audio elements for typical mobile products: mobile phones, PDAs, digital video cameras and hybrids of these devices.

Being competitive requires innovation. Innovation requires change and risk – two things that do not come easy in corporations. Before we could complete our two main goals, creation of a strategy and tools for innovation, we had to bridge the gap between East and West. It took some work and the first steps were a little shaky, however in this case study I will discuss how we satisfied the contracted assignment of creating a global sound strategy and, at the same time, created tools to spark innovation. Rather than follow a strict chronological discussion of the GSP this case study will alternate between narration, which is vital to understanding the project context, and some brief examinations of process and design concepts.

No process is perfect and no project is without missteps, the GSP was no exception. Recognition of our shortcomings early on in the process and responding to client feedback was critical, and examples of such are provided in this article. I hope this approach will provide the reader with some insights into what turned out to be a complex but successful project.

2. Culture, Shock

2.1 Better Aikido than Boxing or, Saying "Yes" when you Mean "No"

A note about working with Korean companies – Samsung in particular. Samsung has employed some of the best and brightest educated people in both Korea and the West. This means that many of the individuals that we worked with spoke English freely and were well acquainted with Western ways. Many were not however.

In Korea Samsung is a well respected corporation. Doing business with them can be, from the Korean point of view, a great honor. From a Western point of view this can at times be viewed as arrogance but it should not be taken as such. Furthermore, do not confuse the politeness and hospitality of Korean culture with a lack of business acumen. They are experienced and ferocious negotiators.

Unlike most business relations in the West, contracts can be viewed as the beginning of negotiation rather than the end. This is not the rule, but it can happen. Such departures or requests for extra work can range from the trivial to the absurd. Even if the client is clearly out of bounds, waving around a stack of paper in their face isn't going to change their mind – unless you are *Bechtel, IBM* or *Sony*. It is safe to say that Samsung is bigger than you and has more lawyers than you. For small requests that don't impact the project schedule or resources (too much) it can make sense to just say "yes" and do the extra work.

Who knows, maybe their request is well founded and will open up some new ideas? For requests that are clearly out of the project scope or are in some other way unreasonable; be diplomatic. We were able to avoid some tight spots by agreeing that request xyz was a great idea but that it might seriously compromise other parts of the project and that we would be happy to perform request xyz at a later date, etc.

This constant process of give and take is as much a part of Korean business as the propose, review, refine, narrow, repeat process that most agencies in the West follow. What does all this boil down to? Keep some design resources in reserve, be flexible and above all never, ever, lose your cool.

2.2 Meetings in Seoul

Although we had worked for Samsung's US offices on other projects, this was the first time we would be dealing directly with the headquarters in Seoul. I hope our experience of dealing with Samsung, specifically native Korean Samsung employees will help the reader understand the cultural issues we were faced with and which played a decisive role in the way the project was conducted.

Our kick-off meetings were rather informal and were attended by user interface designers, middle-managers, and so on. No engineers or industrial designers were present and this made us a little nervous as we had requested the attendance (and interviews) with both. These meetings took place over the first few days in the different offices of departments that had all supported the project we were starting. We met with one of several mobile groups, the global business group, a UI group and so on. We sat through many Powerpoint presentations—some informative, some not so. As we moved from meeting to meeting it was clear that the different departments who had a stake in the project all had different views on what it should be. The next day we visited a manufacturing facility to get a closer look at the products we would be designing for. A meeting with the head of one of the digital-imaging groups had been arranged that would turn out to be one of the most fruitful meetings of the entire project.

2.3 Trip to Suwon

After a breakfast of fish soup and Korean pickles we met up with the head of the sound design group and made for the train station. A short train-ride from Seoul brought us to Suwon, one of Samsung's factory cities. The predominant architecture in Suwon is neat rows of small, city council-style flats with building numbers and Samsung logos painted on the sides 10 meters high. The people that live in these flats, for the most part, all work for Samsung. Nearby is the facility: a sprawling complex of laboratories, fabrication facilities, a product museum and who knows what else. It is huge. At lunch time 30,000+ people all sit down to eat.

Before entering the facility we had to wait in a rather dingy mobile-home/pre-fab style area filled with Samsung employees (waiting for what, we didn't know), a few shabby couches and a water cooler. Behind a scratched counter, and somewhat out of place, stood two immaculately groomed, smiling young women who welcomed us and took our passports. Some words were exchanged with our host who turned to us and said "OK, we wait." What we were waiting for was unclear, however after 45 minutes and several cups of tea another super-clean, uniformed employee motioned to us that it was time to leave and led us to the main entrance of the facility. I never went through Checkpoint Charlie when the wall divided Germany nor have I ever taken a tour of the U.S. Treasury, but I will never forget clearing security to enter the Suwon complex. Steel gates, bullet-proof glass, grim-faced guards—it was all there. Scanned, searched and secured—they taped our laptops shut with adhesives so strong I never managed to get the sticky- blotches off of my *Ti-Book*. Walking into the complex I was reminded no less that five times not to take any photographs or video. Walking around the facility we saw that many of the buildings had huge banners affixed to the sides. The text on the banners was often a mix of English and Korean with phrases like "Microprocessor Group B Leads the Way!" Our host explained that different divisions were often in competition with each other and that slogans, along with boosting morale, were used to identify different projects and teams. I seldom give our projects catchy names but it seemed to be something that was encouraged here. Later we took a cue from the naming concept and applied it to the strategy we created.

What made the trip to Suwon so important was our meeting with the digital video camera group. Many of our prior meetings tended to be uneventful and left us with more questions than answers. Not so with the man we were about to meet. Our host led us into what I later described as the "Mini Digital Video Camera War Room". The walls were covered with blueprints and design diagrams for Digital Video Cameras (DVCs). The tables were piled with torn apart DVCs, electronic components and so on. A man entered the room with two assistants. We were introduced and we exchanged cards. Not waiting for us to be seated he spoke to the translator in rapid-fire Korean, after which the translator turned to us and said: "Mr. (xxxx) wants you to design a better shutter sound for our cameras, it should reflect Samsung's current design positioning and differentiate us from our competitors. What information do you need from us to complete this task?" Wham!

After days of talking in circles this came as a shock. I replied by saying we needed some examples of their cameras, the schematic for the camera's audio-components and whatever research they had done on the competition. She translated this information to the manager, he nodded, jammed his finger down on the phone in front of him and let out another burst of Korean. Two minutes later an engineer hurried into the room and gave us everything we had requested. As we were getting ready to leave our guide turned to us and said "Please make sure that you explain your process to Mr. (xxxx) when you deliver the sound. Oh, and keep in mind he speaks no English."

I cannot emphasize enough the importance of these two events. The first, being given a clear directive, and the second, the requirement that we communicate our work efficiently to someone who understood no English. Section 3 of this document will discuss how we initially ignored the communication requirement and nearly scuttled the project. By the end of the GSP however, the work we did for the DVC department was some of the best of the project.

3. Process, Methods and Deliverables

Our process was simple. Each deliverable supported the others in their phase and each project phase built a platform for the next, culminating in a unifying strategy document and AUI guideline tool. In addition, most of the deliverables could be used as "stand-alone" documents. The GSP was a collection of many different tasks including:

- Brand and positioning review
- Market research
- Trend research
- Competitive analysis and benchmarking
- User research
- Device testing
- Sound design
- Sound branding
- Tool building
- Guideline creation
- Strategy development

4. Communicate with images

Following the meetings in Korea we set to work on the first set of project deliverables—the Findings Documents. These were two of the most comprehensive documents we have ever assembled. They were masterpieces. 100+ pages packed with findings, competitive analysis, sound branding opportunities, cultural highlights, trend research and intelligent achievable next steps and, as far as the client was concerned, failures that could have cost us the project.

What went wrong? Too much text and not enough pictures. We had written relevant and insightful documents that, unfortunately, did not capture the imagination of our client. Why? We asked them to walk uphill. That is, we answered all of their initial questions and fulfilled the responsibilities outlined in the proposal-plan but in such a way that the information was A: difficult for non-native speakers to process and B: far too dense and too lengthy; it did not engage, excite and inspire the reader.

Valuable information or no, after this experience we moved from text- heavy and static to image weighted and dynamic documentation and presenters. Bright, colorful, interesting documents that were able to operate in a stand-alone fashion as well as integrating within a system. When dealing with Samsung less text and more graphics build communication and trust while reducing concerns and questions. It took this mistake to realize that fact. Although the presentation was flawed the two findings documents set the foundation for the entire project and accomplished the following:

– Outlined Samsung's positioning relative to its competitors, in particular a clear mapping of attributes of competitors sound image and sound identity.
– Interpreted Samsung's initial core values in ways that we could attach sonic properties to. This would be used later when we created a design template and strategy for AUI and branded sound elements.
– Showed how the European market differed from the US market. e.g. the relationships between handset manufacturers and carriers.
– Showed that there is no real first mover in audio content–yet.
– Recommended that strategies for sound should be proactive and long-term.
– Showed that emulating competitors would keep Samsung from seeing real opportunities and being a first-mover.
– Introduced the concept-slogan "audio-active". This served as a rally cry for almost all the documents that followed.
– Showed the difference between sounds of Korean and Western origin.
– Introduced the concept of wide regional and cultural variation within the United States. Specifically, the growing population of Hispanic-Americans and their music/audio tastes which varied considerably from most test groups Samsung had previously observed.
– Most importantly, showed opportunity for innovation.

5. User Testing. Device Testing. Making Presenters

5.1 User Testing
Our user testing consisted of a series of focus groups that took place in Germany, Italy, England and the United States. A screener was written based on documentation from Samsung and information gathered from the first project phase that segmented test subjects into 3 different groups. Although it could be argued that many of the issues discussed were universal, it was critical to client acceptance of the data that only the targeted users were tested. The screener was given to recruiting agencies in the respective countries and subjects were then reviewed and selected. For each focus group that took place we used a third-party moderator and supplied a technician to run a playback device for the sounds to be tested. In general we were dissatisfied with the companies that conducted the focus groups. We got usable data but the companies and moderators were not used to talking about sound and it took considerable extra effort to bring them around to our side – even though we were the client. In general one-on-one interviews yield more in-depth results. I completed another user experience (UE) project recently and conducted many in-home interviews that proved insightful.

These issues aside, the focus groups produced a huge body of data that we used to drive the rest of the project. Based on our research in the Discovery Phase we knew that there was a disconnect between Samsung's desired user perception and actual perception.

Statements from the test subjects confirmed this as well as providing a lot of additional information about their perceptions about what are appropriate AUI elements and branded sounds. The focus groups lasted approximately 1.5 hours and were attended by 11- 13 test subjects per session. We tested acceptability of AUI elements, brand sounds and ringtones of Western and Korean (this included sounds by Samsung's competitor, *LG*) origin. Users were asked to rate the sounds they heard on a scale of 1-5 as "better" or "worse" than they had at the time. In addition to the better/worse comparison, test subjects were asked to bring whatever mobile devices they had with them and to tell us what they liked and disliked about the devices.

These data were presented to the client with comment and interpretation by us. We wanted to show not just what sounds were unacceptable but why. Examples were given in the documentation so that the client could click and hear specific sounds along with an explanation about what was or wasn't successful. The users gave us many descriptors that we used later as keywords for creating the strategy documents. A few things the users told us:
– Sounds of Korean origin were unanimously unacceptable for all the groups tested.
– Many users associate good sound with ease of use.
– Short, soft or clear sounds are preferred to sharp, high-pitched or distorted sounds.
– Start-up sounds that were more "song" than "indicator of status" were unacceptable. Such sounds were almost universally rejected by the users and, in the case of users who had some even asked the moderator to help turn the sound off in their own device.

5.2 Device testing
Out of respect for our client I am afraid this section will have to be rather short. Some of our work for device testing consisted of:
– testing a range of Samsung mobile devices,
– showing opportunities for the use of sounds that competitors hadn't used,
– translating these opportunities into specific recommendations in our final strategy document,
– explaining the differences between different types of audio playback systems in mobile devices, i.e. hardware vs. software engines, different speaker types, cavity resonance of different materials etc.

5.3 Developing a better presentation style
Although delivery wasn't scheduled until the end of the project we finished the sounds requested by the forthright DVC-department manager. We built a narrative presenter in Flash that was 90% image and 10% text. We showed our process with still images, some motion and a lot of sound. The text was minimal and, if removed would not affect the intelligibility of the document at all. Early delivery of this presentation style was perhaps the smartest thing we did during the entire project. The response from Samsung was a wholehearted

"yes!" This time we listened and made this presentation style a standard for many of the other documents we delivered. Of course for some documents such as strategy or the AUI guideline discussed next, a 90/10 graphic-image split was impossible but we did make sure to keep our documents engaging and clearer than the first two false-starts.

6. Design for Innovation: The AUI Guideline Tool

6.1 The state of things
From what we saw during our visits and based on the documents we were given, sound design at Samsung was a mess. Samsung's AUI and branded sound development was reactionary to, and derivative of, their competitors and in no way driven by user needs. The existing sound branding strategy consisted of generalized studies for Europe, Asia and North America. Sounds tended to be mapped to features instead of being worked into an information architecture.

There was little standardization of AUI elements or their usage. The elements that did exist were often poor copies of *Microsoft* sounds and various preset MIDI sounds from commercially available synthesizers and samplers. Many of the Korean AUI and branded elements sounded a lot like Korean popular music: chimes, bells, high pitched string instruments. To Western ears these sounds often sound quite shrill. Furthermore, there wasn't much attention paid to sound playback quality – only the apparent volume that the device produced.

Harsh criticism for sure but considering Samsung's stellar performance in semiconductor, design, miniaturization, TFT, etc. the sound design and branding should have been better. What was the problem?

6.2 The problem in general of developing and using AUI elements in devices
Sound designers, project managers, user interface (UI) designers, industrial designers, electrical engineers have three things in common:
1. they all have the opportunity to affect the way sound in used in a device,
2. they are seldom in the same place at the same time to talk about the use of sound in a device,
3. they are unlikely to have a common terminology to address sound related issues.

Without an effective communication about sound in UI/UE context there is a high probability that something will go wrong with the implementation of sound in a device. I have found this to be true in projects prior to the GSP and very much the case during the GSP. We took up this issue as a challenge and one of the best opportunities to spark innovation at Samsung.

7. Presentation: The Good, the Bad & the Mental

Since the delivery process would be almost a week long, we decided to arrive in Seoul two days before our first meeting. In the interest of keeping the budget in order we made the mistake of saving 50 Euro per room and ended up at an absolutely dismal hotel, albeit in an interesting neighborhood. Myself and *Robert Connelly* the other partner at *Receive-Transmit* made matters worse by choosing a room listed as "traditional style" on the hotel's website. Why we thought that sleeping on the floor would enhance our experience still escapes me. Lesson learned: when you fly across the planet to deliver a huge project to a multinational corporation don't radically change what you sleep on the night before you meet the client. Delivery was a multi-step process.

Our project was funded by different departments within Samsung and we were obliged to present to these groups and answer their questions. Furthermore we found out that we had to sell the project again as there would be people attending our presentations who hadn't been involved at project launch.

We knew of this before we travelled and had prepared accordingly. Like the banners in Suwon I mentioned earlier in this article, it was typical for project presentations to be promoted internally. We were told that bringing in decision makers from departments external to the ones we were already dealing with was vital to our project gaining traction after delivery.

To do this we created a small internal advertising campaign that the employees inside Samsung's UI department could implement before our arrival. Our mini- campaign included: a microsite sent to Samsung employees that featured a flash-based DJ/VJ game and meeting announcement, 2 different sets of postcards that referenced the project (these were given away at the meetings as well), and a set of photoshop assets that were used to create announcement posters etc. that were translated into Korean. Such efforts might seem a bit odd but they helped immensely.

When we did finally make our presentations people approached us and told us that they had heard beforehand of the presentation and had taken it upon themselves to find out more about the project and, most importantly, about sound in mobile devices. There were many smaller meetings during the week but our main presentations took place in three separate sessions. The first was frustrated by a host of technical problems the worst of which affected the legibility of our text as it was projected in the conference room.

I exacerbated the problem by talking too fast during the introduction and referenced far too many details without giving the attendees time to absorb a subject that was being presented to them for, perhaps, the first time in their lives.

Long pauses during meetings in Korea aren't a bad thing—they usually mean that people are considering what had just been said. I forgot all this and let my (very American) tendency to get nervous (if there is no immediate response) take control. I talked even faster and confused everyone. Crash and burn.

After the first debacle we had time to figure out what went wrong before our next presentation. Not only had I confused people during the first session I was told that I had actually offended some who had attended. It seems that banging your fist on the table to emphasize a point is unacceptable in Korean business culture. So is placing both your fists on the table and leaning forward, to quote my Australian comrade, "like a bleedin' ape". As funny as this sounds, these actions were affecting the business that we were conducting and things had to change – fast.

So, we fixed the video issues and tested the system twice before the presentation started. As far as the verbal component of the presentation was concerned I wrote myself a script (containing the note to myself: HANDS IN LAP) and followed it as closely as I could. I presented the main points of the project ONLY – "just the hits" you might say. Furthermore I reduced my pace by (silently) counting to five between every sentence. As a result the final presentations were successes.

8. End Thoughts

An AUI or branded element that might be appropriate for one culture might not be for another. In North America and Europe the descending minor third interval is often used to denote a failure or error sound – "uh oh!" in devices. Trying to develop universal sounds or universal branded sounds without considering the way users experience them can be a recipe for at worst, disaster or at best, mediocrity. Consider that the timbral qualities of music and language endemic to any given culture will necessarily inform the perception of AUI and branded elements perceived by users native to that culture. For example Chinese language is sensitive to pitched intervals much more so than in the west.

In short: there are no magic sounds; only magic user experiences. The GSP project created a new set of strategic directions and priorities for Samsung's sound design that built on Samsung's strengths and sparked innovation in its sound design department. Our final report was a platform for strategic sound development – one that met Samsung's goals and enhanced the existing brand identity. This is where I stop but not where the story ends. We just finished another project for Samsung that was built upon the work from the GSP.

"There are no magic sounds; only magic user experiences."

(Aaron Day, 2009)

"As a part of the brand identity, an audio logo should also be able to sustain long-term market processes and not be designed for the immediate market situation."

(Milo Heller, 2009)

The sound of Vattenfall - A brand promise is heard

By Stefan Nerpin, Head of Group Marketing Communication, Vattenfall AB, Richard Veit, Managing Director, Interbrand, Hamburg and Milo Heller, Composer, Hastings Music GmbH

Vattenfall sounds off. The Swedish energy company, which has a strong presence in Northern and Central Europe, has created a new acoustic identity. Since summer 2006, the company has used an acoustic logo and theme as elements of its international identity. Harp tones with violin and cello notes convey the Vattenfall brand values: Easy, empathetic, collegial, progressive and reliable. The players: Vattenfall, *Interbrand* in cooperation with the Stockholm partner agency *Essen* and composer *Milo Heller*.

The Sweden-based Vattenfall Group is Europe's fourth-largest energy company. In 2006, its 32,000 employees achieved a turnover of € 13.7 billion. Vattenfall aims to be a leading European energy company. The holding company Vattenfall AB is fully owned by the country of Sweden.

VATTENFALL

When the Nordic energy markets opened up in the 1990s, the company expanded beyond Sweden's borders. In Germany Vattenfall acquired the companies *Laubag, VEAG, Bewag* and *HEW* and took over *EW* and *GZE* in Poland and lately Elsam in Denmark. The acquisitions were followed by the migration to one Vattenfall brand. Today, Vattenfall is active in Sweden, Finland, Denmark, Germany and Poland.

With its first steps abroad and a dedication to continued expansion, Vattenfall began to invest in its corporate identity. The takeover of several energy companies as a result of deregulation in the respective energy markets dramatically accelerated the company's growth. Vattenfall saw a need to develop a solid, sustainable international brand profile and to implement a monolithic brand strategy. Vattenfall gradually integrated all of the brands and now has a consistent international identity. In this context, the development of a local operator to an international brand within just a few years is a success story.

1. One brand for many target groups and markets

The speed of the international expansion wasn't the only factor which made Vattenfall's brand management so challenging: A central part of the process involved developing the identity for the Group, formerly managed as a national company, which would be unmistakable, relevant and credible for a wide range of target groups on an international arena. It was necessary to design a strategy suitable for the international arena of financial markets and regulatory agencies, which would also work effectively with industrial clients, household consumers and the public opinion.

Vattenfall encountered very tough competition, especially in Germany. Customers recently exposed to the newly deregulated market were bombarded by offers from a wide range of energy brands. After taking over energy companies with long traditions and strong local roots, such as the Hamburg-based *HEW* and Berlin's *Bewag*, Vattenfall faced major challenges in creating one consistent European brand.

Since the beginning of 2004, Interbrand has supported Vattenfall professionals in the international development of the Vattenfall brand together with the Stockholm branding agency Essen. The work involved ranges from strategic consulting and corporate design development to supporting the implementation of the brand identity at all levels of communication.

2. Aim: Enabling people to experience the brand identity

The result is a striking brand identity, which can be experienced on both the visual and acoustic level. The brand has a clearly defined profile and an authentic brand personality at its core. Among competitors with personality characteristics, which can be described as cool and serious, Vattenfall is set on a route to position itself as an empathetic and progressive partner that is reliable and easy to deal with – one committed to provide its customers with a better quality of life. This is a brand which devotes its "heart and mind" to its business.

The purpose and aim of all integrated brand communication is to bring the brand identity to life in all touchpoints and interactions while ensuring that it is always clearly recognizable. The acoustic perception and recognition of the brand represents another element in the creation of an unmistakable brand experience, making it possible to address all target groups in an emotional manner within the sense of hearing.

Stefan Nerpin, Head of Vattenfall Group Marketing Communication:
As our core product – electricity – is invisible and mostly accredited to other end-user brands of household appliances etc., we have to let our brand come alive through all dimensions possible. Therefore Vattenfall is communicating through a wide range of touchpoints. Our brand can

be experienced by almost all senses: heated and lit up bus stops in Poland, customer service centers in Germany, electricity meters in Sweden, mobile services in Finland and group-wide environmental efforts such as the combating climate change initiative and building the world's first CO2-free coal-fired powerplant. All major touchpoints were being thought of. Except one. We wanted to expand the interface to the public and use the emotional strength of the last missing sense, hearing, which led us finally to develop an acoustic identity. Another effect from the acoustic identity we hope for, is also to increase recognition of the Vattenfall identity in all communications investments we's do anyway where sound might be applicable.

3. Experiencing the brand with all the senses

Vattenfall has recognised the increasing importance of effectively utilising images in this age of overwhelming stimulation, especially since Vattenfall's primary product – energy – cannot be perceived directly. As a result, the target groups are forced to seek orientation via other communication measures instead of the product itself. Characteristic acoustic signals help people create associations and recognise trusted, familiar products and brands.

3.1 Sounds enhance brand worlds

Over the last few years, Vattenfall has continuously worked to develop targeted communications that effectively convey authentic, positive experiences and clear messages across all media – with success. Using the sense of hearing and implementing conscious sound design help to refine and expand this brand world. They help to connect content and visual elements with acoustic signals. In the future, this should take place via two central elements:
- via the sound logo, which is used more frequently in connection with visual media (e.g. TV advertisements)
- and via sound themes or soundscapes which communicate the brand in areas where visual means cannot be used (e.g. phone on-hold messages or ringtones) or where a specific atmosphere is to be created (e.g. during events or in customer centres).

3.2 A consistent perception creates distinction

The central element of the Vattenfall corporate sound is the sound logo. Like its graphic counterpart, it represents the personality and promise of the brand. The sound world is created around the sound logo. It is essential that it meet a variety of technical requirements.

It must be possible to reproduce corporate sound in all relevant media - from film advertisements to screensavers. This essential quality factor must be taken into account during the first creation phases. The following illustration shows a selection of relevant acoustic points of contact with employees, customers or the public. The Vattenfall corporate sound should convey a consistent experience across all applications – from the service hotline and sponsoring measures to internal communication.

4. Creating the Vattenfall corporate sound

4.1 The missing acoustic dimension

After the Vattenfall brand position was defined and the corporate design was taken to the next step, the entire chain of experience was reviewed with regard to its completeness and consistency with all aspects of the brand personality.

At this point in time, Vattenfall had introduced the modernized corporate identity in Sweden and Finland. Preparations were being made for the conversion of the brands HEW, Bewag, EW and GZE to the new Vattenfall brand. The number of customers and employees under the Vattenfall brand was to increase considerably in the future. Radio, television and film advertisements were included in the planned communication measures to emphasize the emotional dimension of the brand identity. Events were supposed to expand the brand's chain of experience. Activities and measures targeted towards employees aimed to strengthen the new shared identity. An acoustic dimension of the brand identity was needed in order to implement these communication aims in a consistent manner.

At the end of 2004, Vattenfall's Group Function Communications initiated with the help of *Interbrand Zintzmeyer and Lux* a preliminary selection of possible providers. From three finalists, the agency *Hastings Audio Network* was selected and composer *Milo Heller* entrusted with the creation process. Heller's previous work for top international brands as well as his diverse oeuvre played a decisive role in this decision.

4.2 Inspiration at the headquarters
The task was to develop a comprehensive corporate sound for Vattenfall consisting of a sound logo (incl. variations) and sound themes of varying lengths. A sonic expert team was formed consisting of the Head of Group Marketing Communication, the Marketing Managers of all markets and representatives from the advertising agency *Lowe Brindfors.* Interbrand worked with the Stockholm-based branding agency *Essen* to provide ongoing brand consulting services and project management.

Vattenfall's Stockholm headquarters was chosen as the site of the first team meeting. This way, all of the people involved could get a better sense of the Vattenfall brand. The thematic and visual basis of the Vattenfall brand was introduced, along with sources of inspiration for the creative process: the brand image attributes and brand promise, the anatomy and colors of the Vattenfall corporate logotype and design, the significance of the name Vattenfall, industry-specific associations, the Nordic origins of the brand, etc.

It was decided that the future sonic identity should primarily embody the brand attributes "progressive" and "empathetic". According to studies, these values hold a strong potential for differentiation from the competition. In addition, the new acoustic world should fulfill the brand promise: To devote both heart and mind to enhancing the quality of life for Vattenfall's customers. In this way, the corporate sound would fit perfectly in the range of all communicative measures designed for the brand.

Milo Heller, Composer:
During the first meeting in Stockholm, I gave a general introduction to the topics of corporate sound and the sound logo. My intention was to establish a common basis for our continued work together. It isn't easy to talk about music. First, I wanted everyone to become aware of the process involved in creating corporate sound, to find common language rules and specify evaluation criteria. It is challenging to assess such a short melody. Of course, personal taste does play a role – but shouldn't play such a major role in the decision.

During this first meeting, it was also very important to me to get a feel for the brand and observe the company, the building, the employees. After having given a short impression of music of competitors, I wanted to learn more about the environment of Vattenfall: What national and international campaigns are planned? Will there be a different approach to local markets? Are there company divisions with independent marketing departments?

4.3 Creative workshop: What could Vattenfall sound like?

The creative workshop was held at the Hastings Music sound studio in Hamburg. Milo Heller presented around 30 examples featuring different rhythms, melodies, harmonies and instruments. One important factor: The sounds weren't played on their own, but in a specific context. They were all played at the end of a Vattenfall corporate film in order to evoke an association. The purpose was to limit the creative playing field for the further design process. At first, however, there was a great deal of latitude: Since the participants (group marketing members and marketing managers from all Vattenfall markets) were able to allow their associations free rein and express their wishes and preferences, Milo Heller developed around 100 different variants on the original 30 proposals.

The participants were supposed to wait a few days before providing their feedback. Specific parameters were chosen in advance for their evaluations: Brand fit (consistency with the attributes "progressive" and "empathetic", concurrence with the brand promise), memory factor (distinctiveness), uniqueness (differentiation to the competition and other examples) and overall impression.

The interesting part of this phase involved testing out various sources of inspiration, e.g. integrating themes reminiscent of Norwegian composer *Edward Grieg* or attempting to use typical Scandinavian instruments. This creation phase was important in order to develop an idea which corresponded with the Vattenfall brand.

The result of the creation phase was a selection of ten favorites (short list). It turned out that the attribute "empathetic" was conveyed especially well using string instruments. Other favorites included the clarinets (also "empathetic"), a quick series of electronic sounds which characterized pulsating energy. There were also experimental examples which featured nature sounds, wind, water or bird sounds – attempts which aimed to convey environmental associations.

At this point in time, it was important to include a larger group of people in the current status of the project. The relevant communication departments, such as Marketing, Internal Communications, Public Affairs, Public Relations and representatiion of the Executive Group Management were involved. As a result of this coordination process, four favorites are selected for testing in market research.

Integrating important decision makers was a critical and important factor in ensuring the success of the project. This laid the foundation for gaining a wide consensus for the future sound design.

A qualitative approach was designed to test the four sound logos on the various B2B and B2C target groups in Sweden, Finland, Germany and Poland: 120 test people per country (60 business and private customers each) were surveyed in phone interviews. The aim was to check the sound logo for its communicative power, quality and acceptance.

Once the market research was completed, a decision was made: The current Vattenfall sound logo with the working title "Grieg" only got the second best rating in the market research, but still came out on top. The team of experts felt that it had more communicative power. In contrast to the market research winner, the logo ends in an ascending series of tones which motivates listeners to finish the melody themselves. In addition to the strength in the aspect of "empathetic", this was the decisive moment.

Composer Milo Heller:

With all due respect for market research as a means of insurance, it is better to allow creativity to develop with less restriction. In the process of forming opinions on the audio logo, market research results can be helpful in making decisions. The decision should not be completely dependent on it, because:

– Uninvolved market research participants make more impulsive decisions. Their assessment is always based solely on spontaneous impressions.

– Due to their short duration, audio logos require a willingness on the part of listeners to analyze them carefully.

– The people who truly understand the brand are the involved employees at the company. They have developed a sense of the brand over a long period of time and feel a connection to it.

– As a part of the brand identity, an audio logo should also be able to sustain long-term market processes and not be designed for the immediate market situation.

4.4 "Grieg" creates a unique acoustic position

The new Vattenfall sound logo "Grieg" is an acoustic sequence of four notes featuring plucked harp tones and string instruments (pizzicato). The new sound logo has a timeless, classic and very modern sound, which especially emphasizes the brand attribute "empathetic". This piece has given Vattenfall a unique position.

Milo Heller developed several variations based on an original version. For example, the idea to integrate nature sounds from the integration phase was adopted. In addition, the team considered adding a voice-over – a voice which, pronounces the brand name "Vattenfall" – to the sound logo. In the end, this decision was left to the markets outside of Sweden. In these countries, it may be necessary to communicate the company name as well.

Two different sound themes were also created. These are two- to three-minute compositions which feature the melody, harmony, rhythm and instruments of the sound logo throughout the piece. Since the possibilities for creation were limited by the tempo of the selected sound logo, Milo Heller chose the following arrangements:
– "Theme Splendid" was intended especially for pure listening situations. It should be subtle, relaxing and enjoyable, making it suitable for use on phone messages/hot lines or at the POS.
– "Theme Deep" is suitable for audiovisual applications. It reflects the Vattenfall specifications such as the company size, international orientation, etc.

5. Combining the sound and animated corporate logotype
The sound logo is most often used with the corporate logotype in moving images. In order to strengthen the impact of this interplay, the recommendation was made to synchronize the corporate logotype with the sound logo using computer animation.

In order to avoid interfering with the acoustic design process, the Vattenfall corporate logotype was only animated after the sonic logo was completed. The result involves animated graphic elements in the logotype, which correspond to the rhythm and duration of the sound logo. The animation features the sound logo as the soundtrack and can be used in all audiovisual media. It is never shown as a silent version.

6. Documentation in the Brand Manual
Vattenfall's identity and design is documented in the Brand Manual which is part of the groupwide Management Instruction System. The Brand Manual exists out of a Core Manual,

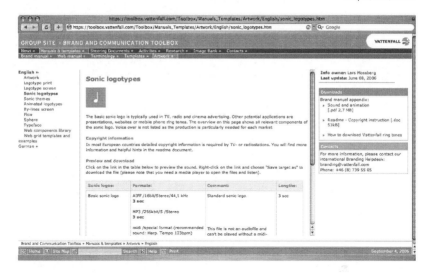

appendices and best practive examples. Together with The "Brand & Communication Toolbox" on the company's Extranet it forms a binding tool for day-to-day work which is updated and expanded on an ongoing basis.

After production was completed, all elements, formats, application principles and technical data including the animated logotype were described in a systematic manner and added to the Toolbox as an Appendix to the Brand Manual entitled "Sound and Animation".

It is possible to download the sound and image files directly from the Toolbox. The Toolbox also contains a description of the role that acoustic identity elements play in the Vattenfall chain of experience. The information in the Toolbox is accessible to all relevant employees and selected suppliers.

7. Legal aspects

Vattenfall will have unlimited rights to use the sound logo and sound themes in any media in relevant markets. For this reason, the usage rights were purchased from Milo Heller. A written agreement with the composer confirms the Vattenfall's right of usage. However, Milo Heller retains the copyright. In addition, Vattenfall registered the sound logo as a trademark, enabling the company to take action against possible imitators.

Milo Heller, Composer:

In my opinion, it is important to ensure the most comprehensive trademark protection possible for a sound logo. I register every logo I develop with the GEMA (= German copyright association). In this way, it is registered as a composition and protected by copyright. This excludes the possibility of plagiarism, at least in the scope of legal possibilities. This protection primarily

8. Summary and lessons learned

Corporate sound represents an extension of the basic elements in the brand identity. In essence, the acoustic logo is a representation of the brand using sounds and notes.

The development and decision process for the corporate sound and animated logotype for Vattenfall took a total of nine months. This is a realistic amount of time to ensure the success of the project. The internal coordination processes involved in this type of work should not be underestimated. Overall, the following points were decisive in the successful development of the new Vattenfall sound world:

A strong intention. Vattenfall has recognized the value of the acoustic logo and expressed a clear intention to create a striking and distinctive solution. Experience the brand. The brand identity is the central starting point to develop the corporate sound. It is an important point of orientation and steers the decision-making process.

A wide foundation. The team of experts was formed of marketing representatives from the holding company and subsidiaries in the respective countries. This constellation made it possible to achieve a wide consensus and acceptance. The team was supported by professional brand/sound identity experts who brought an outside perspective as well as the point of view of the brand into the creation process.

Keep your eyes and ears open. What is the competition doing? What has already been done? It is important to take a look at the market and differentiate yourself from the competition. However, Vattenfall's target groups are also exposed to communicative influences outside of the energy industry as well. Such aspects are to be taken into account to ensure that the company stands out and is not considered an imitator of popular trends.

Use reason to control impulsive decisions. At the beginning of the development process, clear criteria for decision making based on the specified brand identity should be developed. The sound designs should be evaluated according to these in the creation phase.

Define the playing field. It is important not to limit the search at the start of the creative process. Hearing a lot of different sounds, rhythms, harmonies, melodies and instruments makes it possible to gain a feeling for the sound world and future corporate sound of the brand. Over the course of the process, the playing field becomes better defined and the decision options more limited.

Integrate top management. Getting top management involved early on is a factor for success. Once a feel for the characteristic sound world has been developed, the management should listen to what has been achieved so far. At Vattenfall, this ensured that there were no unpleasant surprises at the end of the process.

Set trends. It is important to test the favorites on the market and among the relevant target groups. However, it is important not to blindly follow the results of the market evaluation. When it comes to creating the new acoustic identity, it is difficult for the test people to effectively assess the new sounds. If the team of expert feels that a sound design other than the test winner has greater communicative potential and is better suited to the brand, it is important to trust this feeling.

Protect rights. As a new basic element of the brand identity, the developed sound logo should be protected by copyright. This ensures that the exclusivity of the sound world is protected in the future as well.

Case Study: NBL Team Anthem, WWF India

Shouvik Roy & Anupam Sen Gupta
Anthems, India

1. Background and Brief

The *North Bank Landscape* (NBL) team of *WWF India* is based in Tezpur, Assam; a state that is blessed by Mother Nature in the North Eastern part of India. This conservation team focuses on areas around the Northern bank of the Brahmaputra River. A key challenge for this team is to make sure that the large population of Elephants living in the area can peacefully co-exist with the local villagers. This task has become more and more difficult over the past couple of decades due to a variety of reasons.

Such was the backdrop for a workshop that used music as a tool. This workshop was conducted in January 2007, a short time after the untimely demise of *Pankaj Sarmah*, a core staff member of North Bank Landscape team.

Pankaj was an experienced conservationist and his loss was a serious blow to the conservation work in the area. The WWF Secretariat in New Delhi felt that a good way to lift the spirit of the team would be by using music as a tool as the state of Assam and the North Eastern region of India is known for its prolific musicians. The leadership of WWF India was already exposed to the *ISquare ventures'* 'Anthems' format. So, when they requested the two of us to go to Tezpur and rekindle the undying spirit of the team, we found ourselves there within the next few days.

2. The Key Challenges
Traditionally an 'Anthem' has been defined as a 'hymn' of praise or loyalty. However, over a period of time world over anthems have been used as a flag that binds people together for a common cause. Our endeavour is exactly the same – create an anthem that truly binds the team together towards a common cause. Easier said!

Every 'Anthems' workshop is unique in every way. This one was truly exceptional as it took us far away from our comfort zones to a land that was unknown, people who had diverse taste in music and speak languages that are not known to us. As is widely known, Indians speak several languages and even more dialects. In the North Eastern states in India, English is commonly spoken and understood by many. However, if one gets to the interiors (as we did) English is spoken by a minority. So, language was a great barrier as well. As we found out, it was nearly impossible to communicate with such a diverse audience, leave alone write an anthem that captures the emotions and binds a team together. But, we could not back out after having travelled for over 2000 kms from another part of the country.

3. Team NBL
One of the most fascinating facts about this workshop was the sheer diversity of the NBL team, one which comprised of seasoned conservationists, a shy girl with childlike innocence and a driver who has braved the wild for over 20 years. The head of the NBL team *Anupam Sarmah*, was there to welcome us to the WWF India's Tezpur office (the venue for the workshop). It was a modest house and they had made the main hall as the venue for this workshop. We were introduced to each of the members who thought we were from outer space. They had never in their lives seen people walking into their office with guitars, keyboards and amplifiers! What was visible instantly was the energy that we felt as we entered the room full of people. These people were clueless about what we were there for yet hopeful and extremely positive. When we explained the format of the workshop and what we were there for, some of them, like always, felt that it was impossible to achieve. How can a team with no experience in music compose and sing an anthem in two days!!!

4. The 2 day 'Anthems' workshop format
Having experimented with multiple time durations in the past, we settled in for the 2 day workshop format for this team.

The spread of two days had three key sections:
1) Excite
2) Explore
3) Create

The first two sections usually take about 4-5 hours and the rest of time is spent on 'creating' the anthem.

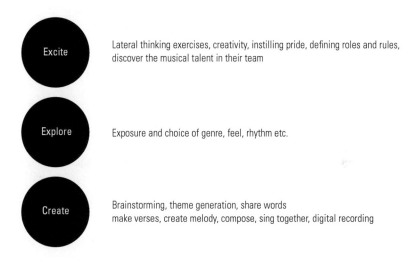

Excite
Lateral thinking exercises, creativity, instilling pride, defining roles and rules, discover the musical talent in their team

Explore
Exposure and choice of genre, feel, rhythm etc.

Create
Brainstorming, theme generation, share words
make verses, create melody, compose, sing together, digital recording

Excite

The NBL team had just experienced a major tragedy and hence it was important for us to be able to 'excite' them. We employed the following means to excite them:

a) Expectation setting: We started the workshop by telling everyone what the outcome of the workshop will be. We made them understand the concept of 'anthems' and what makes an anthem different from the just any other song. The team was expectant and doubtful at the same time.

b) Roles and rules: Here is where we define our role as facilitators and their roles of writing, collaborating and singing, very clearly. This also allayed some fears and concerns about their 'ability' to create an anthem.

c) Discovery: We encouraged them to expose their 'musical' side to others. To our joy and their disbelief, we found a couple of very decent singers. Discovery also works very well as an ice-breaker in diverse teams. This team needed no ice-breaker as they were already in an environment where true camaraderie existed and there were very few barriers between them.

d) Play: There was some time allocated to 'play', be playful, play some music and play some games with each other. This prepared them for some serious action in the forthcoming sessions.

Explore

The real musical sessions began with 'explore'. Here the participants were taken through the origins of music, the origins of a guitar and other musical instruments, introduction to genres using an entertaining show-and-tell format.

At this stage it was important for us to expose them to Eastern as well as Western music. The modern day overlaps of sound worldwide were also critical to convey. The team had a lot of interesting questions in this session, particularly when they heard that an Indian Classical Raga Bhopali and the rock 'n' roll (major pentatonic scale) were played on the same notes.

The show-and-tell format in this section got people on to their feet and they were itching to get started. The team was exposed to multiple genres and style of music from across the world. They were asked to choose a genre that they can easily identify with. And to our surprise instead of choosing a contemporary popular sound, they chose a traditional Folk song format for their anthem. This decision was almost instantaneous and unanimous. Not only was the team clear about the Folk format, they wanted a folk format that they were familiar with and was rooted in their native state of Assam.

As musicians it was challenging for us to instantly be instilled with the folk rhythm of Assam on which we were to create the anthem.

Create

We spent more than half of the time during the two days in co-creating the anthem with the NBL team – a journey that we will not forget for a long time.

The 'Create' section started with us taking them through the components of an 'anthem' and how they needed to choose a theme on which they had to write the anthem, followed by the lyrics and melody and the rhythm. We spent about an hour explaining how an anthem is made and then we straight away got into 'theme selection'. Pretty much like the genre selection, 'conservation' was chosen as an overarching theme for their anthem unanimously.

At that point we made it clear to them that a broad theme like 'conservation' needed to be made more specific for their 'anthem'. This is when we got into the specific areas, landscapes and species that make the NBL team unique.

These areas were highlighted and we later used them to string parts of the lyrics together at a later point in time. Writing the lyrics was the most difficult part of the workshop. The team was free to choose the language they wanted to write the anthem in. How-ever, to our surprise they chose to write an anthem that was bilingual – Assamese and Hindi. We had a working knowledge of Hindi but Assamese was Greek to us. Nevertheless, in keeping with the spirit we told them that we requested for someone to champion the Assamese section and we were delighted when a lady gladly took it.

So, there we were a dozen people and 2 facilitators writing lyrics for the anthem in two languages and more importantly agreeing on the content. The first cut lyrics were ready by about 5 pm and we even managed to put it to a melody that the team liked.

So, we spent about an hour giving it some final shape and we requested everyone to practice the track so that the next day we could start recording onsite. We found that about half of the participants stayed back till 10 pm to rehearse the anthem so that they could sing it better.

Day 2 of 'Create'

The two of us came back ready to record the anthem. On entering the room we felt that all was not quite right. We started by asking if everyone was ready to record. There were only murmurs and not a resounding 'yes'. On probing the reason for their reluctance we found that they were not happy with the 'Assamese' verses in the anthem. Suddenly we felt totally helpless because of our total lack of knowledge of Assamese. We needed to think of some out-of-the-box solution.

So, we asked everyone to break out into two groups and come back with verses they felt work better. There was no way the two of us facilitators could have helped them directly. But, before we split them into teams we gave them a common meter and length to work with. Luckily for us both teams came back with very powerful verses, and the one was chosen over the other. This let us breathe easy.

To make up for the lost time, we made them practice singing the anthem in a group before we started recording. The base track was already put together by us the previous night. They had to sing on that track with the new lyrics. This exercise took about 4 hours and by the end of it they knew their anthem by heart and were all jumping with the joy of creation. Suddenly, they had achieved what they never thought they could do – write, compose and sing their own anthem. As facilitators our role was to guide them through this journey and to make sure what they wrote and sang was heartfelt and truly bound the team together.

Outcome

First and foremost the most difficult part about any Anthems workshop is to create an anthem that the participants feel they own and bond with. The biggest achievement of this workshop was that the end product was something each of the participants owns even today, a year after the workshop.

The NBL team anthem is widely used by the team as a mark of achievement of the team in an unfamiliar area where together they stretch and achieved what seemed impossible. This automatically motivated the team to achieve more in every sphere of life. The NBL anthem is put up on the WWF India website even today as a significant achievement and a flag that binds the team together. It is a prime example of employee branding. The values of the team were captured as were their love for nature in this simple yet provocative anthem. For us, we discovered that Sonic branding principles can be used for Internal branding, retaining the loyalty and motivating members of an organisation most effectively.

The NBL Team Anthem (translated)

These beautiful forests, the gorgeous greenery, let us not lose them.
The Blue Mountains and spring water.
These elephants and bears, tigers and deer, let us not lose them.
We are theirs and they are ours.

From the Sankosh river to the Dibang, many places have we been to.
The grand old river Luit and the blue hills.
We met various people and learnt a lot from all of them.
The Bodo and Adivasi tribes.
With dreams of this green planet and the blue skies.
Let us all move forward in our endeavour.

Glossary

Technical terms audio branding

Brand versus corporate
The term 'corporate' refers to the company as a whole, while 'brand' refers to an individual brand. Thus, the design guidelines of the company *Daimler* are listed in the corporate design manual, whereas the company owned car brand *Mercedes-Benz* has its own brand design. The same applies to 'corporate sound' and 'brand sound' (q.v.). Brands which refer to a company as a whole - e.g. *Lufthansa* – are also called corporate brand (corporate sound).

Acoustic brand management
Management process of acoustic brand communication. Main objectives include circularisation, differentiation and identification of the brand.

Audio branding
(sound branding, sonic branding, acoustic branding)
Process of brand development and brand management by use of acoustic elements (audio branding elements) within the framework of brand communication.

Brand sound, corporate sound
Acoustic dimension of brand design (corporate design). Reflects the acoustic identity of a brand (company) and becomes audible as audio logo, brand song, brand voice etc.

Brand sound identity, corporate sound identity
Form the basis for acoustic brand appearance (corporate appearance) and input of acoustic branding elements. These are expressed in the brand sound (corporate sound) and are the acoustic identity of a brand (company).

Central acoustic idea
Creative idea, deduced from brand identity, for the acoustic design of a brand, analogue to the visual design idea of a brand design (corporate design).

Commercial song
Used as spot background and background music and – as opposed to brand song (q.v.) - is employed only temporarily or just once in an advertising campaign.

Sound style guide
(acoustic design manual, brand sound guidelines)
Set of rules for all brand sound elements (corporate sound elements) and guideline for their use.

Key elements of audio branding

Audio logo
(sound logo, sonic logo, acoustic logo, signature theme, jingle, acoustic signature)
The audio logo is a brand's acoustic identification element and is often used in combination with the (animated) visual logo. Must be concise, distinct, catchy and flexible and fit the brand (brand fit). Special form jingle: Is in effect the musical version of the advertising slogan ("*Haribo* macht Kinder froh, und Erwachsene ebenso / Kids and grown-ups love it so, the happy world of Haribo", "*Mars* macht mobil bei Arbeit Sport und Spiel / Mars makes you mobile, at work, sports and play") and acoustically conveys the advertising message.

Brand song (corporate song)
Piece of music following classic song pattern with verse, chorus etc. Composition or selection is based on acoustic brand identity. In contrast to commercial song (q.v.), it is used over a longer period of time and may vary or be situationally adapted.

Brand voice (corporate voice)
Vocal element of brand communication represents the brand personality and is often part of an audio logo.

Sound objects

A. Sound icon
Sound icons are the smallest or shortest sound elements of audio branding. Characteristically similar, they directly point to the brand performance. In man-machine communication at auditory user interfaces also referred to as auditory icons.

B. Sound symbol
Sound symbols are abstract sound objects that – unlike sound icons – do not resemble the item they are referring to. At auditory user interfaces they are called earcons.

Technical terms sound

Chord
Harmony of at least three notes. These can also sound successively as a broken chord.

Acoustics
Originally, the science of physical sound processes as wave phenomena in solids, liquids and gases based on mechanic molecular vibrations. Today, acoustics also include the science of

sound perception (i.e. psychoacoustics) and sound effects (e.g. physiological changes in the ear resulting from high sound intensity).

Audio-visual
Combination of auditory and visual information. Related to hearing and sight.

Auditory
Of or related to the process of hearing.

Noise
Impulsive perception of a sound without clearly definable pitch. As opposed to sound, noise is based on a non-periodic or pulsed sound process.

Sound
Basis of sound is a periodic sound signal. A sound consists of a key tone and an overtone spectrum (harmonic) comprising multiples of the fundamental frequency. Frequency of the key tone determines the perceived pitch, while number and characteristic of overtones (amplitude) determine the timbre.

Timbre
The perceived timbre is defined by number and amplitude of overtones, i.e. form of the overtone spectrum. The characteristic sound spectra of the musical instruments result in the characteristic timbre. On the basis of the timbre of a language, vowels can be distinguished and speakers identified. Additionally, timbre has strong emotional significance.

Music
According to the current use of language, music is defined as any form of sound expression in the broadest sense. Classifications of music, defined according to purpose (film score, dance music), performance (concert music, family music), cast (guitar music, vocal music) or composition method and technique (twelve-tone technique, electronic music) demonstrate the different characteristics of music, yet do not refer to a superior theoretical system. Equally unfeasible is a differentiation between art music and popular music (fundamentally altered concept of aesthetics of music in the 20th century).

Music genre
Defines different styles of music according to origin, characteristics, instrumentation and distribution (e.g. classical music, electronic music, rock, pop etc.).

Score
Vertically arranged set of all individual parts and voices of a composition allowing the conductor to oversee the entire musical event simultaneously. Scores are also used to store music in a reproducible form.

Psychoacoustics
Includes search for quantitative and generalizable relationships between physical sound impulse (sound event) and sound perception (hearing event), developed as a branch of psychophysics. Physical sound events can cause perception of hearing events which manifest as noise or sound objects.

Rhythm
Organising and formal principle of the chronological process in music, dance and composition.

Soundscape
The term was introduced by the Canadian composer Murray Schafer in analogy to landscape. A soundscape has a rather diffuse background with meaningful foreground elements (sound marks in analogy to land marks). Every auditory environment can be considered a soundscape. The compositional design includes spatial differentiation according to fore- and background as well as the deliberate setting of meaningful elements for the listener's orientation.

Major mode
Definition of a mode encompassing all keys whose scales include 5 whole steps and 2 half steps, namely from the 3rd to the 4th and from the 7th to the 8th step. The major triad consists of key tone, major third and perfect fifth.

Minor mode
The "soft" mode, whose triad is formed by minor triad and perfect fifth (e.g. C - E-flat - G). In the 16th century, the current minor mode developed from the Aeolian, Doric and Phrygian church scales.

Technical terms branding

Branding
Originally, branding referred to the property marking of livestock. Today, the term describes all activities involved in the development of a brand with the aim to set one's own product apart from the bulk of similar ones and to enable distinct association with a specific brand.

Corporate brand
Brand that refers to the company as a whole and which - unlike the product brand which is primarily focused on the customer – is aimed at all contact groups of the company.

Corporate design (CD)
Creative transformation of corporate identity stressing the multisensory unity of a company's image.

Corporate identity (CI)
Intrinsic self-concept of a company, clearly distinguishable from competitors (complete external and internal profile of a company) and – based on existing company culture – expressed in appearance (corporate design), communication channels (corporate communication) and attitude of all members of staff (corporate behaviour).

Brand
Comprises one or several of the following brand elements: name, concept, emblem, symbol and/or design. A brand (formerly: trademark) aims to identify the performance of one or several suppliers and to distinguish it from competitors' offers.

Brand elements (brand components)
Design parameters employed in the marking of a performance include visual, acoustic, olfactory, haptic and gustatory signals.

Brand identity
All characteristics of a brand which permanently distinguish it from other brands.

Brand image
Perception of a brand represented in the brain as brand associations.

Brand equity/brand value
Value of a brand "in the consumers' mind" compared to an non-brand, yet objectively similar item. In financial terms, brand equity/brand value refers to the cash value of future payment surplus generated by the brand. In terms of behavioural theory, it refers to the result of different consumer reactions to marketing methods of a brand versus a fictional brand evoked by specific concepts of the brand which are stored in the brain.

About the Authors

Lukas Bernays

Kai Bronner

The founder and directing manager of audio relation, an agency specialized in manifold communication and corporate sound. He completed his professional training in Communication and Culture Management. He has garnered years of experience fulfilling both client and agency requirements by using integrated communication approaches. However, for over 20 years he has been actively involved with music and audio artifacts: as a musician, radioman and producer - and as a result has acquired considerable related know-how.

In the 90's he made an international breakthrough with the CD "Technomajikal" when he collaborated with Dieter (Yello) Meier and Lee Perry.

Studies in media economics at Stuttgart Media University (HdM) - university of applied sciences. Internships in advertising agency, music production and management of music events. Graduation (graduate engineer) with diploma thesis "Audio-Branding. Akustische Markenkommunikation als Strategie der Markenführung" in 2004. Since then Kai Bronner gained experience in the field of audio branding and sound communication on several projects in collaboration with different partners and companies. He is co-editor of the in 2007 published German compendium "Audio-Branding" and a founder member of ExAM - Expertenkreis Angewandte Musikforschung (expert society for applied music research). His main research interests include sound communication, sound design, multisensory design and music in general.

James Bull

Aaron Day

James co-founded Moving Brands in 1998 after graduating in Graphic Design from Central Saint Martins College of Art and Design (CSM). He was Creative Director on Moving Brands until Jan 2008, when he was promoted to Executive Creative Director.

He oversees the creative output of a multi-disciplinary studio and believes that truly powerful brand experiences are created with a consideration of a brand's Moving, Static, Sonic and Responsive assets (an approach unique to Moving Brands). Such experiences allow brands to thrive and stand out in an increasingly complex world.

In his role as Creative Director, James has created work for Vodafone, The Body Shop, J:Com, Nokia, Keane, Universal Records and Nokia Siemens Networks.

Since 1998 Aaron Day has worked to bring these attributes to interfaces, brands and devices.

Aaron works with multi-disciplinary teams across languages, cultures and continents to address usability and user experience problems for clients in the mobile, online, handheld device, automotive, and medical industries. Through his work with iconmobile, Receive-Transmit and Method, Aaron has developed unique, successful and sometimes unconventional processes and methodologies. His international experience brings extensive client management and business development skills as well as relationships with vendors around the world. Most of all, Aaron's ability to visualize processes and outcomes, along with his improvisational skills in the time domain, give him the ability to create original ideas that have value.

John Groves

Anupam Sen Gupta

John Groves is a Composer, music producer and consultant on the use of sound and music in advertising and communications. In the early 90s he became one of the pioneers of Sound Branding, by developing a structured system for the creation and implementation of brand and corporate Sound Identities. This method has provided the basis for what has become a market standard. GROVES Sound Communications has offices in Hamburg and London with representation in Stockholm, Zurich and Madrid. Their client list contains a number of distinguished brands such as Olympus, Wrigley's, Mentos, Bacardi, Audi, Nivea, BMW, Visa as well as a large number of radio and TV stations. He is president of the Composers Club, Germany, vice president of 'the Federation of Film and Audio-visual Composers of Europe, and board member of ECSA 'the European Composers and Songwriters Alliance', member of the Art Directors Club and deputy for the advisory board of the GVL.

Anupam Sen Gupta started his career in shipping in 1986 and worked for 11 years till he quit following his passion for music. He has been playing guitar since 1980 and has played with various bands. But it was only in 1997, he chose to take up music for a living. Anupam's first band, The Karmic Circle was in the top 12 in India at the Levi's Great Indian Rock in 2002. He opened his chain of music schools, Guitar Workshop and also ventured in alternate application of music. He now offers aural solutions, team building workshops in collaboration with his partner besides offering a wide range of services like consultancy to radio stations, internet radio, logical application of sound in schools, music education, music designing for films and documentaries etc.

Michael Haverkamp

Rainer Hirt

Born 1958 in Gütersloh/Bundesrepublik Deutschland, he studied electrical enginee- ring at the Ruhr-Universität Bochum, with a focus on technical and psychological acous- tics and communications engineering. PhD thesis on physiological influence and perception of vehicle vibration, based on investigations done at the Medical Depart- ment of Universität Mainz, Institute for Oc- cupational Health. Beside long term expe- rience in acoustics engineering and teaching – currently in the automotive industry at FORD Engineering Centre Cologne - studies on cross-modal perception, design, the arts and music are important fields of activity. He is also involved in arts projects and per- formances of improvised music. Numerous publications and presentations on sound and vibration engineering, perception, sound design and synesthesia. His compre- hensive approach on multi-sensory design is presented in the book "Synästhetisches De- sign", published 2008 (in German language).

Born 1979 in Überlingen. He studied commu- nication design at the University of Applied Science, Konstanz (Master of Arts). While still a communication design student, he founded the corporate sound information portal www.audio-branding.de, well-known in professional circle. In 2006 he cofounded Anemono, a agency specialised in Audio Branding with clients like Danone, Symrise or Volkswagen. Rainer Hirt is also author and co-producer of the compendium "Audio-Branding" and has been, since 2007, supervising various research projects with serval universities.

Jasmin Junge

Karsten Kilian

Jasmin Junge holds a degree in economics from the University of Oldenbourg and specialized in intellectual property. She was born in 1981 and has worked with the audio consulting group in Hamburg as a consultant since 2007.

e-mail:
jasmin.junge@acoustic-branding.com
www.acoustic-branding.com

For the last five years, Karsten has been conducting research on brand management at the University of St. Gallen in Switzerland. He studied marketing in the MBA program at the University of Florida and received his graduate degree of a Diplom-Kaufmann (equivalent to an MBA) at the University of Mannheim in Germany. Karsten worked several years as a consultant for Simon-Kucher & Partners. He has contributed to a wide range of anthologies on brand strategy, audio branding, multi-sensory communication, and experiential marketing. Besides, Karsten has built up Markenlexikon.com which has become the most-respected website on brand management in the German-speaking world.
kilian@markenlexikon.com
www.markenlexikon.com

Mark Lehmann

Stefan Nerpin

Mark N.D. Lehmann was born in 1973 in Lübben/Spreewald, Germany. Initially a culinary chef by profession, his interest in music led him to branch out, becoming involved in the music industry in the mid-1990's. In 1999, at that time working as a product manager, he began studying 'business communication'. The study of multi-sensory communication then led him to the field of audio branding. The voice, within the context of brand communication, caught his special interest. His book "Voice Branding" is an in-depth analysis of the voice in brand communication in Germany. Lehmann resides in Berlin and works as a consultant, advising agencies and companies on audio branding. He is visiting professor at the Berlin University of the Arts and teaches in the Department of Sound Studies.

Stefan Nerpin, former Vice President and head of group marketing communications, manager of the Vattenfall group brand strategy, planning and marketing communications, involving re-branding of local brands to one international brand. Stefan previously worked at the global mail and express group TNT at the headquarters in Amsterdam as corporate identity design and communications manager where he led one of the largest re-branding projects in the world during the 1990s. Before that, he worked at TNT as head of communications and marketing for Russia, Baltics and Nordics. Stefan also has a background as Director at the PR firm Burson-Marsteller where he worked as a PR-consultant. Prior to this, he was account director at the Nordic B2B advertising agency Sandberg-Trygg, and started his career with the international marketing research company AC Nielsen as project manager.

Rayan Parikh

Rayan Parikh is the Director of Audio Strategy at Elias Arts. Since joining the practice in 2003, Rayan has expanded the approach and methodology for Elias Arts ID services and partnered with many Fortune 500 clients to develop audio-based branding solutions, including Coca-Cola, Cisco, Sun Microsystems, Orange and Citi.

Prior to joining Elias Arts, Rayan was a Director of Strategic Services at FutureBrand Worldwide, a brand strategy and design consultancy based in New York where he developed multiple corporate identity programs for global brands, including Saudi Aramco, Thrivent Financial and Pricewaterhouse Coopers.

He received an MBA from Georgetown University in Washington DC and a Bachelor of Arts in European History at the University of North Carolina at Chapel Hill.

Hannes Raffaseder

was born in Freistadt 1970, lives in Vienna. Hannes studied Communication Engineering at the Technical University and Computer Music at the University of Music in Vienna. He is head of the Institute of Media Production at the University of Applied Sciences in Sankt Poelten, Austria. His book 'Audiodesign' is published by Carl Hanser Verlag, Munich. He is artistic director of the Komponistenforum Mittersill (kofomi.com), Klangturm St. Pölten (klangturm.at) and einklangrecords.com.

He was involved in the research project allthatsounds.com and published several papers focusing on function, effect and meaning of sound and music in media. He has won several awards and comissions.

Some of his works are recorded on CD, broadcasted and published by Musikverlag Doblinger, Vienna.

http://www.raffaseder.com

Cornelius Ringe

Shouvik Roy

studied business administration at the University of Augsburg with majors in advertising psychology, corporate governance, and human resource management. After some experience in music business at the international marketing division of Universal Music in Berlin he 2005 joined the audio consulting group in Hamburg as consultant. Since 2007 he is lecturer for Audio Branding at the Pop Academy Baden-Wuerttemberg - University of Popular Music and Music Business and holding guest lectures at some other German Universities. As author of several publication concerning audio branding, pop sponsoring and brand-artist-partnership his general field of research is meaning of music in corporate communications.

Shouvik Roy is a Strategic Innovation specialist, Brand Consultant and a Corporate trainer based in India. An engineering graduate from and an MBA, Shouvik has worked in several blue chip companies across New Delhi, Mumbai and Kolkata. Shouvik has been deeply involved in subjects such as Corporate Branding, Brand Architecture and Consumer Behaviour. His love for music led him to partner Anupam Sen Gupta to bring in some cutting edge Sonic Branding and Team bonding tools to India using music as a tool. Shouvik teaches and trains. He is a guest faculty for Brand Management, Consumer Behaviour and Services Management in leading Business Schools in India. Shouvik is an expert for msn India's education portal and he writes for several leading journals and websites.

Holger Schulze

Ralf Sieckmann

Prof. Dr. Holger Schulze, born in 1970, is a cultural theorist and writer. He lives and works in Berlin and teaches at the University of the Arts Berlin, where he is a visiting professor for Anthropology and Ecology of Sound and head of the Master of Arts program in "Sound Studies – Acoustic Communication". He has worked on a three-part volume Theorie der Werkgenese (theory of work genesis): The Aleatoric Game – Heuristics – Intimacy and Mediality. He writes for newspapers, monthly journals, magazines and blogs on electronic music, developments in contemporary art and new cultural life forms. Hes is also the author of sound pieces, experimental texts and stories.

M.Sc., Ph.D. in Chemistry, Partner, Cohausz Dawidowicz Hannig & Sozien, Patent & Law Firm, Duesseldorf Berlin Munich Paris, sieckmann@aol.com, www.copat.de/mn_nl_dus.htm
Studied chemistry, economics and law, (German) Patent Attorney, European Patent and Trademark Attorney. Working for more than 20 years in industrial property rights protection, specialized in patent and trademark law; manage-ment consultancy in IP (patent and trade mark strategies). Specialities: trade marks including new media, chemistry, pharmacy, chemical engineering and related non mechanical fields. Former lecturer on industrial property at Duesseldorf University for Applied Sciences. Co-author of BUSINESS ANGELS (2002), INTELLECTUAL PROPERTY (2006, 2007, 2008), Lessons on Madrid Agreement and Protocol, Community trade marks after publication in INTERNATIONALES MARKENRECHT (2007, 2008), publications and seminars.

Georg Spehr

Richard Veit

*1967, communication engineer and multimedia designer specialized in acoustic design. 1989 - 1998 engineer for professional audio equipment. 1999 - 2002 multimedia designer for crossmedia and internet projects. Since 2002 freelancer for acoustic consulting and multimedia design. 2003- 2005 lecturer at the FH-Potsdam, study course interface design. Since 2006 lecturer at University of Fine Arts Berlin, study course Sound Studies. Speeches and publications in the field of audio-branding, functional sounds and acoustic conception. Consultant for the EU-funded project The Aural City I Die Hörsame Stadt 2008. Georg Spehr lives in Berlin.

Richard Veit is Managing Director of Interbrand, Hamburg. Interbrand is a leading international brand consultancy specialized in brand services and activities, including: analytics, brand engagement, brand design and brand strategy. The branding specialists are located in Hamburg, Cologne, Moscow, Munich and Zurich and belong to the worldwide Interbrand global network. Interbrand's clients include reputable companies such as BMW, Deutsche Telekom, TUI and Schweizerische Post. Interbrand has created Corporate Sound projects for Deutsche Telekom, TUI and Koelnmesse.

Index